Ewing Kauffman Book Fund

The purchase of this book
was made possible by the
friends of Mr. Kauffman

5-10-2005

Scenes of Visionary
Enchantment
Reflections on
Lewis and Clark

Scenes of Visionary Enchantment

Reflections on Lewis and Clark

DAYTON DUNCAN

University of Nebraska Press, Lincoln and London

Acknowledgments for
previously published material
appear on pages 201–2.

Library of Congress Catalog-
ing-in-Publication Data
Duncan, Dayton.
Scenes of visionary enchantment : reflections on Lewis
and Clark / Dayton Duncan.
p. cm.   Includes biblio-
graphical references.
ISBN 0-8032-1724-2 (cloth :
alk. paper)
1. Lewis and Clark Expedition
(1804–1806)   2. West (U.S)—
Discovery and exploration.
3. West (U.S.)—Description
and travel.   4. Explorers—West
(U.S.)—Biography.   5. Overland
journeys to the Pacific.   I. Title.
F592.7 .D86 2004
917.804'2—dc21
2003011752

This book is dedicated to the late

STEPHEN E. AMBROSE

– friend and fellow explorer,

my captain on many unforgettable journeys.

We'll miss your voice along the trail.

Contents

Introduction

Twenty years ago, after a brief initial exposure, I contracted a virulent strain of "Lewis-and-Clark-itis." Almost immediately the symptoms began running their course through progressive stages.

In the first stage, you find yourself wanting to read more and more about the Corps of Discovery and their epic adventure. In stage two, you want to go to as many places along their trail as possible. (These two stages of the disease sometimes present themselves in reverse order, but they always overlap, and they never disappear.)

In stage three, you can't help yourself from talking incessantly about the expedition. And by stage four, you wake up in the morning, see that the calendar says September 3 (your birthday), and instead think: *September 3, September 3 . . . oh yes, they would have been just entering the Great Plains of South Dakota their first year . . . crossing Lost Trail Pass into Montana and about to meet the Salish Indians on year two . . . and, let's see, barreling down the Missouri, just twenty days from St. Louis on their last year.* Depending on your schedule, you might then go to the den and get out the journals to double-check your memory—and hours later be called away into the kitchen, wondering why a cake with candles is on the table.

I'm in stage four now, obviously an incurable case. But many of these essays originated in my stage three period—the talkative one—which began in the late 1990s, roughly fourteen years into my affliction. Luckily for me, a number of organizations apparently wanted to help ease me through this stage and started inquiring whether I'd consider coming out to some spot along the trail to give a speech about Lewis and Clark. Part of the disorder turns out to be an inability to say no to such requests. Off I went—and I'm glad I did.

Those speeches gave me not only another excuse to revisit the Lewis and Clark trail but another reason to revisit their journals. In both cases—the revisiting through travel and reading—I discovered that after authoring two books and writing and producing two films about the Corps of Discovery, I still had more to learn. And more to say.

This book is a way to say it. Covering a range of places along the trail, events that occurred during the expedition, or broader themes that I find particularly significant and compelling, this collection of essays in a certain sense follows Lewis and Clark to the Pacific Ocean and back. But it is not meant to be a chronological retelling of the story. Each essay, I hope, can stand up for itself, and because of that, a careful reader will encounter some occasional moments of overlap between one and another.

Since about half of the collection began as speeches, in converting them into essays (oftentimes by adding more material) I've decided to preserve the more informal tone and grammar of the originals whenever possible—and to extend it throughout all the pieces. My composition teachers from high school and college may wince from time to time, but the English language will survive, just as it survived William Clark's spelling. Likewise, anyone looking here for a scholarly treatment of the Corps of Discovery will be disappointed; fortunately for them, many fine Lewis and Clark books by much better historians than myself already exist and continue to come out.

These essays reflect my opinions, my passions, my interpretations, and my experiences—personal thoughts from someone at least honest enough to admit from the start to be carrying a contagious disease.

I write this as the bicentennial of the Lewis and Clark expedition has just officially opened with a wonderful week at Monticello, a promising beginning for a three-year commemoration during which I hope a wide array of voices and opinions are heard. I also hope it spurs a new generation of Americans to rediscover their country and its history—the dark valleys as well as the peaks, the bracingly cold mornings as well as the golden sunsets. That's what Lewis and Clark did for me. And that's why, after all these years and getting to know them warts and all, I consider them my friends: Lewis, Clark, Drouillard, Sacagawea, York, Sheheke, Cameahwait, Twisted Hair, and on and on—all of them, friends.

Considering people you've never met—and who lived two hundred years ago—as close friends. . . . I believe that's the sign that you're entering stage five.

Dayton Duncan
Walpole, New Hampshire
February 7, 2003

*Scenes of Visionary
Enchantment*
Reflections on
Lewis and Clark

I

An Unsatisfied Curiosity

In May 1997 the newly organized National Council of the Lewis and Clark Bicentennial gathered in Nebraska City, Nebraska, to begin the tireless and selfless task of planning for the two hundredth anniversary of the Corps of Discovery's historic journey. They asked me to deliver the keynote address, from which this essay is taken.

My favorite anecdote from the rich annals of Lewis and Clark and their Corps of Discovery occurred in the spring of 1805. They had passed the mouth of the Yellowstone River, reaching what is now Montana, and were at last pushing forward, farther than any white men had gone before on the mighty Missouri. The riverbanks swarmed with game, and the men were astonished not only at the sheer number of animals but at their relative tameness.

"I think that we Saw at one view nearly one thousand animels," wrote John Ordway, a young sergeant from New Hampshire, using the free-form spelling and grammar practiced by every journalist on the expedition. "They are not to day verry wild for we could go within a 100 yards of them in open view of them before they would run off and then they would go but a Short distance before they would Stop and feed again. . . . Saw a buffaloe Calf which had fell down the bank & could not git up again. we helped it up the bank and it followed us a Short distance."

The first bighorn sheep they had ever seen appeared on cliffs above the river. Geese, swans, pelicans, and cranes flew overhead. Bald eagles were everywhere, and Ordway got the quills from one of them to use in writing his daily journal. Beaver were so numerous that the smacking of their tails on the water kept Clark awake at night. The men briefly made pets out of a litter of wolf pups. "The Game is gitting so pleanty and tame in this country," Ordway eventually wrote, "that Some of the party clubbed them out of their way."

Then he looked down on the ground and saw the biggest paw prints he had ever seen in his life. He and the other men began to get excited—and powerfully curious to discover the animal that could leave such huge tracks. The previous winter, in what is now North Dakota, the Hidatsas had told the explorers about a bear they would meet farther west: big, ferocious, absolutely fearless, and almost impossible to kill. On April 29, Lewis and another hunter finally encountered their first one and killed it. It was the grizzly, never before described for science.

The bear *was* big (weighing at least three hundred pounds though not yet fully grown, Lewis estimated) and, compared to a black bear, "a much more furious and formidable anamal [that] will frequently pursue the hunter when wounded." Nevertheless, Lewis confidently confided to his journal, while he could understand why Indians with bows and arrows might be frightened of one, Americans with muskets had little to fear.

Then they met another grizzly (a "monster" weighing six hundred pounds, nine feet tall from nose to hind feet, claws seven inches long, which took ten shots to kill). And then another, and another. One chased Private William Bratton for over half a mile, even though he had put a bullet through the center of its lungs. Three days later, a hunting party of six men opened fire on yet another grizzly, only to find themselves running for their lives across the open prairie when it turned on them. Two of the hunters-turned-prey tossed their rifles away in panic and jumped off a twenty-foot embankment into the river. The bear jumped in after them. Just at the last moment, a shot to its head brought the beast down. When they dragged him to shore and opened him up, the men found nine musket balls in his body.

Finally, a chastened Lewis wrote in his journal, "I find that the curiossity of our party is pretty well satisfyed with rispect to this anamal."

Over the last twenty years, in pursuit of magazine articles, books, and documentary films, and suffering from a lifelong case of "road fever," I have retraced the Corps of Discovery's route from St. Louis to the Pacific and back four different times. More times than I can count, I've made additional trips to specific locations along their route. I have stood on the deck of a reconstruction of their keelboat as it pushed through the red mist of early dawn and navigated against the Missouri's relentless current, not far from the river's confluence with the Mississippi. In Kansas and Nebraska, I've sweltered in summer heat, been eaten alive by chiggers and mosquitoes. In Iowa, I once witnessed a yellow moon ascend into heaven above the final resting place of Sergeant Charles Floyd. In South Dakota, I watched in wonder as a thousand buffalo thundered over the crest of an undulation in an endless prairie—and then disappeared just as quickly.

One January in North Dakota, when the temperature outside was forty-five degrees below zero and the radio was warning all North Dakotans to stay indoors, I theorized that, well, *we* weren't North Dakotans, so I took a cameraman out at dawn and stood knee deep in snow with him along the banks of the Missouri, shooting footage of a mighty river that had literally frozen solid overnight. (As a reminder of that folly, the frostbite I suffered in my nasal passages that morning still acts up every winter whenever the thermometer approaches zero.)

I've canoed nearly a dozen times through Montana's magnificent White Cliffs, the place Lewis called "seens of visionary inchantment." I've stood in awe at the base of the Great Falls; unfurled a fifteen-star flag at the summit of Lemhi Pass; been caught by surprise by a sudden snow squall in early October in Idaho's Bitterroot Mountains. I've gotten seasick in a boat bobbing and rolling on the swells in the mouth of the Columbia River. And I've spent a truly unforgettable night at Fort Clatsop National Memorial on the Oregon coast, alone with the spirits of the Corps of Discovery. As I read from their journals by candlelight, I could share their mixed feelings of accomplishment and homesickness as they huddled near the Pacific with an entire continent between themselves and their countrymen.

And yet . . . and yet, I must say, "I find *my* curiosity with respect to this expedition is *never* satisfied."

Why is that? What is it about this expedition that keeps drawing me back? I don't believe it can entirely be dismissed as some personal quirk of my own, because I've met too many other people, from all walks of life, with the same abiding fascination and for whom an interest in the Lewis and Clark expedition is the only thing they share in common. Something about this story still grips our national imagination two centuries later. Why? And what does the expedition mean, not just to me and so many other Americans, but to America itself?   ×   ×   ×

It begins, like all enduring stories, with a compelling cast of characters.

There's Meriwether Lewis—the brilliant, but troubled, commander. His journey took him from the comfort of Thomas Jefferson's White House, where he lived at the side of one of our nation's greatest presidents—and greatest minds—to becoming the first United States citizen to reach the Continental Divide, then on to the Pacific and back to Washington DC, where one senator told him it was if he had just returned from the moon. Along the way he wrote some of the finest, most lyrical passages describing an almost indescribable landscape ever written by any explorer—or any writer, for that matter. And his personal journey also took him to a darker rendezvous with his own demons at Grinder's Stand in Tennessee, three years after becoming a national hero, when he took his own life.

There's William Clark—gregarious, steady, trustworthy, a self-taught mapmaker of the highest order, perhaps not as poetic a journalist as his co-commander, but more reliable at recording each day's events and sometimes more enjoyable to read. (He spelled "Sioux" twenty-nine different ways in his journals and in one sentence deployed three variations of "berry.") Clark was the rudder of the expedition, the man who kept things moving forward on an even keel. My own belief is that there could not have been a "Lewis Expedition," even though Jefferson always considered it as such. It was Lewis *and* Clark—the partnership—that succeeded. Lewis *and* Clark—two very different men who nevertheless forged one of the great friendships of all time and are now, rightfully, joined forever in history.

Beyond the two captains lies a supporting cast of almost novelistic diversity and depth, as if this great American nonfiction epic had been written instead by a Dickens or a Tolstoy.

Consider York, Clark's slave, whom the startled Indians, who had never seen a black man, called "Big Medicine"—someone, in other words, who had been raised a slave because of his color, who suddenly found himself in cultures that *honored* him because of his color. Likewise consider Sacagawea, the teenage Shoshone who joined the expedition at the Mandan villages—a young woman traveling with a group of hardened military men, enduring every hardship and facing every danger across every difficult mile with equal fortitude, all the while nursing her baby boy. (Her experience reminds me of what my mother told me was once said of Ginger Rogers: she danced every step that Fred Astaire danced—only backward and in high heels.) Even Dickens or Tolstoy could not have concocted the miraculous plot device of Sacagawea's climactic moment near the Continental Divide, when she is brought in to translate during the crucial negotiations for Shoshone horses—negotiations that would determine the expedition's success or failure—only to learn that the chief who held their fate in his hands was . . . her long-lost brother.

The smaller roles are too many to name, but for the sake of example they range from young George Shannon, whose seeming penchant for getting separated from the others for days at a time undoubtedly gave the fatherly Clark a number of gray hairs, to the more experienced John Colter, destined to become one of America's first "mountain men"—the direct link between the expedition and the next phase of the nation's westward expansion; from John Potts, a German-born miller, to Alexander Hamilton Willard, a blacksmith by trade and scion of a prominent New England family; from Pierre Cruzatte, a one-eyed boatman who played the fiddle while other men danced around the evening campfire and who nearly killed Lewis in a hunting accident by mistaking the captain for an elk, to George Drouillard (like Cruzatte the son of a French father and Indian mother), the master hunter and expert in sign language whom Lewis considered perhaps the most indispensable member of the expedition.

Soldiers and frontiersmen, farmers and tailors, southerners and northerners, immigrants and natives ("natives" in every respect of the word), the expedition reflected everything the new nation had to offer and created its first dramatic example of the military-unit-as-melting-pot, a model Hollywood would later fictionalize to great popular success in so many World War II movies. With the Corps of Discovery, however, fiction isn't necessary. The facts themselves are enough to construct a stirring narrative.

They began the journey as a motley crew—rough and undisciplined, given to disobeying the captains or breaking into the whiskey supply in the middle of the night. For infractions of the rules, they received fifty to a hundred lashes on the bare back. For the inevitable sicknesses—such as dysentery from drinking river water—they were routinely bled by "Doctor" Lewis and then given laxatives of such explosive power that the men no doubt wondered whether the captain's treatments were harder to survive than his punishments. Only three months into the journey—before passing what is now Iowa and having not yet met any unfriendly Indians—two men deserted and another man died, hardly an auspicious start for an expedition planning to span the continent. But by the end, under the extraordinary leadership of the two captains, this unlikely collection of individuals had become a cohesive unit, a community on the move whose sense of shared purpose enabled them to surmount all the odds and achieve great things.

The dramatis personae doesn't end with the Corps of Discovery—a fact too often overlooked. There's an equally diverse and fascinating cast of Indian people the expedition met along the way: from the wise Black Buffalo of the Teton Sioux, who defused a tense standoff that could otherwise have violently ended the expedition before its first summer was over, to the haughty One-Eye of the Hidatsas, who believed the only useful members of the expedition were its blacksmiths and gunsmiths; from Twisted Hair of the Nez Percé, who freely gave the starving explorers food when they most needed it, to Delashelwilt of the Chinooks, who offered to trade for the affections of his women. They and so many others like them left no written record of their own, but they come alive in the expedition journals as vivid reminders that the story of Lewis and Clark has more than one side to it, that it includes much more than the adventures of easterners experiencing the West for the first time, and that Native Americans were never one-dimensional.

The cast would also be incomplete without a person who never made it west of the Allegheny Mountains: Thomas Jefferson. To Lewis he was "the author of our enterprize"; Clark called him "that great Chaructor the Main Spring of the action." The expedition was Jefferson's idea, after all, and through him its story takes on a larger meaning. Intermingled with his dispatching Lewis and Clark, Jefferson purchased the Louisiana Territory, that incredible act of diplomacy that doubled the size of his country, changed the course of American history, and made possible a *continental* United States. We now take it for granted, or naively consider our nation's expansion to the Pacific historically inevitable, but without Jefferson's Louisiana Purchase, our western border could have remained the Mississippi River, St. Louis could still be a "foreign" city, the West could have been carved into other nations, and the United States could have become the North American equivalent of Brazil.

Through Jefferson, the Corps of Discovery is even connected to the race to the moon a century and a half later. Searching for the Northwest Passage, the fabled all-water route across the continent, this was the first official exploration of unknown spaces ever undertaken by the United States. It was prompted by an international race (between Britain, France, Spain, and our nation) for prestige as well as control of those spaces. Jefferson told his rivals the expedition was for science, then sold it to Congress on its potential commercial benefits. It was staffed by the military and employed the latest in technology—an air gun and Harpers Ferry rifles; portable soup, the Tang of the early nineteenth century; and the keelboat, the biggest vessel the Missouri had seen at that point, the Saturn booster rocket that lifted them to the edge of the unknown (the Mandan villages) before dropping back as they pushed forward in smaller vessels. From the unknown, the explorers sent back samples they collected—and although prairie dogs aren't moon rocks, they still generated intense interest among the public. The men returned as national heroes, but some, just like the astronauts who followed, had difficulty adjusting to civilian life after reentry. And, of course, it overran its budget. Throughout it all, substituting for NASA and its scientists and powerful computers, with Monticello as "Mission Control," was the remarkable mind of Thomas Jefferson.

With that, you'd think the story was adequately populated for telling and retelling across the ages: two captains, a black slave, an Indian girl with her baby, and a mixed crew of everyday heroes about to encounter an equally unforgettable array of native characters, while behind the scenes waits not just a president of the United States but a visionary simultaneously setting in motion his nation's push across the continent and, through the model he conceived with the Corps of Discovery, the long trajectory to the moon and beyond.

In terms of raw material, that's more than enough for an epic. But in a stroke of dramaturgical brilliance, Lewis added yet another character to the cast—one guaranteed to hold every schoolchild's (and some adults') interest in the expedition's story when all else fails. Before leaving the East, he purchased a big Newfoundland dog named Seaman and brought it along on the journey.

What else about this story spans the chasm of time, holding our fascination and illuminating our common history?

If you are interested in ethnology, there exists no better record of the amazing diversity of Indian peoples of the West at the dawn of the nineteenth century than the journals of Lewis and Clark. Each tribe's customs, habits, dwellings, food, and other details were studiously recorded in the journals. They are invaluable today, not only to modern scholars but to people in those tribes who wish to reach across two centuries of ceaseless change and recapture part of their own traditions and history.

Some of the tribes they met had never seen white people before, and as Private Joseph Whitehouse wrote of one encounter, "they signed to us that . . . they thought that we had rained down out of the clouds." Other tribes were already well acquainted with whites, such as the Indians of the lower Columbia, who had been in contact with sailors for more than a decade by the time the Corps of Discovery arrived by land. "The persons who usually visit the entrance of this river for the purpose of traffic or hunting I believe are either English or Americans," Lewis wrote. "The Indians inform us they speak the same language with ourselves, and give us proofs of their varacity by repeating many words of English, as musquit, powder, shot, knife, file, damned rascal, sun of a bitch, etc." (That's one thing that hasn't changed in nearly two centuries—a sailor's vocabulary.)

In their journey, Lewis and Clark encountered people from nearly fifty different tribes: people who lived in tepees and followed the buffalo herds on horseback; people who dwelled in permanent villages of earth lodges and tilled the soil; people who lived on rivers and survived on fish; people who braved the ocean, traveling by boat—people who for hundreds of generations had called the land *their* home. People without whose help the expedition would never have succeeded. In return for that help, on behalf of the nation poised to move westward, a grateful Lewis and Clark offered "the hand of unalterable friendship" and promised that "the Great Spirit will smile upon your nation and in future ages will make you outnumber the trees of the forest." Those promises were made in good faith—but as history tells us, and as any visit to a modern Indian reservation will starkly confirm, those who followed Lewis and Clark too often left those promises unfulfilled. If you're searching for a case study in perseverance against continual adversity, the Corps of Discovery certainly provides one; but an even greater example is the survival of native peoples since the time Lewis and Clark passed through their homelands.

If your interest lies in how the natural world has changed in the last two hundred years, again the Lewis and Clark journals are essential, providing a comprehensive baseline inventory of the terrain, wildlife, and botany (even the daily weather) of the West as it existed before the United States overran it—including detailed descriptions of 122 animals and 178 plants never before written down for what Lewis called "the enlightened world."

The unfolding wonders began in earnest in September 1804 as they entered the Great Plains and, as John Ordway marveled, at every turn encountered animals—creatures like antelopes, jackrabbits, mule deer, black-billed magpies, coyotes—"never yet known in [the] U.S. States." They were in what is now Nebraska, only a few hundred miles due north of the geographic center of the Lower Forty-eight. That Ordway and the other journal keepers were already referring to things "back in the States" is, in itself, an exquisitely concise lesson in political history. If our nation's supposed manifest destiny was to overspread the continent, apparently no one had informed Ordway and his fellow explorers.

Like the others, Ordway was especially intrigued by what Lewis called "barking squirrels" and Clark referred to as "ground rats." Ordway's journal for September 7 names them prairie dogs—and history has preferred his choice over the captains'. The expedition caught one alive, somehow sustained it in a cage over the winter, and sent it downriver with the keelboat the next spring to St. Louis. From there it rode a boat to New Orleans, then was shipped around the tip of Florida and up the Atlantic, arriving on the East Coast on August 12, 1805, the very day that Lewis was ascending Lemhi Pass to reach the Continental Divide and the nation's new western boundary. Jefferson kept the little animal in the White House awhile, then sent it on to Philadelphia for public display in Charles Willson Peale's natural science museum, located, of all places, in Independence Hall. Where the Declaration of Independence had first been read aloud, a prairie dog added its distinctive bark and whistle.

Prairie dog villages covering ten acres of ground were astounding enough, but beyond them Lewis and Clark crossed a landscape filled with wildlife in ways none of us will ever see. Grizzly bears and elk living not in isolated numbers in remote mountains, but openly on the plains. Buffalo herds numbering, Clark estimated at one spot, nearly twenty thousand; herds that made him stop his canoes on the Yellowstone for hours as the beasts crossed the river. California condors flying overhead near the Pacific. The Columbia River choked with salmon.

The expedition traveled the entire length of the Missouri and substantial stretches of the Snake and Columbia—*up*stream as well as down—when those rivers were undammed and untamed. They went through grasslands that had never experienced a fence or a plow, forests that had never been touched by a saw. "This immense river," Lewis wrote on his way up the Missouri, "waters one of the fairest portions of the globe. Nor do I believe there is in the universe a similar extent of country." A little farther on, still caught in the thrall of his surroundings, he added: "It seemed as if those seens of visionary inchantment would never have an end." Sadly, many of those scenes *have* ended, although with some searching a few can still be located. But all of them can be found—with great vividness and immediacy—in the expedition's journals.

The journals themselves are another reason (perhaps the principal reason) why the Lewis and Clark story remains so captivating. They are much more than a recitation of the miles traveled and the route followed by the nation's first expedition from sea to sea; more than a firsthand treatise on native peoples; more than a rich database of the natural world that awaited a westering nation—though any one of those would make them invaluable to history and science. Full of quirky spellings and uneven punctuations, but written with a directness by men whose fallible humanity becomes as endearing as their unmistakable heroism is inspiring, the journals invite us to become members of the expedition and join in the journey.

Stretching from St. Louis to the mouth of the Columbia, the Lewis and Clark trail is, in essence, a four-thousand-mile museum through the heart of the country, accessible to anyone who chooses to visit any part of it. But that literal accessibility pales in comparison to the unique access offered through the journals. They connect our imaginations. With the journals along on the modern trail, we can close our eyes and "see" what Lewis and Clark saw, mentally strip away the last two centuries, and somehow touch their experience. Even armchair travelers find themselves pulled in. As the novelist Larry McMurtry has observed, Lewis and Clark and the other journalists of the expedition "accomplished the one essential thing that writers must do: they brought the reader along with them, up that meandering river and over those snowy peaks."

Sent by a young nation that itself would soon embark toward the Pacific, Lewis and Clark took our first transcontinental "road trip," and since that time road trips have held a special place in the American imagination. From Twain's *Adventures of Huckleberry Finn* to Kerouac's *On the Road*, Steinbeck's *Travels With Charley*, and McMurtry's own *Lonesome Dove*, tales of journeys are what we have most readily responded to, perhaps because journeying is so intertwined with our past. "We proceeded on"—the most recurrent phrase in the expedition's journals—also summarizes much of our history.

More than anything else, this is a great *story*—"something simple and immortal," the historian Bernard DeVoto once called it: "a tableau of courage and endurance in clear light, one of the world's heroic stories that seem like myths." Operating as our own national *Odyssey*, it is not only a great epic adventure; it is also filled with hundreds of smaller, equally great stories and moments.

Sad moments—like the death of Sergeant Floyd during the first summer, near what is now Sioux City, Iowa. "I am going away," he whispered to Clark, "I want you to write me a letter." Then, before he could dictate it, he died; and the Corps of Discovery buried their comrade on a bluff that still carries his name. With the advantage of time, we know now that Floyd would be the only expedition member to perish (a remarkable testament to the captains' leadership), but none of the men gathered around his makeshift grave in August 1804 knew it. As they paid their last respects before moving on, it's easy to imagine each one of them thinking, "How many more of these ceremonies will we have? And will one of them be for me?"

Playful moments—like holding footraces and games with the Nez Percé to get in shape for the return crossing of the daunting Bitterroot Mountains. They even played a game of prison base, a precursor of baseball, although the journals don't reveal if the Indians won or lost this spring training exhibition.

Moments of incredible drama—the tense confrontation with the Teton Sioux; Private Richard Windsor hanging on for dear life on a slippery cliff over the Marias River; a flash flood near Great Falls that nearly swept Clark, York, Charbonneau, Sacagawea, and her baby to their deaths; the deadly fight with the Blackfeet; and the exultant moment at Lemhi Pass when Lewis finally reached the Continental Divide, expecting at last to discover the elusive water route to the Pacific, only to be confronted by an unimaginably discouraging vista: endless mountains where mountains were not supposed to exist.

Then came the suffering—physical and psychological—of crossing those unexpected mountains. It was snowing and cold. There was no game to speak of. They ate some of their horses; they even ate some of their candles to survive. "I have been wet and as cold in every part as I ever was in my life, indeed I was at one time fearfull my feet would freeze in the thin Mockirsons which I wore," Clark wrote. "Men all wet cold and hungary. . . . To describe the road of this day would be a repition of yesterday except the Snow which made it much worse." Two days later, camping at what the expedition named Hungry Creek, John Ordway summarized their geographic predicament: "The Mountains continues as fer as our eyes could extend. They extend much further than we expe[c]ted."

At Lemhi Pass, a myth that had begun with Columbus—the myth of an easy Northwest Passage—had been mortally wounded. But in the Bitterroots, in the fallen trees and steep slopes and cold camps without food, in those mountains that Patrick Gass called "the most terrible mountains I ever beheld," the myth finally died, only to be replaced by something equally powerful. Through their failed attempt to find a Northwest Passage, the Corps of Discovery nonetheless succeeded in crossing the continent and then returned home with what DeVoto called "the first report on the West, on the United States over the hill and beyond the sunset, on the province of the American future."

There are other significant moments of American history within the expedition's story—and, I think, important lessons to be learned from them. In a nation that celebrates individual achievement, the Corps of Discovery succeeded through cooperation and teamwork. The captains broke military protocol and shared the command equally. They broke it again at the mouth of the Columbia, when the expedition needed to make the crucial decision of where to spend the winter. Instead of simply issuing an order, the captains decided that the Corps of Discovery would face this issue the same way it had faced every hardship along the way. They would face it *together*—with each person casting a vote.

There they were, this remarkably diverse microcosm of their young nation, beyond the fixed boundaries of the United States, having crossed a continent their countrymen would spend the rest of the century expanding across, and this decision was made democratically, by involving everyone. York voted—a half century before slaves were emancipated and enfranchised "back in the states." Sacagawea voted—more than a hundred years before women *or* Indians were granted the full rights of citizenship "back in the states." It was, I believe, an extraordinary and powerfully symbolic moment, a moment that even now—perhaps now most particularly—reminds us of an essential American promise: from diversity, strength; from different origins, a common destination. *E pluribus unum.*

In some things, it took our country fifty or a hundred years to catch up with Lewis and Clark and to follow their example. In some other things— like their relations with Indians—we never did.

But the example is still there. A Corps of Discovery that stuck to its job in the face of one obstacle after another; a Corps of Discovery willing to bear any hardship to inch ahead, even when it seemed their goal was impossibly out of reach. The struggle up the seemingly endless Missouri. The uncertainty—and potential for disaster—at every unexpected fork in the river. The month-long portage of the Great Falls, with violent hail storms, broiling sun, maddening bugs, prickly pears, and a rough, broken ground that was wearing out their moccasins every two days. Dragging their canoes up the shallow, stony Jefferson and Beaverhead Rivers. The terrible ordeal over the Bitterroots. And those three discouraging weeks near the mouth of the Columbia, pinned down by storms, their clothes rotting and supplies dwindling, just a few miles from the ocean they had already traveled so many miles and suffered through so much to behold.

They captured it all in the three ordinary words that show up again and again in their journals: "We proceeded on"—a simple phrase neatly describing the only way to cross a continent at fourteen miles a day; the only way to push forward and expand the boundaries of knowledge; the only way to overcome daily disappointments and constant barriers to progress and reach a better tomorrow. One step at a time. "We proceeded on."

What does the Lewis and Clark expedition mean to America? What *doesn't* it mean? It means so much because there is so much to it. And because, through the journals, it is so accessible, so approachable, so human.

By November 1805 the Corps of Discovery had at last reached the Pacific, having become the first American citizens to cross the continent by land. Far from home and trapped against the rocks by a relentless Pacific storm that Clark called "tempestous and horiable," they nevertheless found a tangible way to commemorate their remarkable achievement: they began carving their names into the trunks of trees. (Judging from Clark's journal entries, it would seem they did it so many times that few trees near their sodden campsites escaped their knife blades.)

With each cut they seemed to be boasting, "I was here. I made it." Yet there also may have been something less boastful and more pleading in each stroke of their blades, something of a prayer that asked, "Remember me."

Those tree markings—and in most cases the trees themselves—have long since disappeared. But the story that the Corps of Discovery left behind survives. It remains embedded in our national consciousness, and each generation etches it again with a fresh flourish.

Across two centuries of separation, through their words and their example, they still speak to us—reaching from the past, yet calling us toward the next horizon. We can still follow their trail and open their journals to reexperience their stirring adventure. We can find inspiration in their perseverance and courage. We can be reminded by them of what we as a people are capable of—for good *and* for ill. We can mourn what's been lost in the time between their journey and ours, perhaps dedicate ourselves to honoring their promises or to restoring something of the scenes of visionary enchantment they beheld with such awe. We can applaud and maybe even try to emulate their bond of friendship and community.

And we can learn what Lewis and Clark and the Corps of Discovery learned for themselves at the mouth of the Columbia so many years ago. All of us leave some sort of mark on the trail as "we proceed on." But long after that mark has vanished, what's remembered is the spirit with which we made our journey.

2

Great Expectations: Lewis in Philadelphia

This essay comes from a speech I was asked to give in Philadelphia at the annual meeting of the Lewis and Clark Trail Heritage Foundation in August 2003. Without drawing too close a connection between myself and Meriwether Lewis, I can still remember my own culture shock and intellectual awaking upon arriving in Philadelphia in 1967, a young man from a small town in Iowa about to begin my own studies at the University of Pennsylvania. And as a writer, I can also sympathize with Lewis's predicament at the end of his journey—the easy, exhilarating confidence that surrounds the start of any book, quickly followed by those terrible long moments when the words refuse to come and crushing doubts rush in to fill the void.

Two hundred years ago, Meriwether Lewis was working at a "desk job" in Washington DC when his boss, President Thomas Jefferson, made an intriguing offer. Would Lewis be willing, Jefferson asked, to give up his duties as the president's personal secretary and instead do something no American had ever done before? Would he lead an expedition across the continent, all the way to the Pacific Ocean? Map the unmapped? Discover the undiscovered? On behalf of his young nation, would he find the great prize that every explorer since Columbus had been seeking—the fabled Northwest Passage—and open up the wealth and empire it promised for the United States?

Clearly, the prospect Jefferson was dangling in front of his young protégé was more than the chance to get away from paperwork in the White House; this was the opportunity of a lifetime, a chance for adventure and fame, perhaps even immortality. Lewis was twenty-eight years old at the time, a promising army officer, single and ambitious. It's hardly surprising that he immediately accepted Jefferson's offer.

What may seem a little surprising, however, is what he did next. He went to college—and he went shopping. On the verge of departing for places where, in Lewis's words, "the foot of civilized man had never trodden," the young Columbus headed first for the nation's largest and most sophisticated city at the dawn of the nineteenth century, Philadelphia, the undisputed cradle of learning for the United States. There, in the bustling Athens of America, he would prepare himself for the wilderness.

As he rode into the city from Lancaster in early May 1803, Lewis had, in effect, already embarked on his voyage of discovery. The metropolis of Philadelphia would have caused as much shock and wonder to this Virginia country boy as would the Great Falls of the Missouri two years later. At the time, fewer than ten cities in the entire nation had populations over 10,000 — none of them in Lewis's home state and certainly not Washington DC, still more of a frontier outpost than capital city. With roughly 45,000 residents (more than 60,000 counting the two contiguous but as yet unincorporated townships), Philadelphia was ten times the size of almost any town Lewis had ever visited. "If I can make it here," he probably told himself, "I'll make it anywhere."

It's impossible, of course, to know what was going through his mind. But it's easy enough to imagine. The constant clatter of horses and wagons on the cobblestone streets, echoing off the tall buildings; the clamoring crowds of people in the densely packed markets and shops; the great, unending hubbub of a busy port near the city's pulsing heart—these were new experiences that would have placed Lewis in a state of sensory overload.

Add to that the initial purpose of his visit. He had just been entrusted by the president of the United States with a mission of profound national and international importance—at the moment, a mission so sensitive that its true objective was still being kept secret. He had already been to the army arsenal at Harpers Ferry, supervising the construction of a collapsible iron boat frame he had invented—an ingenious device he intended to unveil at the Missouri's farthest reaches, tote a short distance across the Great Divide, and then ride triumphantly down the Columbia to the Pacific. And he had just spent three weeks in Lancaster, Pennsylvania, with Andrew Ellicott, learning how to use celestial navigation to ascertain latitude and longitude—a skill with which he intended to nail down the precise location of the elusive Northwest Passage. Now he had arrived in the teeming hive of economic and intellectual activity that was Philadelphia, carrying letters of introduction from the president to undertake a series of private tutorials from the nation's most brilliant scientists.

Given the situation and the setting—and given the nature of Meriwether Lewis—I think it's probable that he rode down Market Street feeling a little full of himself, as young men on important missions are apt to be. One thing is absolutely certain: every cell of his agile mind would have been on high alert and tingling with unbridled expectations. So it is at the start of any adventure, in that exquisite moment when every hope and every plan have yet to collide with reality and therefore are incapable of failing; when every new horizon glistens with promise; when the gap between what you *think* you know and what you *really* know is at its widest.

The tutorials began immediately, all of them under men associated with the University of Pennsylvania, members of the esteemed American Philosophical Society, and Jefferson's acquaintances.

Talk about unbridled expectations: with Caspar Wistar, the nation's leading expert on fossils, Lewis discussed the possibility of encountering mastodons somewhere in the distant West! Wistar's specialty was anatomy—he had published America's first textbook on the subject—but like his friend Jefferson he was fascinated with paleontology and believed that the interior of the continent still sheltered living, breathing prehistoric animals. After his days under Wistar's tutelage, as he slept in his Philadelphia boardinghouse, perhaps Lewis dreamed of tracking a woolly mammoth to the source of the Missouri and bringing it down at the Continental Divide—thereby simultaneously becoming the first person ever to find the Northwest Passage and the first person in ten thousand years to kill one of the giant beasts. In that dream, the carcass no doubt would then be loaded into his iron-framed boat and transported to the Pacific shore.

From Robert Patterson, vice-provost of the university and a renowned mathematician who lived on the college grounds, Lewis received additional instruction in the painstaking and complicated tasks of determining latitudes and longitudes. Apparently this was not Lewis's strongest subject, and Patterson recommended a few extra days of instruction before passing him.

Benjamin Smith Barton provided the training that turned out to be the most useful on Lewis's expedition: lessons on how to identify, collect, and preserve botanical and zoological specimens. Barton himself was no stranger to youthful high achievement. At twenty-three he had become the nation's first professor of natural history and botany; now, in his mid-forties, he had just published the nation's first botany textbook and (like two of Lewis's other tutors) had recently been elected to the medical staff of Pennsylvania Hospital, also the nation's first. Whether he gave any advice on the proper techniques for dissecting and preserving a recently killed five-ton mastodon is unknown, but he did sell Lewis a copy of his new botany text for six dollars, loaned him a book called *The History of Louisiana,* and even talked briefly of accompanying his eager student as far as Illinois for additional training in the field.

And then there was Dr. Benjamin Rush. Given the advantage of hindsight from two hundred additional years of medical breakthroughs, it's hard now not to poke some fun at a doctor who believed that the medical cure-all for any ailment, from fevers to dislocated bones, was the same: draw some blood from the patient and administer a few doses of Rush's bilious pills— eruptively powerful laxatives better known as Rush's Thunderbolts, fifty dozen of which Lewis purchased for five dollars and then liberally dispensed to his fellow explorers at every turn during the next two and a half years, with no noticeable benefit to their health but surely putting their intestines at some risk, not to mention the water quality of the Missouri and Columbia watersheds.

But in 1803, Dr. Rush was without question the nation's eminent physician and was passing along medical knowledge that for its time was "cutting edge" both figuratively and, in the case of the bloodletting, literally. Rush was also revered as one of the signers of the Declaration of Independence, an enduring feat he had achieved at the age of thirty-one—Jefferson, the author, had been thirty-two—facts which no doubt reminded Lewis that in terms of great accomplishments his own biological clock was ticking.

Lewis obviously held Rush in great esteem, as his slavish devotion to the efficacies of bloodletting and purging a patient's innards would prove during the expedition. But it's worth noting that the good doctor had a number of other suggestions for maintaining good health, enumerated in a long list, which the Corps of Discovery almost uniformly ignored on their trek across the continent:

• "In difficult & laborious enterprises & marches," Rush warned, "*eating sparingly* will enable you to bear them with less fatigue & less danger to your health." Lewis and his men, on the other hand, preferred a daily portion of nine pounds of buffalo meat—per person—to fuel their labors across the Great Plains. They certainly ate sparingly in crossing the Bitterroot Mountains, but that was by necessity, not choice, and during the ordeal Lewis noted their health falling away with each day.

- "Washing the feet every morning in *cold* water," Rush advised, "will conduce very much to fortify them against the action of cold." I wonder if Lewis read this one to his troops each morning in western Montana when the men bitterly complained about having to wade into the icy Jefferson River and drag their canoes through water that had been mountain snowbanks only a few days earlier.
- "The less spirit you use the better." They ran out of whiskey on the Fourth of July, 1805, about halfway into their journey. No further comment necessary.
- If your feet are chilled, "it will be useful to wash them with a little spirit." I imagine any man who poured whiskey on his feet during the expedition would have been court-martialed by the rest of the group and sentenced to one hundred lashes.

I'm sure the men would have appreciated Rush's injunction:

- "When you feel the least indisposition, do not attempt to overcome it by labour or marching. *Rest* in a horizontal position."

But the captains, it seems, did not pass along this advice. (Nearly a century later, however, another famous American apparently adopted this part of Rush's Rules for Good Health. Mark Twain said that whenever he got an urge to exercise, he liked to lie down until the feeling passed.)

When he wasn't studying botany, mathematics, paleontology, and medicine with his tutors, Lewis was busy spending money. Congress had secretly appropriated $2,500 for the expedition, and Lewis left virtually all of it in the tills of Philadelphia merchants. At the time, Lewis thought his expedition would include only fifteen men—another expectation soon to be shattered; the size of the group leaving St. Louis a year later would be three times larger—but outfitting even the smaller number for an anticipated two-year journey (oops, one more overly optimistic estimate) proved to be a prodigious undertaking. With the aid of Israel Whelan, the purveyor of public supplies, he appears to have left no store in the business district untouched.

They got twenty-five dollars' worth of fishing tackle from George Lawton; ninety dollars of medical supplies—including Rush's pills and lancets for bloodletting—from the druggists Gillaspy and Strong; flannel and calico shirts (at roughly $1.50 each) from Matilda Chapman; two pounds of Hyson tea from Priscilla Logan; and thirty gallons of strong spirits from

David Jackson—enough, if Lewis intended to follow Dr. Rush's formula, to provide two gallons for foot washings for each man.

It's often said that the $250.75 Lewis paid the watchmaker Thomas Parker for a new chronometer (a timepiece necessary for calculating longitude and latitude) was his single biggest purchase. But he shelled out $289.50 to Francis Bellet for 193 pounds of "portable soup," that horrid reduction of beef stew to be used when no other food was at hand. The chronometer wound down early in the expedition, making its readings suspect, and the men despised the portable soup so much that they turned to horse flesh and dog meat instead when game was not available, so an argument could be made that the money for both items might have been better spent.

On blue beads, for instance. Lewis paid a total of $669.50 to a variety of merchants for Indian presents—combs and looking glasses, silk ribbons and ornamental bells, thousands of sewing needles and fifteen dozen scissors, brass kettles, corn mills, 130 rolls of tobacco, pipe tomahawks, and colorful beads by the pound. Used as gifts and later as barter for food, these supplies would be essentially depleted by the time the expedition reached the Pacific, where blue beads—of which they had none—commanded the highest exchange rate. I'm sure more than one of the men pondered how much easier life would have been at Fort Clatsop if the $289.50 spent on the 193 pounds of inedible portable soup (that's $1.50 per pound) had instead been put toward cheap blue beads back in Philadelphia.

They would have been grateful, however, especially on those sticky summer nights along the Missouri, for the $15.50 their captain had dedicated to buying mosquito curtains. And the $182.08 spent on arms and ammunition—augmented by supplies from the government arsenal—provided them with more than enough lead and powder to survive the journey.

In all, Lewis accumulated 3,500 pounds of supplies and spent $2,160.14 during his shopping spree in the big city. Had he stayed any longer, I'm sure the chamber of commerce would have gladly named him Man of the Year. If he was worried about spending most of Congress's appropriation so quickly, he never mentioned it. He had little reason to pinch pennies; after all, his mentor, Thomas Jefferson, was renowned for often living beyond his means—in fact, he had dispatched Lewis for some personal purchases in Philadelphia: bottles of fine wine, a leopard skin for saddle covers, watch repairs, fleecy socks, and a robe of Peruvian sheep's wool—and upon Lewis's return to Washington would present him with an extraordinary, open-ended letter of credit, personally signed by the president and promising the full faith of the United States for requisitioning any additional supplies or services he might need on the journey he was about to begin.

Before leaving Philadelphia, Lewis also received a rough draft of Jefferson's meticulous instructions for the expedition. Grand expectations again. Anyone reading them today has to be impressed with the breathtakingly broad intellectual ambitions Jefferson held for his Corps of Discovery in terms of ethnology, geography, zoology, botany, mineralogy, and meteorology, not to mention his clearly enunciated goals for the expedition's impact on relations with western Indian tribes and the delicate balance of power between them, the United States, and foreign powers in the all-important international trade in furs. This had not been conceived as some simple wilderness endurance test, as Lewis already understood and as his time with the Pennsylvania savants attested.

But seeing it all laid out on page after page after page of detailed orders must have brought home to Lewis as never before the daunting prospect before him, if he hoped to live up to the great faith his president had placed in him. At a time when Lewis's mind was already reeling from azimuths and lunar timetables, from the Latin nomenclature of species classification and medical procedures, and from unending checklists of supplies and the buzz of a busy city, Jefferson's intimidatingly specific instructions must have given him at least a momentary pause to wonder if he was capable of rising to what had become a momentous challenge as well as a historic opportunity.

I believe this because immediately upon his return from Philadelphia Lewis would contact his former commander William Clark, a seasoned frontier officer four years his elder, and make the astonishing offer of co-command of the expedition. He had just purchased supplies for fifteen men, and now he planned on two of them being captains? That suggests at least the seeds of doubt in an outwardly confident young man.

Yet as he rode out of Philadelphia for a brief stop in Washington before finally setting off for the unknown West, the journey ahead still resided firmly in his dreams, a happy string of untested expectations. The trip would take just two years. Fifteen men would be enough. The iron boat would be a success and become recognized as a revolutionary invention. Mastodons, mammoths, and who knew what other exotic species would be brought back as trophies. The Northwest Passage was waiting for its coordinates to be fixed by a well-trained, well-supplied American Columbus. Philadelphia, the nation, and the world would soon know his name and sing his praises.

And if he couldn't make these dreams come true on his own, maybe William Clark could help him.   × × ×

The Meriwether Lewis who returned to Philadelphia in the late spring of 1807 was a different man. He had packed a lifetime's worth of experience into four years, leading a group of men across a rugged continent and back, molding them into a team and—with Clark's invaluable assistance—holding them together in the face of innumerable obstacles. Armed with the theories and book learning he had acquired at the feet of Jefferson and the Philadelphia scholars, he had ventured into the dreamworld where the sun sets to test their great expectations in the harsh light of midday. And as those expectations wilted one by one, he had been forced to dig within himself for new answers, been required to improvise, to trust his instincts, and, far from the comfort of libraries and classrooms, to make decisions that would determine not just success or failure, but life or death.

The journey had taken him three years, not two, and had required up to forty-five men, not fifteen—but he had brought them all back safely except one, who had died from causes no medicine of the time could have cured. The iron boat—his beloved *Experiment,* as he called it—had leaked water its first day and had to be buried in sight of the mountains without ever being used; no matter, he had crossed the mountains without it. He had learned there was no Northwest Passage, and no mastodons either, but he had brought back descriptions (and some specimens) of 178 plants and 122 animals new to science, and he now possessed firsthand information on what had previously been a great blank in maps of the continent. He had learned, his president proudly told the nation, "the character of the country."

And in the crucible of leadership he had gone through to accomplish it all, I imagine he had also learned something about himself and his own character. At the very least he had learned to rely on Clark, his trustworthy co-commander and now his closest friend in the world.

One of his great expectations had been met. When he arrived in Philadelphia in April, his name was on everyone's lips. *Governor* Lewis was his title now, having been chosen by Jefferson and confirmed by the Senate to administer the vast new territory west of the Mississippi. As a further reward, Congress had given him sixteen hundred acres of his choosing and four thousand dollars in double pay to spend as he saw fit (twice the amount in government funds he had brought to the big city on his first trip). Four years had made quite a difference for Meriwether Lewis.

He sat for Charles Willson Peale, who wanted to add Lewis's portrait to the "Gallery of Illustrious Personages" displayed in Independence Hall. Peale later begged to be allowed to make a wax figure of the national hero, and Lewis consented—then consented again when Charles B. J. F. de St. Mémin asked to draw his likeness in crayon.

Lewis's elevated status was equally evident by his attendance at three meetings of the American Philosophical Society, which had elected him as a member in absentia during his journey to the sea. Acolyte no more, he took his place alongside his former tutors Patterson, Wistar, Rush, and Barton. No doubt he derived special pleasure in writing a personal inscription in the borrowed book he returned to Barton, having taken it to the Pacific and back—*The History of Louisiana,* now woefully out of date because of his own achievements.

He lingered in the city through May and June and was there when Philadelphia celebrated the nation's thirtieth birthday on the Fourth of July. Perhaps he went to Independence Hall, the birthing room of the Republic, and in Peale's museum on the second floor told the story of July 4, 1804, when he had presided over the first Independence Day ever celebrated west of the Mississippi, and then, as the crowd eagerly leaned forward to hear more, regaled everyone with the hilarious tale of how it took the efforts of his entire crew to capture the solitary prairie dog that he had sent back, live, to Jefferson, and which only recently had been the museum's greatest curiosity. Maybe he strolled the few blocks to St. Peter's Church—where a handful of Osage orange seedlings, which Lewis had collected in Missouri, were now growing on the edge of the cemetery—and told whoever would listen of a place just beyond Missouri where you could turn in every direction and see forever, without a single tree between yourself and the far horizon.

To be sure, he was no longer an anonymous army officer, the country boy wandering the streets of the metropolis, but just as in 1803, Lewis's mind was once again on fire with great expectations. He wanted a wife—and as the nation's newest celebrity he had every reason to believe he would find a proper one when he returned home to Virginia. As the governor of the Louisiana Territory, once he reached St. Louis he could anticipate being in on the ground floor of a land rush and economic boom in this newest section of the country, could rightfully dream of adding to his sixteen hundred acres and becoming wealthy in the burgeoning American fur trade along the Missouri.

Most of all—and this was the main reason he had returned to Philadelphia and spent so much time in the city—he expected to cement his place in history (and make still more money) by publishing an account of his historic journey. "It is a work that seems to excite much attention," Charles Willson

Peale wrote to a friend that spring, "& will I hope have a great sale & give considerable profit to this bold adventurer."

After signing a contract for the work with the Conrad publishing company on Chestnut Street, Lewis paid a man named Varnum ten dollars to begin distributing a prospectus to potential subscribers. It promised three volumes of nearly five hundred pages each, plus a "map of good size" of "the most direct and practicable rout across the continent of North America."

The first volume would be a narrative of the journey, with descriptions of "some of the most remarkable places in those hitherto unknown wilds of America." The second would focus on geography, the Indian tribes and their customs, prospects for the fur trade, and a weather diary noting the daily rise and fall of the major rivers. The third would be "confined exclusively to scientific research"—botany, zoology, mineralogy, some thoughts on the origins of the prairies, and why the Missouri was so muddy.

All three volumes were to be lavishly illustrated, especially the final one, "as it is intended that every subject of natural history which is entirely new, and of which there are a considerable number, shall be accompanied by an appropriate engraving." The first two volumes were being offered for a combined price of ten dollars; the third (with more engravings) would cost eleven dollars by itself; the map was priced at ten dollars.

Having publicly promised to have the first volume available by the first of January, with the others to follow in quick succession, Lewis busied himself with preparations in Philadelphia. Peale agreed to draw many of the natural history portraits for the final volume, augmented by Alexander Wilson, a specialist in bird drawings. Mémin was hired for $83.50 to draw the Indian portraits. John James Barralet was paid $40.00 for two engravings of waterfalls. And Ferdinand Rudolph Hassler, a mathematician, received $100.00 to double-check and correct Lewis's calculations of longitude and latitude.

The actual writing, on the other hand, was not a job he could so easily farm out. Two other members of the Corps of Discovery—Sergeant Patrick Gass and Private Robert Frazer—had already advertised their intention to publish accounts of the expedition, and Lewis, presumably out of both monetary concern and a legitimate reporter's fear of being "scooped," had gone to great lengths to assure the public that he, the captain of the enterprise, was the only person in a position to present the complete story—not just the adventurous tale of crossing the continent, but the important details about new animals and plants, the proper coordinates of significant landmarks, the diplomatic nuances of relations with a multiplicity of Indian tribes. After all, it was *Lewis* who had specifically prepared himself for this very task, however briefly, at the feet of the nation's top minds in Philadelphia—certainly not an Irish carpenter like Gass, nor a lowly private like Frazer. Not even Clark— equal in all other respects, Lewis happily conceded, to every credit for the expedition's success—was capable of writing the official version of the Corps of Discovery's epic, with the necessary literary flourishes in describing a new landscape and with the correct scientific background in describing new species.

This was something Lewis needed to do himself. Jefferson expected it of him. The world was waiting. It was now July, and the first volume was due for publication in six months.

Did Lewis harbor any doubts this time that his expectations—of romance, wealth, and literary fame—might be unrealistic? Had his experiences in the West taught him not to believe too heavily in dreams hatched in Philadelphia boardinghouses?

Somehow, I think not. We all know, because history tells us, that his repeated attempts at romance were about to fail miserably; that his spec- ulations in Missouri lands would be equally unsuccessful; that within two years he would die by his own hand, unmarried, heavily in debt, cornered by the cruel and fickle circumstances of life, surrounded by the hounds of self-doubt, and feeling helpless to do anything about it except to hope that Clark might come to his rescue. We know also that with him on that sad night would be the original journals from the expedition, still in their raw, unedited state, with not one single word written for the great book that he had so confidently predicted would take six months to complete.

We know all this, but in the summer of 1807, Lewis didn't—and had little reason to suspect. He was, after all, wiser and more experienced than he had been during his dreamy student and shopping days in Philadelphia four years earlier. Could finding a wife be harder than finding your way through the Bitterroot Mountains, that jumble of peaks whose "eternal snows" had mocked the dream of a Northwest Passage? Could managing to amass wealth in a boomtown be more difficult than figuring out how to keep a company of men supplied with necessities after all your trade goods had become depleted thousands of miles from home? And if you had conquered a continent and filled in its blank spaces, could filling in blank sheets of paper really be much of a challenge?

Lewis's first experience in Philadelphia had taught him the values of preparation and purposeful study. Then the expedition had taught him that you can't anticipate and prepare for every eventuality fate throws in your path. Expectations can be easily overblown. But at the start of any worthwhile endeavor, great expectations are sometimes the fuel that gets you moving.

So as he rode out of Philadelphia for the second—and final—time, I imagine the future seemed brighter than ever for Meriwether Lewis, brighter even than it had in 1803, when he had been an inexperienced captain, not a seasoned explorer, governor, and national hero. In his mind, he probably could see himself with a beautiful wife and happy family, living a prosperous and contented life in St. Louis, with his good friend Clark nearby. And tomorrow, he could tell himself, he would finally get started on the first chapter of his masterpiece.

3

Days of Discovery

Over the course of many years on the trail, it's been my pleasure to get to know men and women who devote their free time to reenacting Lewis and Clark's experience as authentically as possible for "living history" demonstrations—people who, bless them, like to put on buckskins and spend a weekend hollowing out a dugout canoe or setting up a campsite on a mosquito-infested riverbank. As a proud, though strictly honorary, member of many of their organizations, I salute them and dedicate this essay to them.

America's greatest expedition got under way on a dreary day in the midst of a hard spring rain. On the afternoon of May 14, 1804, a small crowd gathered on the Illinois side of the Mississippi River to watch "The Corps of Volunteers for North Western Discovery" set off from their winter encampment in a big keelboat and two smaller pirogues. A booming shot from the small cannon on the keelboat's bow signaled their departure. Perhaps a farewell shout rose up from the shore and was answered by the men who, according to the journals, were in "high spirits" despite the rain that must have soaked them to the skin and made every chore more difficult and uncomfortable to accomplish.

There would have been a flurry of activity and more noise—barked orders, the grunts of men straining into setting poles to get things moving out of the shallow water, then the creak and splash of oars. The boats' sails were finally hoisted, and the canvas sheets would have flapped before they filled and stiffened from a gentle northeast breeze that pushed the small flotilla across the Mississippi and into the mouth of the Missouri, whose distant and mysterious source was an important yet intermediate goal on the explorers' ambitious itinerary. Final destination: the Pacific Ocean—and back. Miles traveled that first day: four and a half. No one had promised it would be easy.

It may be an abject admission of imaginative failure on my part, but the truth is that I had already followed the Lewis and Clark trail several times and had written one book about it before the scene of that first day ever really occurred to me in any detail. My initial interest in the expedition had focused on other things—the grand adventure of it all, Meriwether Lewis's complicated personality and tragic fate, and the highlight reel of dramatic moments. As I got to know the story a little better, my background in politics drew me toward examining the extraordinary vote the expedition took at the mouth of the Columbia, as well as toward chronicling the choices our country had made that accounted for the difference between the West that Lewis and Clark experienced and the one I encountered so many years later. Following their trail awakened in me a profound fascination with American history. I fell in love with the western landscape. My abiding joy in the open road found a new excuse for exercise.

All of which is just another way of saying that I usually skipped over the day-to-day stuff. Maybe it was an old habit from my reporting days: news, by definition, focuses not on everyday occurrences but on either the out-of-the-ordinary or the significant event, and that's where my first instincts took me with Lewis and Clark. In my mind they departed on May 14, 1804, "under a jentle brease" (Clark's spelling was more interesting than the fact of the wind)—and that was enough. I was ready to fast-forward to something with a little more action, something a little more unusual. Private Alexander Willard's court-martial and subsequent lashings on July 12, perhaps, or Sergeant Charles Floyd's death a month later (even though it initially seemed rather undramatic, being from sickness, after all, rather than a bullet to the chest or a buffalo stampede), or those amazing days in early September when every animal seemed to be a new species, or the standoff farther upriver with the Teton Sioux, when swords were drawn, arrows were notched, the cannon was readied for a much less celebratory purpose, and the fate of enterprise hung in the balance. Then on to being chased across Montana by grizzly bears, or facing starvation in the Idaho mountains, or . . .

Impatient for Lewis and Clark to reach the next moment of particular interest, I often skimmed through the journals to get there faster myself, and in doing so unconsciously I sped them along without fully appreciating how long it actually took them, how much effort it required, and how significant the sheer day-to-dayness of the journey was to understanding their experience. From the mouth of the Missouri to the Three Forks that form it turned out to be 2,848 miles, according to Clark's estimates. The total distance they traveled to reach the Pacific was 4,162 miles. Which meant the return was another 4,162 miles. This was a journey of 8,324 miles that began with a first day that covered four and a half miles. And then that day was followed by 862 more. Obviously, I was overlooking something.

I realized my oversight after my friend Ken Burns and I began work in the mid-1990s on a documentary film about the Corps of Discovery. We were filming a crew of dedicated Lewis and Clark buffs trying to manhandle a reconstruction of the expedition's keelboat at Lewis and Clark State Park near Onawa, Iowa. (They called themselves Friends of Discovery, from Onawa, and The Discovery Corps, from Omaha.) The first day, as we tried to get just the right shot of the fifty-five-foot boat being moved by the use of setting poles, they toiled up and down a mile-long oxbow lake (once part of the Missouri), silhouetted against a blood-red sunset. Every time they thought they were done, we'd ask them to do it once more. The temperature was in the high nineties. So was the humidity. We kept them at it until the stars came out.

The next morning they were back before dawn, so we could shoot the keelboat being towed by a rope, this time silhouetted against the yellow ball of a rising sun. We got our camera into position, the men on deck jumped into the shallow water, stretched out the cordelling line, began pulling with all their might, and the heavy wooden craft slowly moved by. We asked them to do it again (so we could get tighter shots). They did. We asked for another pass (for a wider shot). They complied—though this time one man pulled a leg muscle straining against the rope and the thigh-deep water. Before we were done, the crew had made four or five more passes, the sun was two hours above the horizon, and the heat was already as oppressive as the day before. I'll never forget their shout of joy when we radioed through our walkie-talkies that the shoot was over—and then their second shout when a south wind suddenly rose, allowing them to sail effortlessly all the way from the far end of the lake to the dock.

I remember thinking to myself that now I understood why the expedition's journals never failed to note those days (or even parts of days) when the wind conditions permitted the sails to replace the poles, oars, and rope. To them, a fresh wind from the right direction would have been an event of tremendous significance. That thought led to another. These bone-tired men who had been helping us had every right to be exhausted. We had worked them hard for an evening and a morning in stifling heat. But they had been maneuvering their keelboat in a currentless *lake*, and tonight they would sleep in their beds at home and then tomorrow return to their regular jobs. The men of the original Corps of Discovery had the untamed, unstoppable, land-chewing, tree-spitting, boat-swallowing Missouri River to contend with—a brutish, indifferent force of nature that met them every morning to renew the fight for every inch the explorers dared to gain toward its headwaters.

Suddenly the math in Clark's daily chart of courses and distances took on new meaning: four and a half miles the first day (a late start), nine and a half miles the second, nine miles the third; some favorable days covering seventeen or eighteen miles, some unfavorable ones making only a few, some necessary days of rest making no progress at all. Every day a struggle. Nearly three thousand miles to the Three Forks. Four thousand miles to the sea. Perhaps there were moments of higher excitement or more lasting significance, but this was drama in itself—and no less dramatic simply because it was repeated day in and day out.

Our filming brought us into contact with other groups dedicated to replicating Lewis and Clark's experience. At the mouth of the Missouri, Glen Bishop had built his own keelboat and equipped it with a hidden motor so it could be safely taken out onto the big river. His group—the Discovery Expedition of St. Charles, Missouri—rowed their boat past our camera (and past it again and again and again) during one long sunset, and then sailed through one of the prettiest sunrises I've ever witnessed while we shot from a shoreline so sticky and oozy that when we tried to move, the mud sucked off our boots.

In Nebraska, some reenactors set up a Lewis and Clark campsite along the river for us to film at night. When we returned the next morning for the dawn shoot—they had dutifully slept at the camp, we had retired to an air-conditioned motel—we found them with puffy faces and their eyes swollen shut from mosquito bites. Farther upriver in Montana, where the Lewis and Clark Honor Guard of Great Falls prepared another camp for us, it struck me just how complicated the logistics could be to get everything unpacked and set up for three dozen people; how cranky tired men can become if there's a delay in getting fed; and how quickly they can unwind around a blazing fire with some whiskey in their gullet and a brisk fiddle tune filling the night air. The next day they strapped harnesses to their shoulders and dragged a ponderously heavy dugout canoe back and forth along the crest of a barren hill until we were satisfied that anyone who watched our film would not just see but *feel* how difficult the expedition's portage really was.

Lewis's journal entry from June 23, 1805, had greater meaning for me now. "At every halt these poor fellows tumble down and are so much for-tiegued that many of them are asleep in an instant," he had written during the portage. "In short, their fatigues are incredible. Some are limping from the soreness of their feet, others faint and unable to stand for a few minutes . . . yet no one complains, all go with cheerfullness." (When we were through filming, the exhausted but still remarkably good-humored men of our own crew insisted that Ken, Steve Ambrose, and myself put on the harness and try it ourselves, while they chanted, "Just one more time. Just one more time.")

What these experiences had taught me was much more than a few practical demonstrations of what the Corps of Discovery faced in trying to ascend what Lewis called "the mighty and heretofore deemed endless Missouri." Being with those groups helped me see the Lewis and Clark story in a new light. It slowed down my sprints from one climactic moment to another and prompted me to read the journals again to enter their world as *they* experienced it, one day at a time. It taught me to recognize the simple heroism of hard work inherent in the expedition's historic accomplishment. It broadened my perspective, encouraging me to pay as much attention to what the journal-writing enlisted men had to say as I had to Lewis and Clark's entries, reminding me again that this is a story told by many voices, each with its own point of view.

Two friends—the historian James Ronda and Gerard Baker, a Mandan-Hidatsa from North Dakota—had already widened my field of vision to see the Corps of Discovery from the perspective of the Indians they encoun-tered. My time with the modern expedition reenactors widened it again, inviting me to get out of the captains' tent, where the decisions were being made, and join the circle around the campfire, where the working stiffs were talking about how hard the river had fought them that day and what they would be having to eat and drink before falling off to sleep in preparation for yet another day of difficult labor. It made me consider the group dynamics of men on the move. And it forced me to notice the "smaller moments"— of sweat and toil, rest and simple pleasures, weather endured and miles traveled—that I had previously consigned to relative unimportance in favor of the "big moments."

Most of all it reignited my imagination about a story I thought I already knew, convincing me that not only does each new generation reinterpret Lewis and Clark according to its own interests, but each person is capable of coming back to the story again and again—like men pulling a keelboat or dragging a canoe in front of a camera—until he or she gets it just right.

I am still attracted to moments on the expedition I find particularly dramatic or significant or revealing, and I'm still drawn to themes and lessons from the story that I consider especially important. But I also now find great pleasure in occasionally picking a single ordinary day from their journey to study. If I'm headed to some place along their trail I like to dive into the journals and see what happened there two hundred years ago. (Locating the proper entries is much easier than it used to be, thanks to the helpful footnotes in Gary Moulton's magisterial, thirteen-volume *The Journals of the Lewis & Clark Expedition*.) I'm never disappointed from the exercise.

In the spring of 1997, having been asked to meet with a group beginning to plan for the national commemoration of the expedition's bicentennial, I traveled to Nebraska City, Nebraska, about forty miles south of Omaha. On the way I opened the journals for July 19, 1804, and joined the Corps of Discovery for the day they passed through the immediate area.

They had been gone two months by this point and were already well acquainted with the Missouri. The daily struggle against its relentless current had already settled into what must have seemed to the men as a never-ending, backbreaking routine: rowing with oars, pushing with the setting poles, or wading on the slick banks and shallows and straining with a cordelling rope—trying to move the ten-ton keelboat a little farther upriver; suffering from mosquitoes Clark described as the size of houseflies; suffering from occasional heatstroke and dysentery and boils where their perpetually wet and unwashed clothes rubbed against their skin; suffering again when Lewis treated nearly every ailment by drawing blood or dispensing his medicine of choice, those pills he had bought in Philadelphia from Dr. Benjamin Rush— laxatives so powerful that everyone called them "Rush's Thunderbolts." The backs on a few of the men would have been sore from something more— lashings meted out as punishment for breaches of discipline.

They had not yet reached the Platte River (the modern border of Iowa had only been crossed the day before), but to many of the men it must have seemed that they had already been gone a lifetime. Nonetheless, they all realized they were still in the earliest stages of their long journey.

William Clark wrote in his journal for July 19 that breakfast that morning was roasted deer ribs and a little coffee—and that he named an island they passed Butter Island, "as at this place we made use of the last of our butter." Nearing the mouth of the Platte, the Missouri was braided by a greater number of sandbars, he observed, "and the quick & roleing Sands much more danjerous." During the early part of the day, he left the keelboat and was walking through some woods onshore when he came across the fresh sign of elk (*elk*, roaming free in the Midwest). Following the elk tracks led him up through the trees in the river valley until he "Came Suddenly into an open and bound less Prarie, I say bound less because I could not See the extent of the plain in any Derection. . . . [T]his Prarie was Covered with grass about 18 Inches to 2 feat high and contained little of any thing else."

These were men from Kentucky, Ohio, Virginia, Pennsylvania, New Hampshire—forested places with mostly vertical vistas. Now they were just beginning to enter a strictly horizontal world, for which they were totally unprepared.

"This prospect was So Sudden & entertaining," Clark noted, "that I forgot the object of my prosute." Now, William Clark was not the kind of man who forgot the object of his pursuit, however momentarily. But his first sight of a boundless horizon, this first intimation of the West and what would soon enough become a common sight, literally stopped him in his tracks. It is a remarkable—almost poetic—moment, even through the straight-to-the-point prose style of Clark.

Lewis was the writer more likely to wax rhapsodic over a scene like this, but if he was keeping a journal on this day it hasn't been found—July 19 occurring in the middle of one of the greatest gaps in his daily record, a void essentially from May 14, 1804 to April 7, 1805, with a few exceptions. (From the expedition's departure to its return, more than four hundred days are missing a description from the captain President Jefferson had personally ordered to make sure complete—and redundant—journals were kept.) At noon on July 19, however, Lewis did get out his octant at what he scribbled down as "Point of Observation No. 23" and calculated that they had reached latitude 40 degrees, 29 minutes, 50 seconds. From Clark we're told that Lewis walked onshore during the afternoon (one of the captains normally stayed with the boat—and most often it was Clark). Perhaps Lewis, too, was enthralled by the tall grasses waving in the wind as far as his eyes could see, and this was a day that remained fresh in his mind eight months later when he wrote his mother about a treeless expanse "fertile in the extreem, the soil being from one to 20 feet in debth, consisting of a fine loam, intermixed with a sufficient quantity of sand only to induce a luxuriant growth of grass."

From the journal of Patrick Gass we learn that the expedition had set out at sunrise on this day and that they gathered choke cherries during their stop for lunch.

Charles Floyd noted that the bushes of choke cherries were "about as High as a mans hed" and that they named a nearby creek Cherry Run. The river current they were fighting all day was, in his words, "strong."

John Ordway also mentions the cherries; he adds that William Bratton came across a large quantity of a plant they called sweet flag.

Joseph Whitehouse provides the most details. The weather that day was clear, he wrote, and in the shallow water near shore they saw two catfish—the "largest siz'd catfish" he calls them, "which had hold of each other" and could not let go. One of the French-Canadian boatmen shot them to add to the evening meal's larder.

According to Whitehouse, the cherries they picked were along a creek they called Butter Run (probably North Table Creek or South Table Creek in Nebraska City), and not only did they delay until three o'clock there, they used some of their resting time to stuff the wild cherries into the whiskey barrel.

Whitehouse also reveals the method of propulsion for the day, saying they rowed the keelboat for what he estimated to be twelve miles. Clark called it ten and three-quarter miles, and is probably more accurate, but then again he was lost in rapture out on the prairie during the morning, not bending to the oars from dawn to dusk. Whatever the distance, they encamped that evening at the head of a willow-covered island called "the crying Island," Whitehouse wrote, "& near a River call'd the crying Water" (about three miles north of Nebraska City).

George Drouillard arrived from his daily hunt with two deer and reported seeing great numbers of young geese. William Bratton, hunting on the other side of the river, apparently had less luck; he stripped off his clothes, left his gun on the bank, and swam across to join the others on the island for supper.

I can see them around their campfires that night, the low and steady rustling of the Missouri's tenacious current mixing with the pop and sizzle of burning driftwood, the buzz of omnipresent mosquitoes punctuated by irritated slaps to the skin. It would be their first night without butter, but they would no doubt be enjoying their meal of venison and catfish, and the warm glow in their throats from whiskey with a cherry aftertaste.

They would be tired from their labors, but I imagine Clark's report of that boundless prairie he had so suddenly stumbled into would have filled them with curiosity about what lay ahead. They wouldn't know, for instance, that within a month their comrade Charles Floyd would be dead; that farther on, they would run out of more things than butter: whiskey, then tobacco, and that there would be times when a good night's meal would be the flank of a horse or a roasted dog. And though some of them had joined the expedition with hopes of gaining what John Ordway called "great rewards"—in land, double pay, and fame—I can't imagine that any of them could have conceived that two hundred years later their nation would be officially commemorating the bicentennial of their journey and that people would be parsing their journals for every possible additional scrap of information.

On that warm July night at the head of Crying Island, as they dipped their quills into ink and scratched their quaintly spelled words across a page, I doubt they gave special attention to their descriptions of the ten-mile day that had just transpired. It had been another day of struggle, another day of discovery. But it was nearly three thousand miles to the Three Forks. Four thousand miles to the sea.

4

Independence Creek

One of my prized possessions is an authentic replica of the Corps of Discovery's flag that we used in every production trip while making our documentary film. Only at the end of the project did I realize that our well-traveled companion, now faded and worn and fraying at the edges, is probably the only fifteen-star United States flag in two hundred years to have traced the entire length of Lewis and Clark's historic route and flown over every significant site along the way.

The first Independence Day ever celebrated west of the Mississippi began in what is now Atchison County, Kansas, at sunrise on July 4, 1804, with the firing of the keelboat's cannon "in honour of the day," according to Sergeant Patrick Gass. Once the salute was over, however, it was back to business for the Corps of Discovery. Like the nation whose twenty-eighth birthday they were marking, Lewis and Clark and their expedition were restless to keep moving westward.

The wind was favorable for awhile for the sails and oars, but "the day [was] mighty hot when we went to toe," Joseph Whitehouse reported. So hot, he wrote, that the sand scalded their bare feet until some of the men dropped the cordelling rope to retrieve their moccasins. When they stopped for lunch, Joseph Field was bitten on the ankle by a snake and Lewis applied a poultice of Peruvian barks to the swelling wound, in case the unidentified serpent was poisonous. When the bite proved harmless, Clark named the spot "Jo Fields Snake Prarie" in lighthearted remembrance of the event. Later he named a small creek they passed "4th of July 1804 Creek."

By evening they had rowed and towed fifteen hard miles up the Missouri and decided to make camp near the mouth of a twenty-yard-wide stream flowing in from the west, which they named Independence Creek. "We Closed the [day]," Clark wrote in his journal, "by a Discharge from our bow piece, an extra Gill of whiskey."

On behalf of the young nation that would eventually follow them across the continent, Lewis and Clark "planted the flag" for the United States in the West—figuratively *and* literally. Tucked away among the tons of equipment they brought with them on their epic journey was a supply of American flags, one of the earlier designs of Old Glory, with fifteen stars and fifteen stripes.

The captains used the flags for a variety of purposes. One fluttered over their big keelboat as they ascended the Missouri, signaling that a new nation now claimed the land watered by the mighty river. Others were presented to Indian chiefs, along with a message from their new "Great Father" promising that "when you accept his flag and medal, you accept his hand of friendship, which will never be withdrawn from your nation." A Yankton Sioux chief was thankful, he said, because the flag was "large and handsome, the shade of which we can sit under," and Lewis is said to have wrapped a newborn Yankton baby in a flag, declaring the child "an American."

The flag was carried by an honor guard accompanying the remains of Sergeant Charles Floyd on August 19, 1804, when he was buried on a hill that now bears his name near Sioux City, Iowa. On Christmas morning of 1804, north of what is now Bismarck, North Dakota, having just completed their winter quarters, the entire crew began the day by firing off their guns, drinking a round of brandy, and then hoisting the Stars and Stripes. "Its first waving in Fort Mandan," added Sergeant Gass, "was celebrated with another glass." And it was waving on the next Fourth of July, near Great Falls, Montana, when the celebration also marked the last of their whiskey supply.

A flag was flying with Lewis on August 12, 1805, when he ascended Lemhi Pass, becoming the first United States citizen to reach the Continental Divide. And it was with him the next day, when he became the first white man to reach the homeland of the Shoshones, whose willingness to provide horses to total strangers would determine the success or failure of the whole expedition. Conspicuously leaving his rifle on the ground, Lewis advanced alone and on foot toward sixty mounted Shoshone warriors, carrying only the flag, he wrote, "as an emblem of peace."

Lewis and Clark proudly flew their fifteen-star banner over Fort Clatsop in Oregon, even though Great Britain was also claiming the Pacific Northwest as its own. And long after running out of nearly everything else—whiskey, salt, tobacco, and trade goods—the expedition still had plenty of their nation's flags. Clark used one to purchase food from some Indians on the return trip. Lewis presented one to some Blackfeet warriors, but then pointedly reclaimed it from their corpses after a deadly fight. And Sergeant John Ordway mentions displaying one as they all sped down the Missouri in September 1806, just a week before their triumphant arrival in St. Louis.

Symbol of empire, token of peace; provider of shade, food, good cheer, and solemn ceremony; talisman of both promises made and promises broken; banner of exploration, reminder of home: the Star-Spangled Banner not only went everywhere with Lewis and Clark, it became, in effect, one of the most important (and versatile) members of the Corps of Discovery.

A point of high ground near the expedition's campsite of July 4, 1804, caught Clark's attention that evening. On it rested the abandoned site of a large Kansa Indian village. "This Town appears to have covd. a large Space," he wrote. "The nation must have been noumerous at the time they lived here, the Cause of their moveing to the Kanzas River, I have never heard, nor Can I learn; war with their neighbors must have reduced this nation and Compelled them to retire to a Situation in the plains better Calculated for their defence and one where they may make use of their horses with good effect, in persueing their enemey."

Change, of course, was nothing new in the West. For generations upon generations newcomers had been showing up—other Indian tribes, the French, the Spanish, the British—with their own dreams and designs and claims, their own willingness to displace someone else if necessary. In a certain sense, these men in a slow-moving boat with a fifteen-star flag were merely the latest unit in a passing parade. But an observation a number of them took pains to repeat in their journals that evening suggests that the people they represented had something more than passing through in mind.

Let Charles Floyd's entry speak for them all, since he had so little time left to record his impressions. "We camped at one of the Butifules Praries I ever saw," he wrote, "open and butifulley Divided with Hills and Vallies all presenting themselves." They may have signed up to be explorers, but they came from a population of farmers with an insatiable hunger for land,

and they recognized fertile ground when they saw it. Once the expedition was over, some of them would be coming back—and bringing a nation with them.

The fifteen-star flag the expedition displayed on that Fourth of July next to Independence Creek was already having trouble keeping up with a republic that counted seventeen states in 1804. Now the pace of American expansion was about to quicken even more. The ink was still wet on the treaty incorporating the huge Louisiana Purchase, but it had suddenly become more likely that the small cluster of white stars in Old Glory's corner of blue might someday become a firmament.

5

The Alexander Hamilton Willard Expedition

When I was asked by Bison Books to write a new introduction for the re-publication of *The Men of the Lewis and Clark Expedition*, I used the opportunity to explore the nature of the Lewis and Clark journals—and to highlight the exploits of one of my favorite, lesser-known members of the expedition. Sometimes in my fantasy trips with the Corps of Discovery, I fancy myself as one of the captains; but more likely I'd have been someone like Willard.

A few years ago, I was helping my friend Stephen Ambrose lead a group of people along some of the most scenic stretches of the Lewis and Clark trail. On a warm summer evening, after a pleasant day of paddling canoes on the Missouri River, we camped in the midst of the eerie and majestic White Cliffs of north-central Montana, close to the exact spot where on May 31, 1805, Meriwether Lewis wrote one of his most lyrical journal passages about the wondrous landscape he and his men were encountering. "As we passed on," Lewis concluded, "it seemed as if those seens of visionary inchantment would never have an end."

Nearly two centuries later we found the enchantment equally palpable as we sat around the campfire and gazed at the silent cliffs reflected in the river, tinged pink by the setting sun. There were about thirty of us, roughly the same number as the original Corps of Discovery. Beyond that one feature of our trip—and the geographical location—most of the similarities between the two expeditions ended. On average our group's members were about thirty years older than the young men under the command of Lewis and Clark (along with one teenage Indian woman and her infant son). We had paddled *down*stream to our camp (which was tiring enough for people our age), but nothing we did compared to dragging bulky dugouts day in, day out against the Missouri's relentless current. Unlike the Corps of Discovery, we had no concerns about grizzly bears (they disappeared from the river a hundred years ago), getting lost (we had precise maps and an experienced outfitter), or finding horses when the canoe portion of our journey ended (a chartered bus was hired to take us back to our parked cars). Having studied the history of the expedition in some detail, we also had made sure of another important difference: unlike the Corps of Discovery, we were absolutely *not* going to run out of whiskey.

That evening, after Steve and I took turns reading aloud from the journals, he spoke for a few minutes about teamwork. It's a point he had eloquently made three years earlier in the documentary film Ken Burns and I produced for public television: how after so many days together in their struggle to cross the continent, members of the Corps of Discovery eventually became so close to one another that they could hear a cough in the night and know who it was; they recognized each other's footsteps; they knew who was best at hunting, at starting a fire, or at any other task; they even knew who liked salt on their meat and who didn't. Such detailed knowledge about everyone else's personal habits and strengths—a simultaneous acknowledgment of individuality within a group that itself has begun to act more and more as a single, organic unit—is the natural by-product of the intimate bond of teamwork so crucial to the success of any expedition.

Everyone around the campfire nodded in agreement, then headed for their sleeping bags. The next morning I told Steve he could add another item of familiarity to his list. After only one night camping together, I said, we already knew who snored and who didn't—and we would be pitching our tents accordingly for the remainder of the trip.

Did any members of the Lewis and Clark expedition snore? If so, which ones? Was it a gentle sawing sound that encouraged the others to sleep, like the gentle croaking of frogs on the riverbank? Or was it a series of erratically erupting snorts and rasps, perhaps even a grand anvil chorus of a dozen or more men that reverberated out of the tents, echoed over the hills, and alarmed the wild beasts of the plains? Did their non-snoring campmates ponder (as that other great American adventurer Huckleberry Finn would) the age-old conundrum, the "curiosest thing in the world": why is the snorer, the person closest to the sound, the only one undisturbed by his snoring? Did they kick or shove or toss sticks at the offenders? Or did they simply lie there, wide awake and murderously sleep-deprived, silently calculating how hard it would be to slip a few doses of Rush's Thunderbolts (that super-powered laxative) into someone's breakfast?

We don't know the answers to those questions because our primary source, the expedition's journals, doesn't provide them. But it's a safe bet that every single member of the Corps of Discovery could have answered them at the time, and probably in elaborate detail.

The men considered some disruptions of slumber important enough to mention in their journals. The night before the expedition entered the White Cliffs, for instance, a buffalo bull stampeded into the sleeping camp, rampaged around the four fires, bent a rifle and one of the blunderbusses with its pounding hooves, and, according to Sergeant John Ordway, came "within a fiew Inches of Several mens heads" before Lewis's dog, Seaman, chased it away. "It was Supposed," Ordway added, that "if he had trod on a man it would have killed him dead." This puts the issue of being awakened by snoring in a different perspective. Or consider the night of July 26, 1806, on the return trip, when a vicious wolf sank its fangs into the hand of Sergeant Nathaniel Pryor—the kind of disturbance that might rouse anyone from even the deepest dreams.

Both captains reported times when the worries of leadership prevented them from sleeping: William Clark, when the entire crew was required to spend the night on their keelboat, surrounded by hundreds of potentially hostile Teton Sioux warriors; Lewis, when he camped near Lemhi Pass with a band of Shoshones, whom he feared were about to abandon him before he could purchase any of their desperately needed horses. Seaman the dog had his own share of what Lewis called "wristless nights"—constantly patrolling the campsite after dark in bear country to warn the men of approaching grizzlies, as if the responsibility to allow others some well-earned rest was his alone.

Most of the other recorded bouts with insomnia, though far less dramatic, are nonetheless helpful in providing a fuller picture of the expedition's experience. At a site west of the Yellowstone River the beaver were so numerous that the slapping of their tails on the water kept some men from nodding off; near the mouth of the Columbia, huge and noisy flocks of geese and brant did the same thing. Along the Missouri mosquitoes caused at least two sleepless nights (and probably innumerable others unrecorded); fleas were the problem at Fort Clatsop. Among the Nez Percés in Idaho, after the nearly starved men had unadvisedly gorged themselves on salmon and camas root, Clark dutifully noted in his journal that the feast "filled us so full of wind, that we were scercely able to Breathe all night" (and then, thankfully, left any additional details of the evening to our imagination).

But nowhere in the journals—among the hundreds of thousands of words that chronicle every day of the historic, two-and-a-half-year expedition and brim with a remarkable accumulation of information—do we learn who among the Corps of Discovery snored his way across the continent and back.

Obviously, the issues of sleep and snoring are hardly the most critical points of consideration in the epic journey of Lewis and Clark and their fellow explorers. But they do lead to larger, more important ones.

First, despite the incredible wealth of details in the expedition's journals, much went unrecorded for posterity. (This is not so much a complaint as an observation.) Embarked as they were on an arduous trek into unmapped territory, where every bend in the river and every new horizon might spell discouragement, disaster, or defeat, the insistent priorities of mere survival could easily have overwhelmed the more prosaic task of taking pen to paper every evening. That they wrote at all—let alone created such an enduring classic in the annals of exploration—stands as a stunning achievement in itself, a testament both to Jefferson's farsighted instructions that "your observations are to be taken with great pains & accuracy, to be entered distinctly & intelligibly for others as well as yourself," and to their diligence in carrying out those orders, even in the most difficult situations.

Journals from six men have survived—by Captains Meriwether Lewis and William Clark, Sergeants Ordway, Patrick Gass, and Charles Floyd, and Private Joseph Whitehouse. Taken together their commentaries leave no day of the expedition unrecorded, and for most days they provide multiple perspectives from which to triangulate events. Sergeant Pryor and Private Robert Frazer are presumed to have kept journals as well, but these are as yet unrecovered. What has been lost from not hearing their voices? How much more would we learn from the personal accounts of others on the expedition, such as York, Clark's black slave; or Sacagawea, the young Shoshone woman, and Charbonneau, her French-Canadian husband; or the other enlisted men? It's impossible to tell.

This leads to a second issue: the nature of the journals themselves. These are not the diaries of teenage girls, full of emotion and juicy gossip, meant as an outlet for personal feelings and destined to be kept under lock and key for fear of embarrassment. Nor are they the journals of mature adults as we might expect them to be written today, recording a day's activities as a springboard for someone's innermost thoughts and contemplations. These are the journals of busy military men writing under orders from the president of the United States, recording information meant to be useful to him and the rest of the "civilized world," and fully anticipating that what they set down would be published in some form or another. In other words, the more personal the information—from the trivial (naming names about snoring habits) to the profound (private desires and misgivings or frank assessments of other expedition members' strengths and weaknesses)—the less likely the Corps of Discovery's chroniclers are to reveal it.

On a few occasions, Lewis displays a histrionic yearning for glory or alternately provides brief glimpses into the darker recesses of his soul. Clark sometimes whines about his health or exhibits a fatherly concern for the welfare of his men. Ordway's descriptions of the most dangerous moments come the closest to expressing outright fear, just as his entries about Christmas and his longing to return home seem the most heartfelt. In general, though, the information they provide exists within a fairly narrow range: miles traveled, the day's weather, locations of campsites, new species and new landscapes encountered, Indian tribes met and the prospects for trade, brief accountings of the day's highlights, and so on. All the things, in other words, that Mr. Jefferson so anxiously awaited. He wasn't interested in reading a novel of western adventure, he wanted facts. The Corps of Discovery obeyed by returning with a prodigious number of them.

If Jefferson had added in his instructions, "Take equal pains to tell us more about yourselves and your traveling companions, your own habits, beliefs, and customs, &c.," the journalists might have taken a soldierly stab at it— though it is as hard to imagine them doing so with much enthusiasm as it is to imagine the shy and secretive president wanting that kind of information in the first place. His priorities were clear: he wanted facts, not story.

Nevertheless, from the unelaborated facts alone a dramatic narrative emerges, chock full of more heart-pounding near misses than most novels of the day would have dared attempt: a crumbling riverbank nearly overwhelms the keelboat; Lewis nearly falls to his death from a cliff; a confrontation with the Teton Sioux nearly turns deadly for both sides; men nearly freeze to death on the northern plains; buffalo nearly trample them and grizzly bears nearly catch them; a pirogue containing the most valuable cargo nearly capsizes; the expedition nearly takes a disastrous turn up the wrong river; a violent hailstorm nearly kills some of the men, while a flash flood nearly sweeps Clark to his death; Sacagawea nearly dies from sickness; her people, the Shoshones (with their all-important horses), nearly abandon Lewis; while crossing the Bitterroots, nearly lost, everyone nearly starves; the Nez Percés nearly decide to kill rather than befriend the weak and starving strangers; Columbia River cascades and then ocean swells nearly swamp the small flotilla of dugout canoes; Blackfeet warriors nearly leave Lewis and a few men horseless and gunless in hostile territory; Lewis is shot and nearly killed in a hunting accident. And, unbeknownst to the expedition, Spanish war parties dispatched for their annihilation nearly intercept them.

Just as facts overshadow feelings and personalities in the journals, the repetitive drumbeat of dramatic moments eventually drowns out the details of the more mundane day-to-day routines and the quiet heroics of getting up each morning for yet another exhausting day of moving only a few more miles across a seemingly boundless continent. What's captured in the bargain is undoubtedly the most important information, as well as the most stirring moments. But what's lost is a fuller sense of the participants in this historic event, and perhaps some greater insights into how they succeeded so spectacularly. It's like embarking on an epic adventure without really getting to know everyone else along on the trip.

Exacerbating the problem with all this lost potential is the way in which the captains overshadow everyone else. From the very start this historic enterprise has tended to be viewed from the top down. Jefferson, for instance, always considered it the "Lewis Expedition," reflecting his notion that Lewis was the only one to whom he had delegated authority and who therefore was solely responsible for the outcome. Lewis knew better. He was the first to add Clark to the expedition's name, and always insisted that his trusted friend share in the fame (just as he had shared in the decision making throughout the hard journey). So successful were these two remarkable leaders at melding their talents that they now seem historically joined at the hip, two very different men who cast an even larger shadow because they stand together. They are unquestionably the "stars" of the story and the ones we most readily recognize, not only because they were the leaders but also because they are the story's principal narrators. Despite the existence of other journals, we turn to the captains' version of events first.

From time to time in the story a few other members of the expedition threaten to emerge as personalities in their own right, however fleetingly. The lavish attentions and honor Indians paid to York because of his black skin prompt the journalists to take note of it, too, although for most of the expedition his presence—and its social ramifications—goes unremarked. Did some of the men (many were from slaveholding states) resent those attentions? Did any consider him their friend and equal? And what were York's thoughts? As they all paddled furiously down the Missouri toward home in 1806, was he expecting that whatever newly found freedoms he had gained from the journey (if there were any) would be extended to him once they reached St. Louis?

Similar questions could be asked—and left unanswered—about Sacagawea, the only woman, mother, and full-blood Indian on the expedition. She figures prominently in some of the more dramatic moments, such as the near capsizing of the white pirogue and, of course, the Shoshone negotiations with a chief who miraculously turns out to be her brother; and we get a few hints at her character, such as when she insists on being taken to see the beached whale on the Oregon coast, or when she presents Clark with a Christmas present of two dozen white weasel tails. But she is absent from the recorded story as often as she is in it, and her own point of view is available only through speculation.

What Sacagawea and York have in common—and, to a lesser extent, what Charbonneau, George Drouillard (a mixed-blood of French and Shawnee descent), the baby Jean Baptiste, and even the dog Seaman also share—is what sets them apart from those we call simply "the men." That's merely another way of saying "everyone else." While these few occasionally stand out as individual characters in the saga, most often "the men" come across as an undifferentiated whole, a single unit comprised of interchangeable parts rather than a collection of individuals, each with his own distinct personality, his own foibles and strengths, his own role to play, his own unique perspective on the larger experience. History has tended to lump them all together as "the men" and left it at that.

Clearly *they* didn't see it that way. As military men, they recognized the authority and leadership of their captains and no doubt accepted the enterprise as the "Lewis and Clark Expedition." But as human beings—and, equally pertinent, as Americans in the first generation of independence—each man surely considered it *his* expedition, in experience if not in name. "The men" were individuals with individual names, individual attributes, and individual stories to tell.

Charles Clarke's *Men of the Lewis & Clark Expedition*, published in 1970, was one of the first books about the expedition to remind the world of that self-evident but too-often-overlooked fact. As he wrote in his introduction, Clarke's purpose was "to bring these men into being again and to rescue them from oblivion so far as is possible at this late date." *So far as is possible at this late date.* Unfortunately, for the many reasons already cited—the missing voices, the circumscribed nature of the journals' focus, the dominance of the captains (and a few others) as individual characters—what "is possible at this late date" carries special weight and places severe constraints on a noble and eloquently stated goal. If "the men" have not exactly been fully brought back into being in Clarke's book, the reason is a simple lack of documentary raw material.

But they can be rescued from complete oblivion. By providing biograph-ical sketches of fifty-one expedition members and then arranging a synopsis of each day's events with an emphasis on those things directly relating to each one, Clarke performed a valuable service. One by one "the men" struggle to emerge as the individuals they surely must have been. Yet the facts—or, more precisely, the lack of enough facts—constantly limit their complete resuscitation. Enough exists to reassemble a skeleton and perhaps a bit of flesh, but, *so far as is possible at this late date*, breathing real life and blood into them is now probably best left to historical novelists. As for the rest of us, we can string together the available facts about an individual expedition member to hint at a fuller portrait and, with a little imagination, at least point ourselves toward a fuller understanding of what it must have been like to be on the greatest expedition in American history.

Consider, for instance, one of my personal favorites, Alexander Hamilton Willard, one of the many men about whom there's much more that we don't know than what we do know. Born along the Connecticut River in Charlestown, New Hampshire (just a few miles from my home), Willard was twenty-five years old, apparently a skilled blacksmith, and a private in the army when he joined the Corps of Discovery at its camp in Illinois the winter of 1803–4. What prompted him to volunteer for the expedition? How did he fit in with the other young men who tended toward rabble-rousing that first winter? What were his expectations for the journey? Fevered excitement? Foreboding? Feigned ambivalence? These are all unknown. Aside from a few passing references—a jumbled list of recruits, a notation of who got drunk on New Year's Eve, a mention of bringing in a pair of hinges—Willard's name rarely appears in the early months of the journals.

As the expedition began ascending the Missouri, it appears Willard spent at least some days onshore riding horseback with George Drouillard, the expedition's chief scout and best hunter, which suggests that the captains recognized in him some level of competence with a gun and horses. Someone raised along the Connecticut would have been familiar with rivers, but the mighty Missouri's size, power, and soon-to-be-legendary treachery must have amazed Willard. Perhaps he was thankful to be assigned to hunting duty rather than fighting the Big Muddy with the others. Did he and Drouillard exchange stories from their very different backgrounds? Was there an implicit competition between them over who supplied the most fresh meat to the hungry men? Did the primeval hardwood forests of Missouri, with their majestic stands of hickory and oak, hearken him back to the gentle hills of New Hampshire, blanketed with trees as they might have been when Willard's ancestors had first arrived in New England? We can speculate, but we can't know. The journals only report for certain that he and Drouillard were responsible for the horses in late May, that on at least one occasion he and other hunters killed three fat elk bucks, and that, in the organization of the party, he was assigned to the squad of Sergeant Ordway, a fellow New Hampshire native. It takes a careful reading of the journals to be even aware of Willard's presence.

But on July 12, 1804, at Camp New Island, just north of what is now the Kansas-Nebraska line, Willard burst onto center stage in the expedition's narrative. He did it, ironically enough, by sleeping. During the first months of the expedition the captains had worked to instill military discipline on a group of young men who seem to have been particularly reluctant to accept it. There were cases of drunkenness (Willard's had been but one of many such infractions), open disobedience, men going AWOL, and night guards helping themselves to supplies (that is, the whiskey). In each case Lewis and Clark had convened a court-martial of enlisted men to hear the charges, judge the facts, and mete out punishments, usually consisting of fifty lashes.

On July 12, however, the captains themselves composed the court-martial because of the seriousness of the offense: falling asleep while on night guard, the kind of lapse that might endanger the entire expedition's survival in the wrong circumstance and obviously something Lewis and Clark wanted to make sure never happened again. The few facts we know of the incident are confined to the four terse paragraphs Lewis and Clark entered in the expedition's orderly book: Willard had been assigned as night sentinel the previous evening; his sergeant, Ordway, accused him of "lying down and Sleeping on his post"; the offense was considered "*Capatol Crimes*, and under the rules and articles of *War* punishable by *Death*." Acting in his own defense, the report says, Willard made what I would consider to be the first attempt at a plea bargain west of the Mississippi River: "*Guilty* of *Lying Down*, and *not Guilty of Going to Sleep*."

Whether or not he had actually been asleep a few hours earlier, by the time these proceedings were under way Willard must surely have been fully alert. His life potentially hung in the balance as the captains weighed their decision and then announced it: guilty of both charges. An extra jolt of adrenaline must have rushed through his system in the brief moment between verdict and sentencing: not execution (an obvious relief) but one hundred lashes on the bare back (a quick, reflexive tensing of shoulder muscles) to be administered in equal amounts over four nights.

It would be interesting—and informative—to know the other men's reaction to the trial, the verdict, and the next four evenings at each successive campsite, when Willard would have stepped forward to strip down his shirt and turn his face away to receive his nightly dose. Perhaps some of the men, by now friends since spending their seven months together, turned their faces away, too. Maybe others relished the sight, harboring either some personal grudge against Willard or a belief that he truly had endangered their survival and deserved a stricter punishment. Once again the journals are of no help in creating a complete sense of the event. Gass, Whitehouse, and Floyd make no mention whatsoever of the court-martial, let alone the nightly lashings. Ordway devotes only a single sentence to the incident ("one Sentinel a Sleep on his post last night, and tried by court martial this day"), omitting not only that Willard was the accused but that Ordway himself was the accuser. Is the near silence about the matter in the enlisted men's diaries significant? It's impossible to say.

Equally lost to history is Willard's point of view. If wrongly accused he could have been justifiably resentful toward his sergeant and commanding officers; if caught fair and square, he might have considered himself properly chastised, perhaps even lucky to have escaped with whatever skin was left on his back at the end of the fourth evening. Did Lewis, the chief dispenser of medicine, treat Willard's wounds each night? Did the floggings leave lasting scars? Was Willard comforted or shunned by his mates during the next few days? Was he brought back into the company of men with, perhaps, a few jokes, a friendly word, a helping hand during a task made difficult by a sore back? Answers to those questions would explain much about the dynamics of the Corps of Discovery—between the commanders and their men, between noncommissioned officers and their squads, within the group as a whole, or between individual members—but only if we had more details. Instead we are left to wonder, extrapolate, speculate, yearn for fuller information, and, in the end, be thankful for at least the few facts from which to populate this epic expedition with more than simply names on a list.

We know with certainty that July 1804 was not a good month for Private Willard, because he surfaces next in the journals on July 29 when he was dispatched back to the previous night's campsite to retrieve a tomahawk he had forgotten, and then, while crossing a creek on a log, had lost his balance and dropped his rifle into the deep water. We know also that Reuben Field was sent to rescue the gun from the creek's muddy bottom. Willard probably never forgot that humiliating day: the look in the captains' eyes or the sound of their voices after he admitted to misplacing his tomahawk; the long walk to retrieve it; the moment on the log when he thought he would fall in, and the next moment, right after dropping his rifle, when he probably wished he had; the sight of Reuben Field disappearing underwater and his reappearance moments later with his prize; the talk and the looks of the other men when he and his sodden companion returned to camp and retold the story; the sinking feeling that perhaps he shouldn't have volunteered for the expedition in the first place. Regardless of how memorable the day was for Willard, the journals' mention of his part in it slides by in a few short sentences. We are told more about the weather (dark with occasional rain, cold wind from the west-northwest), the state of the river (more bends and slower current north of the Platte, the banks lined mostly with cottonwoods now, many of them ravaged and broken by a violent storm in the recent past), and the day's provisions (some huge catfish and jerked meat from Drouillard's fresh kills) than we are told about any particular person.

And so it goes for the remainder of the "Willard Expedition." For the rest of the journey, he sporadically appears in tantalizing shards of information, the DNA of a fuller story, suggesting (but only suggesting) the unique quality of one man's unforgettable experience—and through him a better knowledge of the larger organism known as the Corps of Discovery. He appears, then just as quickly disappears, leaving us to fill in the blanks or connect the dots.

And what dots there are to connect:

- September 14, 1804. Willard accompanies Clark in a vain attempt to locate a volcano (a volcano!) rumored to exist somewhere nearby (they are in South Dakota); along the way, Clark kills their first antelope, an animal unknown to science at the time, and Willard hauls it back.
- Winter, 1804–5. Willard and John Shields become indispensable to the expedition's survival by trading their blacksmithing work for corn and meat from the Mandans.
- June 18, 1805. Dispatched to bring in a load of freshly killed buffalo meat

during the portage of the Great Falls, Willard is attacked and nearly caught by a grizzly bear, which chases him to within forty yards of the camp.

- August 15, 1805. Clark names a creek in southwestern Montana "Willard's Creek." A special moment of pride, perhaps? Or even less than a matter-of-fact occurrence, since during the preceding four months so many other creeks had been named for other expedition members? (In 1862 a prospector would discover gold on the creek—renamed Grasshopper Creek—and touch off the Montana gold rush.)
- September 18, 1805. During the terrible ordeal in the Bitterroot Mountains, Willard's "negligence" (Lewis's words) causes a delay in the morning's start: his unattended horse is missing. Lewis sends Willard back to find the horse and marches off with everyone else. Late in the afternoon, Willard finally catches up with the expedition, without the horse.
- February 10, 1806. Willard returns to Fort Clatsop from the saltworks on the seashore with a serious injury. While butchering some elk he had killed, he "had cut his knee very badly with his tommahawk," according to Lewis.
- February 20, 1806. Like a number of the men, Willard is reported sick: "a high fever and complains of the pain in his head and want of appetite," writes Lewis, who treats him with "Scott's pills" the next day. On February 27 he is still reported as "very unwell"; on March 8 he is "yet complaining and is low Spirited"; on March 20 he "remain[s] weak"; and on March 21 he still does "not seem to recover" and is taken by a "violent pain in his leg and thye." Not until March 29, nearly a week after they have all departed for home from Fort Clatsop, is Willard considered "quit well" by his captains.
- April 19, 1806. Halfway up the Columbia, near the Dalles of Oregon, Willard once more allows his horse to wander off. "I repremanded him more severely for this peice of negligence than had been usual with me," a piqued Lewis writes. (Can words sting as much as a physical lashing?) But by May 9, back with the Nez Percés, Willard has apparently regained his captain's confidence and is sent with Chief Twisted Hair to retrieve the expedition's large horse herd, which the Indians had kept over the winter. By the end of May it appears that Willard is one of the few privates entrusted with the all-important trade for food going on with the Nez Percés.
- August 4, 1806. In eastern Montana, where Willard has once more become one of the regular hunters, he and Ordway kill two deer and a large grizzly (revenge from the near-death experience of a year earlier?) and set

out in their canoe to catch up with the others. Darkness falls, but they decide to continue down the Missouri by moonlight, only to be pushed by the current into a thick tangle of driftwood that knocks Willard into the rushing water. As Ordway frantically maneuvers the dugout to safety, Willard clings to a limb. Somehow he grabs two small logs, ties them together, places his clothes on them, and then floats with them about a mile downstream and finally to shore. "It was fortunate for Willard," Lewis writes of the accident, that unlike many of the other men on the expedition, "he could swim tolerably well."

- August 28, 1806. In South Dakota, Willard is among a small group dispatched by Clark to kill an antelope so its skeleton and skin can be preserved for President Jefferson (others are sent out for prairie dogs and magpies). On August 29 he returns empty-handed but tells Clark he did manage to measure the White River a few miles upstream from its mouth: two feet deep, two hundred yards wide. His method of measurement: wading.

- August 30, 1806. Just before midnight a violent thunderstorm erupts, whipping up such ferocious winds and waves that the men are ordered to hold onto the canoes to prevent them from being blown off the sandbar where the expedition is encamped. Two canoes that had been lashed together nonetheless break loose—with Willard and Private Peter Weiser in them, powerless to do anything but hang on for dear life—and are blown across the river. Ordway and six men set out in the small pirogue to effect a rescue. By 2 A.M., during a lull in the storm, they all finally make it back to camp, where it rains until daylight, leaving everyone, in Clark's words, "wet and disagreeable."

With that notation Willard exits from the journals forever. What a pity because, as this brief outline suggests, *The Adventures of Private Alexander Hamilton Willard* would have been an epic in itself, if only he could be brought back to life to tell it in detail from his own point of view. Part *Pilgrim's Progress*, complete with valuable lessons learned on the road, and part *Perils of Pauline*, full of close calls and comic mishaps, it would also add immeasurable depth to the larger story of the Corps of Discovery. If fully fleshed out, Willard's tale—of a lowly and sometimes hapless private who suffered lashings, injuries, illnesses, and accidents, yet persevered to earn his commanders' trust and his nation's thanks—would humanize the expedition in a way that the existing accounts never will.

Lacking that, the mere outline of Willard's journey at the very least demands that we resist the temptation to think of "the men" of the Lewis and

Clark expedition only in passing or predominantly as a single entity. *So far as is possible at this late date*, they should be remembered in the way their captains thought of them and in the way they knew each other: as distinct and fallible human beings. In realizing their individuality, the key to their success—their unity—appears even more remarkable. By admitting their fallibility, their heroic achievement becomes that much more inspiring.

Alexander Willard lived to the ripe old age of eighty-seven—long enough to serve his country several times more (as a government blacksmith for the Sauk, Fox, Delaware, and Shawnee Indians, and in the War of 1812); long enough to marry and raise twelve children (one given the name Lewis, another Clark); long enough to be alive during the invention of photography and have his picture taken, his back proud and erect, his eyes fixed with confidence straight ahead; long enough to play his part in yet another national transcontinental endeavor, the covered wagon migrations to the gold fields of California, where he died in 1865.

There is a faint suspicion that he did, in fact, keep a journal during his expedition with Lewis and Clark and the Corps of Discovery. Certainly he must have told and retold his adventures to his children and grandchildren in the many years that followed. How I wish that journal could be discovered in someone's attic or even that one of Willard's descendants had transcribed his reminiscences. (There is always hope. Segments of Whitehouse's journal came to light in 1903 and 1966; Ordway's journal wasn't discovered until 1916; and Clark's field notes were uncovered in 1953.)

But even if such accounts were miraculously discovered, I doubt they would settle a detail which, in the absence of conclusive facts to the contrary, I've decided to believe about Alexander Willard. I believe he *was* asleep during night guard duty back on Camp New Island in 1804. And I think I know how Sergeant Ordway discovered him and then knew immediately that Willard was both lying down *and* sleeping. He was snoring.

6

Of Hearths and Home

On June 5, 1999, smoke rose from the chimneys of Fort Mandan for the first time in 195 years—the result of work by the North Dakota Lewis and Clark Bicentennial Foundation to make the reconstruction of the fort a more historically accurate replica of the original. This essay comes from the speech I gave that day at the ceremonies dedicating the new chimneys and fireplaces. It was a beautiful summer afternoon along the Missouri River. While I was speaking, a bald eagle rose over the cottonwoods and circled in the sky above the fort.

We tend to think of Lewis and Clark and their Corps of Discovery on the move, under an open sky, following the sun on its daily westward journey, camping under the stars, and then pushing on again at first light; embarked, Lewis explained to every Indian tribe he met, on "a long journey to the Great Lake of the West, where the land ends and the sun sets on the face of the great water."

Over the course of 863 days, as they crossed the West from St. Louis to the Pacific and back, the Corps of Discovery made roughly 620 separate camps—the vast preponderance of them for only one night. They would arrive after a toilsome struggle that had moved them perhaps fourteen miles, set up their tents, cook a meal, fall into a much-needed sleep, and then set off once more in the morning toward the next horizon. But for five solid months, one stationary place was each day's starting point and each day's destination:

the place the expedition named Fort Mandan, near what is now Washburn, North Dakota.

On November 2, 1804, Lewis noted that the captains had picked a site—and a name—for the fort; on November 3, Clark wrote, "we commence building our cabins"; and on November 4 he scribbled the words "Fort Mandan" next to the date of his diary entry for the first time. On April 7, 1805, he would write those two words, "Fort Mandan," as his temporary address for the last time.

November 2 to April 7: five months in the same place. Along the entire four-thousand-mile Lewis and Clark trail, no other site would make such a claim on the restless band of explorers. To them, this wasn't just another campsite. And despite its name, to them—hardened soldiers that they were—it wasn't just another military fort, either. Fort Mandan was something more to the Corps of Discovery. During the long, epic voyage that would take them so far from their friends and families, so distant from what all of them referred to longingly in their journals as "back in the states," Fort Mandan would become the closest thing to home. And like all homes—especially in those days, and even more especially in winter—its life naturally centered around the fire and the hearth.

But first, the chimneys and fireplaces had to be built. Sergeant John Ordway tells us that work on the chimneys began right away—November 7—and the next day, he wrote, "we continued building with as much haste as possable in order to Git [inside] before winter sets in."

By November 13, snow was falling and ice was running in the river—"considerable fast," according to Ordway. Lewis and six men took one of the pirogues upriver, through the flowing ice, to collect stones for the backs of the chimneys. Let Ordway recount the story: "Capt. Lewis returned with his party much fatigued. They got [stuck] on a Sand bar & had to be out in the water abto. 2 hours. the Ice running against their legs. their close frooze on them. one of them got 1 of their feet frost bit. it hapned that they had some whiskey with them to revive their Spirits."

Eight days later the men were still searching for more stones, still working feverishly on their fort. On November 22 the chimneys were finally complete—and just in time, as it turned out. The wind shifted to the northwest, and temperatures began to plummet. By November 29, ice had closed the river near the Mandan villages upstream and the snow was already thirteen inches deep in the wooded river bottoms.

December brought even colder weather—"colder," Ordway wrote, "than I ever knew it to be in the States." This from a native of New Hampshire!

For the Virginians and young men from Kentucky, it must of have seemed unbelievably frigid: twelve below zero on December 8, according to Clark; twenty-one below on the eleventh; a mind-boggling, body-numbing forty-five degrees below on the seventeenth. So cold, according to Ordway, that the guards were relieved every hour—then every half hour—to keep from freezing. So cold, he says, "that we did nothing but git wood for our fires."

But thank God for those fires. "Our Rooms are verry close and warm," Ordway noted with some relief in the midst of the December onslaught, "So we can keep ourselves warm and comfortable."

"Warm" and "comfortable"—and, he might have added, *"alive."* During their time at Fort Mandan the explorers would record forty-nine sunrises when the mercury was below zero. Adding in the constant winds—"winds of astonishing violence," as Clark called them—those temperatures were even colder still.

In the simplest, starkest terms—in terms that each member of the Lewis and Clark expedition understood, in ways that we today cannot; and in terms that they never forgot, nor should we—the fireplaces at Fort Mandan meant survival. Without the chimneys and the fires they made possible, life at Fort Mandan for the Corps of Discovery during the brutal winter of 1804–5 would not have been merely unpleasant or uncomfortable; it would have been impossible.

But the chimneys were built in time; the wood was cut; the fires were kept blazing—and life at Fort Mandan became not just possible, but, to quote Ordway again, "warm and comfortable."

On Christmas morning, the yuletide logs burned particularly bright. Private Joseph Whitehouse tells it best: "We ushered [in] the morning with a discharge of the swivel [gun], and one round of small arms of all the party. Then another from the swivel. Then Captain Clark presented a glass of brandy to each man of the party. We hoisted the American flag, and each man had another glass of brandy. The men prepared one of the rooms and commenced dancing. At 10 o'clock we had another glass of brandy, at one a gun was fired as a signal for dinner. Half past two another gun was fired to assemble at the dance, and so we kept it up in a jovial manner until eight o'clock at night, all without the company of the female sex."

By my count that's three glasses of brandy and a dance party before 10 A.M.; then dinner (and who knows how much more to drink with that); then another six hours of dancing (with, one can imagine, something more to drink during that time).

The hearths of Fort Mandan would have witnessed it all—in fact would have been the center of the celebrations, cottonwood logs popping and crackling and blazing on the hearth, illuminating the small rooms with a fickle, dancing light and casting a warm embrace toward the farthest wall. And the fires would have been the last sound the men heard that night when they went to bed, as Ordway wrote, "all in peace & quietness."

On the other hand, think of everything the *fireplaces* heard during those five long months.

First of all, they heard a multitude of languages. With a population of forty-five hundred—more people than lived in St. Louis or even Washington DC at the time—the Mandan and Hidatsa villages were the undisputed "big city" of the northern plains in the early 1800s, a natural gathering place of many peoples, a "trade mart" for dozens of Indian tribes, an intersection of international commerce and intrigue. I like to imagine it as something like the scene in *Star Wars* when Obi-Wan Kenobi brings young Luke Skywalker to rent a spaceship in a crowded bar whose dizzyingly diverse patrons come from every corner of the far-flung galaxies. The same diversity could have been found at Fort Mandan.

Here were the Mandans and Hidatsas, of course, "our friendly neighbors," as Lewis called them; but that winter Arikaras and Cheyennes, Assiniboins and Crees gathered around the fort's fireplaces as well—all speaking different languages, all wearing their own distinctive clothing, all pursuing their own agendas with the strangers from the East.

Scotsmen like Hugh McCracken and Charles Mackenzie would have rolled their "R's" as they conversed with the captains about the trade policies of the North West Company and Hudson's Bay Company. François Antoine LaRoque, Jean Baptiste LaFrance, and Joseph Gravelines would have added their French to the rich linguistic brew.

In front of those fires, Toussaint Charbonneau applied for a job as interpreter—using his Shoshone-speaking wife, Sacagawea, as his principal recommendation—then backed out of the deal, then begged once more to be hired on. In February 1805 those fires heard Sacagawea gasping in pain during a painful first childbirth; heard René Jusseaume patiently explain to Lewis the use of rattlesnake rattles for inducing labor; heard the potion being ground up and then swallowed; and minutes later heard the very first sounds to emerge from one of North Dakota's most famous native sons when Jean Baptiste Charbonneau—half Indian, half French Canadian, 100 percent American—drew his first breath and cried for his mother. Who knew then that one day Sacagawea would have more statues in her honor than any other American woman in history? And who would have guessed that she and her baby boy would one day grace a new dollar coin minted by the United States government?

It was in front of those fires that Black Cat—a Mandan of "integrety, firmness, inteligence and perspicuety of mind," according to Lewis—recounted what Clark called "Indian aneckdotes" during his seventeen visits to the fort. Here it was that the generous Sheheke told the captains, "If we eat, you shall eat," and another Mandan chief, Little Raven, arrived to trade bushels of much-needed corn and buffalo meat for an iron pot and an axe. The same fires would have cooked the kettle of summer squash, beans, corn, and chokecherries that Little Raven's wife presented as a gift outright, which the captains pronounced quite "palitable."

Those fires listened to Hidatsa warriors explaining the landmarks the Corps of Discovery could expect farther west, drawing rough maps on the floor as they talked, even trying to describe the powerful sound of the Great Falls of the Missouri.

And despite the famous Charley Russell painting to the contrary, it was in front of those fires—not in an earth lodge—that the proud Hidatsa chief Le Borgne (or One-Eye) arrived to test the skin of Clark's slave, York. "The chief observed that some foolish young men of his nation had told him there was a person among us who was quite black, and he wished to know if it could be true," Clark wrote in his journal. "We assured him it was . . . and sent for York. Le Borgne was very much surprised at his appearance, examined him closely, and spit on his finger and rubbed the skin in order to wash off the paint; nor was it until [York] uncovered his head and showed his short hair that Le Borgne could be persuaded that he was not a painted white man."

Le Borgne had not been impressed by the captains' array of telescopes and mirrors, and he had boasted that his warriors could handle the soldiers of the expedition like "so many wolves" on the prairie. But York was something else entirely. To the men from Virginia, he was a slave, something to be owned. To Le Borgne and the amazed Indians, he was someone to admire; he was "Big Medicine."

Around those fires, other types of medicine were discussed and practiced—"medicine" of all kinds. The hearth of Lewis's fireplace became the Fort Mandan outpatient clinic. Two men cut themselves in accidents with their axes. John Shields suffered from rheumatism. Nathaniel Pryor dislocated a shoulder, requiring four attempts to pop it back in place. Walking on the snow-covered plains on bright days, some of the men developed sun-blindness; Lewis treated them by holding their faces over a hot stone and tossing on snow to make steam. He treated them for venereal disease with injections of mercury. He lanced one Mandan boy's abscess and gave another one a dose of that powerful laxative, "Rush's Thunderbolts," for a fever. Yet another Mandan boy was brought in, so severely frostbitten that Lewis had to amputate his toes without the benefit of anesthesia or a surgical saw.

Over in the enlisted men's quarters, the talk around the fireplace was of a much different type of "medicine." It's easy to guess how the conversations went, late into the night, when some of them returned from the Mandan buffalo calling ceremony, that great "Medisan Dance," as Clark called it, designed "to cause the buffalow to Come near" by offering young women to tribal elders and powerful strangers.

And the talk would have had a different tone when the topic changed to a report that filtered up from the Arikara villages in February—news that the Teton Sioux were planning a springtime war against the Mandans and their new friends. "They Say if they catch any more of us they will kill us," Ordway wrote in his journal, "for they think that we are bad medicine."

I'm sure the men shared other stories around those fires. There's something about a fire that tends to bring out stories from those gathered around it, and especially when the days are so short, the nights so long, and the temperatures so cold, there's plenty of time and plenty of reason to sit near a hearth and just talk.

They surely discussed all the new experiences they had shared traveling up the Missouri—the battles with the river's current, the immensity of the treeless plains, the staggering abundance of new animals, the wide diversity of Indian peoples along the way.

They also had new experiences in North Dakota to talk over—a brilliant display of Northern Lights, double suns appearing over the frozen prairie, a total lunar eclipse on January 15, frost coating the entire grove of cottonwoods on the river bottom, the fatigue—and exhilaration—of hunting buffalo in the snow, and of course, just how damn cold it really was only a few feet from the fires' warmth.

As the days wore on, and those stories got stale and worn out from the retelling, the sounds around the fire would have become more mundane: the ring of the blacksmith's hammer near the charcoal kiln; the whisper of needle and thread making moccasins for the road ahead; the scratch of a quill pen on the rough paper of a journal or a letter home; the call of the magpie and the whistle of the captive prairie dog in their cages, waiting to be shipped back to President Jefferson; perhaps an old familiar tune played on the mouth harp or Pierre Cruzatte's fiddle.

And then, I think, they would have started talking some more, this time about themselves, perhaps, or their families "back in the states." It happens that way on long winter nights in North Dakota—or anyplace on earth where the sun goes down at 4:15 in the afternoon and doesn't reappear for another sixteen hours. Talking around a fire can become absolutely necessary to a different type of survival. It's either talk and grow closer, or surrender to "cabin fever" and splinter apart.

This is particularly true for a large group in close quarters, like the Corps of Discovery and the five months they spent Fort Mandan, 1,609 miles (Lewis noted with great specificity) from what had only recently been the farthest border of their native land.

But just how far they had come could be measured in something other than miles. On February 10, Thomas Howard was court-martialed for climbing over the walls of the fort when he returned after hours from one of the Mandan villages. He was found guilty and sentenced to fifty lashes. During their trip up the river in the summer and fall of 1804, the punishment would have been automatically meted out. Their first winter, at Camp Dubois, had been a disciplinary disaster, with disorder, drunken brawls, and open disobedience, and for the next nine months the captains had employed the lash with a certain regularity to enforce their rules.

But this time, the court of Howard's peers recommended mercy—and the captains decided to forgive the punishment. Significantly, this would be the last time a court-martial was convened during the entire expedition—even though there were still thousands of miles and twenty more months to go. Something had obviously changed. Something was different now and would never be the same. And it had happened around the fires at Fort Mandan.

My friend Jim Ronda, a historian, has written that during the winter in North Dakota the Lewis and Clark expedition changed from being an unruly group of soldiers and frontiersmen to becoming something of a family. I believe that's true; that, and something more. Here, I believe, for the first time they truly became a Corps of Discovery in every sense: fully prepared to move forward into what to them was the complete unknown, capable of taking on any challenge and overcoming any obstacle because now they were ready—without coercion or even admonition—to work together.

The captains understood this change that had occurred during the winter, and Lewis expressed it best in the letter he sent to Jefferson in the spring: "At this moment, every individual of the party are in good health and excellent spirits; zealously attached to the enterprise, and anxious to proceed; not a whisper of discontent or murmur is to be heard among them, but all in unison act with the most perfect harmony. With such men I have everything to hope, and but little to fear." He wrote those words by the light of one of Fort Mandan's fires—the very same fires that had helped forge this "most perfect harmony" in the first place.

It's said that travel changes a person. But in the case of these peripatetic travelers, whose most common phrase was "we proceeded on," I think it may have been the five months at Fort Mandan, remaining in the same place, that changed the Corps of Discovery the most. More than any other spot on their long trail, they had made it a home. Here they had talked for hours and drawn closer together. The fires, the hearths, and the chimneys had made it all possible.

April 7, 1805, dawned with a fair sky and the temperature at twenty-eight degrees—warm by Fort Mandan standards, and set to rise to a balmy sixty-four by midafternoon. According to the captains' weather journals, ice had stopped running in the big river on the first of the month. A flock of brant had passed northward on the fourth, followed by an even larger flock of cedar waxwings on the sixth. The ducks and swans they had seen flying south when they first started building the fort had already come back. "All the birds that we believe visit this country," the captains noted, "have now returned."

So had the bugs: troublesome gnats they began noting with increasing displeasure. I suppose the smoke in the fort's quarters might have provided at least a little relief from those pests—one last parting gift from the fires that had seen the men through an uncommonly harsh winter.

It was time to move on. At 4 P.M., the big keelboat pushed off downstream for St. Louis, carrying the prairie dog and the magpies, the collection of skins and skeletons that would reach the East Coast four months later and thrill Jefferson and others in Washington as great curiosities from this newest section of the young nation. There were Indian artwork, Indian vocabularies, and Indian tobacco Jefferson would plant and turn into cigars; maps and a copy of Clark's journals; and a letter from Lewis to his mother, describing the verdant beauty of the Missouri River valley and telling her not to worry about his safety.

At the same time the keelboat headed downstream, Clark and the rest of the "permanent party" headed upriver in six freshly carved dugout canoes and the two trusty pirogues. Lewis was the last to leave the fort. He needed some exercise, he wrote in his journal, and so he intended to walk to what would be the expedition's first campsite in five months.

If there was any tinge of sadness about leaving their temporary home behind, no one mentioned it. Far from it. This was a day of looking forward, not back. Lewis—after comparing himself to Christopher Columbus—captured the palpable sense of anticipation in words: "We were now about to penetrate a country at least two thousand miles in width, on which the foot of civilized man had never trodden; the good or evil it had in store for us was for experiment yet to determine, . . . [yet] entertaining as I do, the most confident hope of succeeding in a voyage which had formed a da[r]ling project of mine for the last ten years, I could but esteem this moment of my departure as among the most happy of my life."

Did he check to make sure the fires were out before closing the door for the last time? Did he look back over his shoulder as he walked toward his destiny? We don't know. The words "Fort Mandan" essentially drop from the journals on that day.

More than a year later, on August 17, 1806, after departing the Mandan villages to begin the final, headlong rush to St. Louis on the return trip, Clark at least stopped very briefly "to view the old works," as he now called the place. Their real homes were beckoning, so this temporary home had been relegated to a lower standing—"the old works"—and there was no need for the entire group to delay for a prolonged visit simply out of nostalgia.

Some pickets by the river were still standing, Clark reported, but most of the rest of the fort was gone. All but one of the rear huts had burned down by accident. The chimneys had done their work—and done it well—when they had been sorely needed, but with the fort abandoned they apparently had given up once they no longer felt a sense of purpose.

Two centuries later, in the reconstruction of Fort Mandan, the chimneys have finally been rebuilt and the fireplaces put back into good working order with a renewed sense of purpose. It's this: that generations gather once more 'round the hearths of Fort Mandan and tell the stories of the Corps of Discovery and the winter of 1804–5, the time when a band of United States soldiers lived as friends and neighbors to the Indians surrounding them; when a black slave was treated with reverence and dignity; when an unknown Native American girl could give birth with the president's top assistant acting as midwife; and when the prospects for the future were as boundless as the western horizon, because the group of individuals who stared across those fires at one another finally saw in the embers' glow the faces of America, ready to act in unison and live in a "most perfect harmony."

As the rising smoke is my witness, that is the story of the fires of Fort Mandan. It was a true story then. It can be true again.

7

"This Long Wished for Spot"

In September 2000 the Fort Union Trading Post National Historic Site, at the confluence of the Yellowstone and Missouri Rivers, hosted a fur trade symposium and asked me to address their final banquet with some thoughts about Lewis and Clark. This piece comes from that speech. It was a wonderful feast that fall evening in Williston, North Dakota, although I do not think anyone there consumed anything close to nine pounds of meat.

At noon on April 26, 1805, an unlikely flotilla of six dugout canoes and two large pirogues slowly made its way against the cold and rising current of the Missouri River and arrived at the point where the Yellowstone empties its snow-fed waters into the Big Muddy. It was William Clark and most of the Corps of Discovery, who now set about making camp even though the day was only half over.

Everyone would have been busy on this brisk April afternoon—a day that had dawned at thirty-two degrees and, although sunny, reached only sixty-three. Clark immediately began measuring the width and depth of the two rivers. Hunters were dispatched. A few men and a canoe were sent up the Yellowstone for Meriwether Lewis, who with four men had reached the river by foot a day before and had camped two miles from the confluence.

Despite this flurry of activity, the explorers must have paused long enough to enjoy the scenery, because all the journalists made sure to mention it that night in their diaries. Private Joseph Whitehouse called it a "handsome

point." Sergeant John Ordway deemed it "a handsom place" with "a beautiful country around in every direction." For Sergeant Patrick Gass it was "the
most beautiful rich plains I ever beheld." Lewis, who arrived later in the day
after taking celestial observations, wrote of the abundance of red berries, service berries, gooseberries, chokecherries, purple currants, rosebushes, and
honeysuckle on the river bottoms. Clark was less poetically descriptive, but
he used the word "butifull"—spelled in his own, distinctive style—five times
in the same journal entry.

Even more impressive than the scenery was the wildlife. "Emence numbers of antelopes in the forks of the river," Clark wrote. "Buffalow & Elk &
Deer is also plenty. beaver in every bend." Lewis found the game so abundant,
he said, that two good hunters could easily supply a regiment with meat—no
mean feat, since each of these hardworking men was consuming an estimated
nine pounds of meat per day. Nine pounds per person sounds impossible
today, but such were the caloric demands of men exerting themselves so
strenuously and with little else to supplement their diet; other explorers
and *voyageurs* of the era reported similar rates of meat consumption.

A large herd of buffalo, standing on a sandbar near the point, quickly
provided the hungry men with four calves, which, they said, tasted as good
as the finest veal. Ordway had stolen six goose eggs from a nest. Someone
else brought in a trumpeter swan from a nearby pond. Seaman, Lewis's
Newfoundland dog, had caught an antelope in the river and dragged it to
shore. Magpies, Canada geese, ducks seemed everywhere. Lewis thought
there were more bald eagles than anywhere else in the country.

Joseph Field arrived from scouting farther up the Yellowstone to say
he had encountered a species of animal they had never seen before, the
Audubon mountain sheep, and had even found one of their huge horns,
which he now displayed as a great curiosity. Even more curious was a buffalo calf that had naively followed him for eight miles—all the way back to
a camp where thirty-three people had just finished feasting on buffalo veal.

"All in good health," Lewis wrote of his party that evening, "and much
pleased at having arrived at this long wished for spot, and in order to add
in some measure to the general pleasure which seemed to pervade our little
community, we ordered a dram to be issued to each person; this soon produced the fiddle, and they spent the evening with much hilarity, singing &
dancing, and seemed as perfectly to forget their past toils, as they appeared
regardless of those to come."

Whether or not the stray buffalo calf stuck around for the festivities or
wisely slipped away when the dancing began, the journals don't tell us.

That must have been quite a night at the confluence for the Corps of Discovery: their bellies full, their heads a little tipsy, their ears ringing with music and laughter, their bodies warmed against the April chill by their campfire and their dancing feet. They were celebrating a major milestone of their journey. "This long wished for spot" represented the edge of the unknown to them, the place where their map went blank and beckoned them to begin filling it in.

Less than a month earlier, upon departing from Fort Mandan, Lewis had compared himself to "those deservedly famed adventurers" Christopher Columbus and Captain Cook. Here at the mouth of the Yellowstone, with everything to the west representing terra incognita, he had every expectation that he would soon be joining their ranks by discovering the fabled Northwest Passage, the coveted prize that had been eluding the world's greatest explorers for three centuries.

Lewis, Clark, and all the rest of the expedition were acutely aware that Indians had previously been here and beyond—in fact, they had just spent the winter voraciously consuming whatever geographic tidbits the Hidatsas, Mandans, and Assinniboins could furnish. But in the name of discovery, that could be easily overlooked. Every other explorer in history certainly had. And even if they had known (which they didn't at the time) that three French-Canadian fur traders had probably reached the Yellowtone years ahead of them, it still wouldn't have dampened their spirits that night. *They* were the Corps of Discovery and, if all went well, *theirs* would be the first report to reach what Lewis called "the civilized world" with news about the wonders of the West and the passage to the Orient. To *them* would go the glory and reward.

And so, poised as they were on what they considered the dividing line between the known and the unknown, the explored and the unexplored, they danced into the night. Tomorrow, their dreams and great expectations might be tested against reality; tonight, the future could be whatever their imaginations wished it to be. If that isn't the perfect setting for a party, I don't know what is.

The next day, the expedition moved on. Incredibly, the wildlife now became even more abundant. "We can scarcely cast our eyes in any direction without percieving deer Elk Buffaloe or Antelopes," Lewis marveled several days later, adding, "the quantity of wolves appear to increase in the same proportion." Bighorn sheep became common sights. A goose was shot that Ordway estimated at eighty pounds.

And the beaver, too, were not only more numerous but larger. The men trapped them at night, shot them along the riverbanks during the day—and ate them with delight. "The flesh of the beaver is esteemed a delecacy among us," Lewis wrote. "I think the tale a most delicious morsal, when boiled it resembles in flavor the fresh tongues and [bladder] of the codfish, and is usually sufficiently large to afford a plentifull meal for two men."

It must have seemed as if they had entered some sort of hunter and trapper's paradise, a "peaceable kingdom" where the wildlife existed in numbers that staggered the imagination of these backwoodsmen from the East. Reading the journals nearly two centuries later, it's even harder for us to fully comprehend. "It is now only amusement for Capt. C. and myself to kill as much meat as the party can consum[e]," Lewis confided on May 6. "We can send out at any time and obtain whatever species of meat the country affords in as large quantity as we wish." By May 9 he noted that the men were now throwing sticks and stones at the buffalo simply to move them out of the way.

Then they ran into their first grizzly, and the "amusement" soon ended. The captains had been properly warned by the Mandans and Hidatsas about ferocious bears beyond the Yellowstone—bears the Indians dared not attack in groups smaller than ten, and even then with an expected loss of life—but the explorers had discounted it as exaggerated tales told around a campfire by poorly equipped natives. At this point in their journey they were still perfectly willing to believe that the western mountains would be no bigger than the Blue Ridge of Virginia, that an easy half-day portage would take them from the Atlantic to the Pacific watersheds, and that the West might be populated by woolly mammoths or blue-eyed, Welsh-speaking Indians— all because Thomas Jefferson's books back in Monticello said so. But the notion of a bear that considered humans as just another article of diet, even when it was described by Indians with firsthand experience, seemed too far-fetched to take seriously. It appears that the men of the expedition were expecting (in fact, eagerly anticipating) a slightly larger, perhaps somewhat tougher version of the common black bear. What they met instead was North America's biggest, fiercest predator.

In incident after incident—roughly fifty encounters in the space of two months as the expedition moved from the Yellowstone to just beyond the Great Falls—grizzlies continually astonished the Corps of Discovery with their size, their strength, their aggressive instincts, and their absolute refusal to die quietly, even under a hail of bullets. Enraged grizzlies, some with five to ten musket balls lodged in their chests, chased the men across the plains, into the river, or up trees. Hugh McNeal was treed for three hours after being surprised by a grizzly, having averted instant death by breaking his musket over its head. Joseph Field had two miraculous escapes from the beasts. Clark, Lewis, Drouillard, Willard, Charbonneau, and many of the other men had similar close calls. Even Lewis's dog, Seaman, was reduced to "a constant state of alarm with these bear and keeps barking all night," his master wrote.

Because of grizzlies, the captains had to issue orders that no man wander off alone and that everyone sleep with his rifle close at hand. "These bear being so hard to die reather intimedates us all," Lewis noted in early May. "I must confess that I do not like the gentlemen and had reather fight two Indians than one bear." By the time they passed through grizzly country again on the return trip in 1806 (and encountered roughly another fifty bears), Lewis had come to view the grizzlies in precisely the way the Mandans and Hidatsas had originally portrayed them. "These bear are a most tremenduous animal," he wrote. "It seems that the hand of providence has been most wonderfully in our favor with rispect to them, or some of us would long since have fallen a sacrifice to their farosity."

In a way, their experience with the grizzlies pretty well summarizes the Corps of Discovery's journey from the confluence of the Yellowstone to the Pacific and back to the same spot: Virtually everything about the West, it seemed, turned out to be a lot more difficult than they had initially imagined.

The waterfalls they had expected to portage in half a day took a month to get around. The mountains they anticipated to be no larger than the Blue Ridge turned out to be the Rockies—higher, broader, and much more difficult to cross; "the most terrible mountains," Patrick Gass would write, "that I ever beheld." The ocean they planned on seeing in late summer wasn't reached until November. The sailing ships they hoped would replenish them with trade goods on the coast never showed up. And most of all, the Northwest Passage they had counted on finding—the easy water route across the continent whose discovery was their prime objective—didn't exist. So, when the explorers returned to the mouth of the Yellowstone in August 1806, they were a wiser, leaner, more experienced group than the one that had danced at the junction of the two rivers more than a year before. Lewis's revised opinion of grizzly bears was merely one example of what they all had learned in the interim.

Clark reached the confluence first, on August 3, having descended the Yellowstone for more than six hundred miles. His group set up camp at the point once more. Most of his journal entry that night is devoted to outlining the reasons why a trading post on the Yellowstone—at the mouth of the Bighorn or Clark's Fork—would be more successful in attracting mountain tribes like the Shoshones than would a fort on the Missouri at the mouth of the Marias, near the home of the Blackfeet.

Back at Travelers' Rest (*all* the way back, near what is now Idaho), Lewis and Clark had separated in early July, agreeing to meet at the Yellowstone confluence in a month. Few modern tourists, equipped with maps and credit cards, would even consider splitting up west of Missoula on the blithe assumption that they could find their separate ways roughly 750 miles across the entire length of Montana and rejoin at the North Dakota border. But that's what Lewis and Clark did—which means it was a "long wished for spot" on the return trip as well, since it now represented reuniting the entire expedition instead of entering the unknown.

But that rendezvous was thwarted by another vicious, unrelenting critter that mercilessly drove Clark's group from the point in less than twenty-four hours. No, it wasn't grizzlies again. It was something much more impossible to defeat. It was . . . the mosquito. Clark, who spelled "mosquito" nineteen different ways in his journals without once getting it right, called them "excessively troublesom" as he waited for Lewis's contingent to arrive down the Missouri. So troublesome that the men couldn't work on making sorely needed clothes from elk skins. So troublesome that Clark found it impossible to hunt. So troublesome that little Jean Baptiste Charbonneau, Sacagawea's baby, had a swollen face from all the mosquito bites. So troublesome that on the next day, August 4, Clark hurriedly scratched out a note to Lewis, tied it to a pole that he stuck into the sand, ordered the men to move camp farther downriver—and then kept moving, day after day for several days. Imagine: some of the bravest men in the annals of American history fleeing one camp after another, routed into continual retreat by a swarm of bugs.

On August 7, Lewis and his contingent reached the confluence, stopped only long enough to get Clark's note, and kept paddling. Five days later, about six miles south of what is now Sanish, North Dakota, and nearly a hundred miles downstream from the mouth of the Yellowstone, they finally caught up with Clark and his mosquito-crazed crew.

By the end of September they were all back in St. Louis—appearing, one startled resident wrote, like Robinson Crusoes, and hailed as heroes. Now they had the delicate and, I imagine, somewhat unpleasant task of writing Jefferson to break the unwelcome news about the Northwest Passage. "In obedience to your orders," Lewis wrote the president, "we have penitrated the Continent of North America to the Pacific Ocean, and sufficiently explored the interior of the country to affirm with confidence that we have discovered the most practicable rout which dose exist across the continent by means of the navigable branches of the Missouri and Columbia Rivers." So far, so good. Then came the fine print.

Instead of a Northwest Passage or short portage, this "most practicable rout" included a 340-mile overland stretch between rivers. And 140 of *those* miles, Lewis admitted, were "over tremendious mountains which for 60 mls. are covered with eternal snows." So much for Jefferson's great dream. "We . . . fear," Lewis added, "that the advantages which it offers as a communication for the productions of the Eeast Indies to the United States and thence to Europe will never be found equal on an extensive scale to that by way of the Cape of Good hope."

To sweeten this bitter pill, Lewis subtly changed the subject. The upper Missouri and all its tributaries, he claimed, "abound more in beaver and Common Otter, than any other streams on earth, particularly that proportion of them lying within the Rocky Mountains." And although the route he and Clark had outlined might not be good for transporting bulky and breakable goods *from* China, it was perfectly suitable—and probably quicker—for furs heading *to* the Orient. "The productions [of] nine tenths of the most valuable fur country of America," he promised, "could be conveyed by the rout proposed to the East Indies." He then went into details about how to schedule the shuttles of goods over the mountains, about how to keep the British from taking over the Missouri fur trade, and, in a separate note, about his vision of the future for the mouth of the Yellowstone.

"We examined the country minutely" at the confluence, Lewis said, "and found it possessed of every natural advantage necessary for an establishment, it's position in a geographical point of view has destined it for one of the most important establishments both as it regards the fur trade and the government of the natives in that quarter of the continent."

Meanwhile, other letters were also leaving St. Louis—letters of a more unofficial nature; letters from townspeople announcing the expedition's arrival and sharing what information they had gleaned from the men. Many of those letters would end up being published in newspapers around the country. None of them carried the headline: "NO NORTHWEST PASSAGE" or "Lewis and Clark Bump Into Tremendous Mountains on Water Route to China." None of them drew the connection, "Bears and Mountains Both Bigger Out West."

Instead, these common-folk correspondents focused on other things. First, they all proclaimed the simple fact that Lewis and Clark had crossed the continent. That in itself was big news. Americans had reached the Pacific by land—and they had returned alive. Brave and resourceful they were, but if the Corps of Discovery could do it, it meant others could as well. Lewis himself had said as much in his letter to Jefferson: "In the course of ten or twelve years a tour across the Continent by the rout mentioned will be undertaken by individuals with as little concern as a voyage across the Atlantic is at present."

The letters fanned out steadily, eventually appearing in virtually every newspaper in the United States (even in the local paper in my tiny hometown of Walpole, New Hampshire). Each correspondent added a little nugget guaranteed to attract the readers' attention.

"The Indians are represented as being very peaceable," one said, adding, "The winter was very mild on the Pacific." Another mentioned the great number of horses owned by western tribes: "It is thought to be a very poor Indian that did not own 300 horses." Several talked of the "curiosities" the explorers had brought back, including a ninety-pound horn from the Audubon sheep. (A Connecticut newspaper even used the headline: "More Wonders. Rocky Mountain Sheep Beats the Horned Frog All Hollow.") Virtually all of them found the profusion of fur-bearing animals important to note.

Good climate; good grazing; friendly Indians; and boundless opportunities in furs—all in a West that was no longer quite as unknown and quite as unreachable as before the Corps of Discovery had set out. That, as far as the reading public was concerned, was what Lewis and Clark had discovered, not the absence of a Northwest Passage.

The prospect of furs had the biggest immediate impact. On their way down the Missouri, the expedition had already encountered more than a hundred traders eagerly heading upriver into this newest section of the nation, even before Lewis and Clark could report their discoveries. In that kind of atmosphere, then, just imagine the effect in the taverns of St. Louis— and in all the other taverns of the land as the expedition's members filtered home—when they began talking about the land just beyond the mouth of the Yellowstone, where the beaver were big and fat, where sheep grew ninety-pound horns, and where the elk, deer, antelope, and buffalo were so thick you literally had to club them out of the way.

Without even bothering to return to St. Louis, John Colter had left the expedition in North Dakota in order to guide two trappers back into this treasure-house of wildlife on the Yellowstone. He would go on to become more legendary as a mountain man than as a private in the Corps of Discovery. In the spring of 1807 at least three more expedition members—George Drouillard, John Potts, and Peter Weiser—signed up with Manuel Lisa to ascend the Missouri and the Yellowstone to build a trading fort at the mouth of the Bighorn (precisely one of the spots Clark had recommended).

How many other Corps of Discovery members joined the burgeoning fur trade in the wake of Lewis and Clark isn't known for sure, but no doubt more than those four found their way back west. Operating out of St. Louis, Clark became a partner in the fur business; so did Lewis's brother, Reuben. Lewis himself may have been a secret investor. And years later, little Jean Baptiste Charbonneau, whose face had become so puffy from mosquito bites at the confluence, grew up to be a mountain man, too. In 1842, John C. Frémont would run into him on a sandbar in the middle of the Platte River, where Baptiste showed the Pathfinder his boatload of furs and offered him boiled buffalo tongue and a mint julep.

In many ways, then, it was an almost seamless transition from the United States' first exploration of the West to the nation's next phase of exerting dominion over the land: the western fur trade and the era of the mountain man. Jedediah Smith—the "mountain man's mountain man"—would travel, it's said, with a copy of Lewis and Clark's narrative in his saddlebag, taking them, in spirit at least, into other, ever more remote corners of the West. Maybe the book was with him when he came across South Pass, the spot that would soon become the favored route for hundreds of thousands of settlers and gold seekers bound for the Pacific coast (usually with ex-mountain men for guides), as the fur trade era made its transition into yet another phase of American expansion.

More trading forts would be built at the strategic points the captains had been first to recommend—including the imposingly impressive Fort Union, the undisputed hub of international trade that rose up at the confluence Lewis and Clark had correctly predicted was destined for such importance.

With Fort Union built, there would be many more nights when the sounds of fiddle and dancing would mingle with the soft murmur of Yellowstone waters embracing the Missouri's. But none of those evenings, I think, would ever quite compare with the night of April 26, 1805, when the Corps of Discovery celebrated at "this long wished for spot"—that night so brimming with expectancy, so pregnant with possibility and so blessedly unburdened by any foreknowledge of everything the future held in store.

That night, they didn't know what ordeals still awaited them in their search for a passage that in fact was just a myth. And farther into the future, they could not have foreseen all that would transpire as the nation would follow their footsteps and rush across the continent, changing forever what they had seen with such fresh eyes.

They wouldn't have known that in the space of only forty years, the beaver, whose size and abundance so amazed them, would be overtrapped to the brink of extinction; that the elk and the grizzlies would be driven into the mountains; that the Audubon sheep would be hunted out of existence; and that in 1887, fearing that the buffalo, too, were in danger of disappearing, and looking for a specimen to stuff before that happened, the curator of the American Museum of Natural History would arrive at the very place where the Lewis and Clark expedition had found it necessary to club them out of the way. He would scour the area for three exhausting months and then head back East without having seen a single one.

None of that—and so much else, for good and for ill—would have seemed possible to the group dancing on that spring night where the two rivers meet. It's for us, not them, to weigh the losses against the gains of history. So give the Corps of Discovery the unalloyed pleasure of their festive and joyful evening at the confluence. But let us remember, there were—and always are—grizzlies of some kind just around the next bend.

8

"Seens of Visionary Inchantment"

I wrote this essay in memory of Stephen Ambrose. Its first seeds came from brief remarks I gave at his memorial service in New Orleans in October 2001 on the front steps of the National D-Day Museum he had founded. When millions of Americans remember Steve, they probably think of World War II and the beaches at Normandy; I think of Meriwether Lewis and the White Cliffs.

Of all the spots along the four-thousand-mile Lewis and Clark trail, the one that has worked its way most deeply into my heart is the White Cliffs of the Missouri River in north-central Montana. I love the place for its wild yet exquisite beauty. I love it because it is remarkably unchanged over two centuries, making it one of the few Lewis and Clark sites where a modern traveler can read from the expedition's journals, look up, and see *exactly* what the explorers were describing—without also seeing power lines, highways, subdivisions, dams, or any other distractions. Over the years I have also come to realize that perhaps the most compelling reason I love it is because of the cherished times I have spent there with old and new friends, as well as my family. And since the White Cliffs is such a special place to me, that makes May 31, 1805—the day the Corps of Discovery first encountered it—a special day on my Lewis and Clark calendar.

It began like almost every other day for the expedition up to that point: rise early to renew the daily struggle with the Missouri, the brawling, bully of a river whose insistent current had been trying to push them back to the Mississippi for more than a year. The temperature was forty-eight degrees at dawn (it would rise a mere five degrees by 4 P.M., according to their weather diary), and a light rain soon started falling that would continue throughout the morning. The captains and some of the crew set off with the two pirogues while the rest of the men took the six dugout canoes to retrieve the meat of two buffalo that had been killed late the previous evening a little ways off the river. Work and finding the food to fuel the work—these were the two quotidian constants of the Corps of Discovery.

The work was particularly difficult this day. The Missouri contained so many shallow rapids and riffles—what Sergeant John Ordway called "Shoaley places"—that the pirogues and canoes could only be inched forward by means of towropes. When the men tugging the ropes walked onshore, Lewis wrote, they found the footing "so slippery and the mud so tenacious that they are unable to wear their mockersons," but then sharp stones cut their bare feet. A quarter of the time, he noted, they had to do their towing from the river itself, sometimes up to their armpits in the frigid water. "In short," Lewis continued, "their labour is incredibly painfull and great, yet those faithfull fellows bear it without a murmur." The towrope for the trouble-plagued white pirogue broke at one particularly bad rapid, and the boat, with the captains' most important possessions (including the journals), nearly capsized.

At noon the captains ordered a brief halt to rest their tired crew and give them lunch. As a special reward for the morning's toil, each man was permitted a dram of whiskey, "which they received with much Chearfulness, and well deserved all wet and disagreeable," according to Clark. The rain stopped, and Lewis and a small group went for a short hunt, killing three buffalo (although one was swept downriver) in the space of an hour before everyone moved on together.

For a number of days now they had been passing through the Missouri River Breaks, a terrain so rugged and broken with its mazes of bluffs and coulees that the Hidatsa Indians usually avoided it in their yearly forays to the Great Falls and Three Forks to hunt buffalo or raid the Shoshones. Which meant that the Hidatsas hadn't described this particular section of the river to the captains back at Fort Mandan. With neither maps nor informal Indian descriptions to aid them, for the first time since leaving St. Louis Lewis and Clark were traveling without any advance knowledge of what to expect around the next bend of the river. That's when they entered the White Cliffs. Suddenly, they found themselves in a natural wonderland of white sandstone bluffs rising hundreds of feet above the river, eerie formations carved from the soft stone by millions of years of erosion, with dark igneous rock outcroppings and lava dikes punctuating it all—an incomparable land-scape made all the more astonishing by its unexpectedness.

To Sergeant Patrick Gass, a carpenter by trade, the "very curious cliffs and rocky peaks, in a long range . . . seem as if built by the hand of man, and are so numerous that they appear like the ruins of an ancient city." Private Joseph Whitehouse noted not only the white cliffs but the high pinnacles and "some very high black Walls of Stone, lying on each side of the River, which appeared curious." Ordway thought the long, thin, remarkably straight lava dikes resembled the stone walls of his native New Hampshire and marveled that "in some places [they] meet at right angles." But Lewis was the prose stylist of the expedition, as he proved that night in his journal, rhapsodizing for pages about the scenic splendor surrounding them:

The hills and river Clifts which we passed today exhibit a most romantic appear-ance. . . . The water in the course of time in decending from those hills and plains on either side of the river has trickled down the soft sand clifts and woarn it into a thousand grotesque figures, which with the help of a little immagination and an oblique view at a distance, are made to represent eligant ranges of lofty freestone buildings, having their parapets well stocked with statuary; collumns of various sculpture both grooved and plain, are also seen supporting long galleries in front of those buildings; in other places on a much nearer approach and with the help of less immagination we see the remains or ruins of eligant buildings; some collumns standing and almost entire with their pedestals and capitals; others retaining their pedestals but deprived by time or accident of their capitals, some lying prostrate an[d] broken othe[r]s in the form of vast pyramids of connic structure bearing a sereis of other pyramids on their tops becoming less as they ascend and finally terminating in a sharp point. nitches and alcoves of various forms and sizes are seen at different hights as we pass . . . the tops of the collumns did not the less remind us of some of those large stone buildings in the U' States . . . for here it is too that nature presents to the view of the traveler vast ranges of walls of tolerable workmanship, so perfect indeed are those walls that I should have thought that nature had attempted here to rival the human art of masonry had I not recollected that she had first began her work.

"As we passed on," Lewis wrote, in what has become one of the expedition's most famous passages, "it seemed as if those seens of visionary inchantment would never have an end." (Clark wisely saw no need to waste time trying to top his friend and co-commander's descriptive effusion and copied Lewis's words directly into his own journal—with, of course, a few inevitable variations in spelling. Ordway seems to have cribbed a few phrases, as well.)

They camped that evening near the mouth of what they called Stonewall Creek, on what Whitehouse described as "a handsome bottom" covered with cottonwoods, the only growth of timber they had seen that day. Whether they picked the spot for the trees (easy firewood), for the creek (fresher water), or for the fact that they had covered eighteen hard miles (the Missouri's current hadn't relented just because the scenery was pretty), it also happens to be the best campsite within the White Cliffs in terms of stunning views, a fact that would have become evident when, as Whitehouse notes, "in the evening, the weather cleared off, and became pleasant."

The hunters came in with more meat to add to the buffalo already killed that day—an elk, a mule deer, and two bighorn sheep whose impressive curled horns the captains preserved, according to Whitehouse, "in Order to carry them back with us, to the United States." Warmed by cottonwood fires, the tired men would have had plenty to eat. Their bonus dram of whiskey earlier in the day would not have prevented them from receiving the four-ounce "gill of ardent spirits" that was standard issue every evening. (Did anyone notice that there was now only a month's supply of whiskey left?) If Cruzatte pulled out his fiddle, his music would have echoed off the sandstone palisades directly across the river, giving the effect of a larger string section playing for the men's enjoyment.

Lewis and Clark both made short explorations on foot before sunset, collecting specimens of the sandstone and noting the appearance of coal in some places. On the bluffs, Lewis observed a species of pine (the limber pine) he had never seen before, and in the distance he saw "the most beautifull fox that I ever beheld" with distinctive colorings of "fine orrange yellow, white and black." Shortly after nightfall—excepting the night guards and whatever journalists were still busily trying to write down the day's experience—I would imagine everyone was sound asleep.

With a Northwest Passage to find and a continent to cross, the Corps of Discovery could not linger amidst these scenes of visionary enchantment. The next morning, Ordway says, "we Set out at an eirily hour and proceeded on as usal with the toe rope." In other words, back to the daily grind. "But fiew bad rapids points to day," he notes, "the wild animels not So pleanty as below." They made an impressive twenty-four miles, and long before stopping to camp they had left the White Cliffs behind. The scenery had become more mundane, yet worth recording nonetheless: great numbers of yellow and red currant bushes, chokecherries, and wild roses and prickly pear cactuses in full bloom. And off in the distance, something less enchanting but equally compelling to their eyes: "a range of high mountains . . . covered with snow."

My first encounter with the White Cliffs came in May 1983, when I was working on a freelance magazine article and following the Lewis and Clark trail for the first time. Bob Singer, a former music teacher from Fort Benton, Montana, who had started Missouri River Outfitters, took pity on a reporter with no advance reservations and less money and gave me an abbreviated tour in a small boat. Even though I had already seen the series of beautiful paintings of the White Cliffs done by the Swiss artist Karl Bodmer in the 1830s, seeing the real thing was nearly as startling for me as it must have been for Lewis and Clark.

I had stepped back in time. What I saw was precisely what Bodmer had painted and what the Corps of Discovery had described. Over the course of time, roads and highways had avoided the area for the same reason the Hidatsas had: the traveling is much easier on the flatter plains away from the river breaks. While giant wheat farms and a few small towns could be found on the flatlands, only a scattering of cattle populated the breaks. Clark had predicted as much in 1805. "This Countrey may with propriety I think be termed the Deserts of America," he had written on May 26, "as I do not Conceive any part can ever be Settled, as it is deficent in water, Timber & too steep to be tilled." A proposal to build a dam for irrigation had been abandoned after a lengthy battle in the 1960s, sparing the stretch of river from being inundated, like so much of the rest of the Missouri. Congress even offered a modicum of protection as a "wild and scenic river," limiting access to people in boats, preferably without motors, who were willing to put up with barebones campsites and the complicated logistics of putting onto the river at one place and taking out at another many miles downstream. Remoteness, climate, terrain—and a little legislative help—had spared the White Cliffs from the wholesale changes wrought along the rest of the trail.

Two years after my first visit, I was back. This time I had a book contract and more time (though not much of an advance) to spend. Bob Singer gave me another unscheduled quick visit, but I told him I could get more material for my book if I could go through the White Cliffs more slowly and with a group. Would he let me earn my way by helping with the support work? He looked at his schedule and said to show up again in three weeks ready to tote bags and coolers, clean up camp, and paddle a canoe. A tour group of thirteen had signed up for a three-day trip, led by some professor from New Orleans.

The professor turned out to be Stephen Ambrose. At the time he was hardly the celebrity historian he would become. He had written his well-respected multivolume biography of Eisenhower and was in the midst of a Nixon trilogy, but his best-selling World War II books were yet to come. And it didn't take long in his presence to realize that he had another deep-seated historical passion. He was, as he unabashedly told me, in love with Meriwether Lewis. For nearly a decade he had been taking his family on summer trips along the Lewis and Clark trail. He had commemorated the nation's bicentennial on July 4, 1976, camping at Lemhi Pass. He had spent a night alone, sleeping in his car, parked next to Lewis's grave site on Tennessee's Natchez Trace. He had read aloud from Lewis's journals at his daughter Stephenie's wedding. He made what my friends already considered my own "Lewis and Clark obsession" seem like a passing interest.

That first night we camped at Stonewall Creek, the same spot where the Corps of Discovery had camped on May 31, 1805. Before dinner, Steve insisted that we all sit facing the river while he, sitting behind us, read us Lewis's journal from that day. I can still hear his voice, raspy and gravelly and gruff like a drill sergeant's who has shouted out too many orders, yet caressing the passages as if he were reciting stanzas from a lyric poem. It was a magical moment that made me wonder whether the journalists of the expedition ever shared their work aloud with the rest of the party. Somehow I doubted it, but listening to Steve's recitation at that campsite made me hope that Clark (and Ordway) got the idea to copy down Lewis's words after hearing them from the author himself.

We made the three-day trip paddling downriver under a merciless summer sun, temperatures in the high nineties, a hot wind often in our face. No one complained. As Steve's readings of the journals reminded us (he read to us at breakfast, on the water, at lunch, back on the water, and every evening), this was nothing compared to what the Corps of Discovery had gone through to see the same scenery. In fact, in something of a reverse image of the expedition's experience, my canoe mate, Steve's college buddy from Wisconsin, Jim Wimmer, and I took every possible opportunity to immerse ourselves up to the armpits in the Missouri; it did wonders warding off the heat. With Steve's daughter and son-in-law, Stephenie and John Tubbs, and their dog Curly, I clambered up to the Eye of the Needle, a graceful sandstone arch perched on a sheer bluff nearly two hundred feet above the river—a landmark directly across from Stonewall Creek that Bob Singer had first shown me, from which he and I had witnessed a chevron of white pelicans flying below our feet. All of us—the Ambroses and the Tubbs (with Curly) and the Wimmers—made an hour-long hike to the Hole in the Wall, an even loftier vantage point from which to overlook the ribbon of river snaking through the White Cliffs.

Like the "faithfull fellows" of the expedition, we got to know one another through our shared experience. We became good enough friends that Steve asked me to stand in for him during one of the evening journal readings, something his children said he had never done before; and one afternoon, as our small flotilla floated in close formation while Steve rhapsodized from the journals yet again, his beloved wife, Moira, leaned across the gunwales and confided, "If I hear him say 'scenes of visionary enchantment' one more time, I may tip the canoe over." I retold our adventure in my first book, *Out West*, and I take some measure of reportorial pride that I had identified on paper the passion that, eleven years later, Steve would pour into his masterful biography of Lewis, *Undaunted Courage*.

I brought along an old friend on my next visit. Ken Burns and I were working on a Lewis and Clark documentary film for public television, and it was my great pleasure not only to introduce my buddy to Montana but to bring him to the White Cliffs. I can still remember the size of his eyes when we floated past a cottonwood tree where a bald eagle sat undisturbed on a branch overhanging the Missouri. His eyes got even bigger when we rounded the bend of the river that revealed the Stonewall Creek section.

We set up camp there with longtime colleagues Buddy Squires and Roger Haydock, the cinematographer and assistant cameraman for the film; Larry Cook, who had taken over Missouri River Outfitters after Bob Singer's death, and who carried on Bob's love of the upper Missouri and its stories; and Larry's assistant, Dave "Parch" Parchen, a high school art teacher who in a previous incarnation surely must have been a wild-eyed mountain man. Clouds barreled in from the west in the late afternoon, snuffing out our plans for filming the sunset, and late that night a thunderstorm erupted overhead. Ken and I lay awake in our tent, counting the time between the lightning bolts (which illuminated our tent poles like an X-ray of a skeleton) and the thunder that followed. When the lightning and thunder hit at the same time, we knew we wouldn't be going to sleep. Because of the turn in the weather, we left the next day without having gotten the film equivalent of Lewis's descriptions, but rather than being discouraged we were secretly thrilled. It meant we would have to come back. And we had a great thunderstorm survival story to tell our children.

The weather was more cooperative on our return trip—although fierce thunderclouds towered ominously on the northern horizon as we boated down the river in a vessel I calculated would make a perfect lightning rod. Worried about the prospects of another storm and therefore working furiously to take advantage of the dramatic late-afternoon light, we filmed the White Cliffs glistening in the sun, the Eye of the Needle arching high across from Stonewall Creek, a magnificent lava dike displaying "tolerable workmanship," and a full moon rising dreamily above the Hole in the Wall. Then, with our filming complete, we decided to just keep on going to our pull-out spot, using the full moon as our lamp—an unforgettable night voyage that even a hardened river rat like Larry Cook still refers to with reverence each time we meet.

Every subsequent trip I've made has been equally memorable. In 1998 my family finally came along. We joined a group of friends who have made retracing part of the Lewis and Clark trail a yearly summer ritual. After celebrating the Fourth of July in Great Falls with the Ambroses, we all set off downriver from Fort Benton with Larry and Bonnie Cook and Parch under ideal weather. My two favorite images from that voyage both come from Stonewall Creek. One is of our daughter, Emmy, frolicking in the river at day's end with Bonnie, who was patiently trying to show her how to squirt a powerful jet of water with a quick squeeze of her fist. The other is of Will, our son, talking excitedly as he hiked through a defile called the Narrows with Larry and Parch and myself, finding a magpie feather on the trail, and thereby being given the name Magpie—in honor, Parch said, of his and the bird's shared traits: intelligence, unquenchable curiosity, and the gift of gab.

Two visits were part of longer Lewis and Clark tours put together to help Steve Ambrose raise money for the World War II museum he was hoping to start. Steve's son Hugh ran the tours' logistics. Another son and daughter-in-law, Barry and Celeste Ambrose, catered the meals—exquisite affairs of fine food and finer wines for the prospective donors. Steve was the star attraction. I was asked to help provide "expert" commentary. I remember one trip for the weather at Stonewall Creek. It stormed even harder than it had when Ken and I had been there, and I remember telling my new tent mate, a federal judge from New York City, that these Montana thunderstorms could be fierce monsters, but they blew through quickly. Each time the wind picked up, sounding like a Boeing 747 buzzing the cottonwoods, and we braced our bodies at the upwind side of the tent to keep it from sailing off, I would assure him that the storm was nearly over and the stars would be coming out soon. I was an "expert" so he believed me—at least for the first few hours. But by dawn, when it was still blowing and pelting rain and showed no signs of letting up—and despite the fact that ours was one of the few tents still in its original position—I think my status had lowered in his eyes.

On the other tour, Steve and I uncharacteristically declined the chance to make the short climb to the Eye of the Needle. It had recently been destroyed by vandals, and neither of us had the heart to inspect the damage firsthand. Larry Cook, who had discovered the wreckage on a previous trip, described it for us. Someone apparently had climbed the bluff and pried loose the top four feet of the ten-foot-high arch, leaving behind only some broken beer bottles, the marks of a crowbar, and the rubble of an exquisite landmark that nature had taken eons to sculpt. It was a senseless, sickening act, as if someone had smashed off the head of the Jefferson Monument. An investigation had been launched, aided by a sizable reward posted for any information leading to a conviction of the perpetrator, but the most it had turned up were persistent rumors with no proof. (The maximum penalty for the crime is ten years in prison and a fine of $250,000, although some of us suggested a better punishment would be the one meted out for offenses during the Lewis and Clark expedition: fifty to a hundred lashes on the bare back.)

There was also talk of having a mason reconstruct the arch, and the Bureau of Land Management (BLM) was seeking public opinion about the idea. It seemed to me an understandable reaction to the loss of a Montana land-mark but wrongheaded nonetheless, especially considering Lewis's initial, awestruck reaction to the White Cliffs. Their beauty and wonder, he be-lieved, stemmed precisely from the fact that, though they appeared at first to be the work of man, they were actually the work of nature. *That* is their special magic. Camping in the shadow of the Eye of the Needle, he had been forced to admit that nature not only did her work first but also was often better at it than mankind.

Rebuilding the arch would not only miss Lewis's point but violate it as well. Hard as it was to imagine the Eye of the Needle gone forever, I argued, its broken remains should be left alone to serve as an additional, but different reminder: of the ease with which mankind can thoughtlessly destroy nature's handiwork; and of the responsibility we all share to make sure that scenes of visionary enchantment never have an end. × × ×

My last visit to the White Cliffs turned out to be the last adventure Steve Ambrose and I would share on the Lewis and Clark trail, though neither of us knew that to be the case. By this time he and I and our families had accumulated memories at nearly every significant spot along the expedition's route—from dedicating a statue in Kansas City to paddling a bulky (yet amazingly tipsy) dugout canoe on the Clearwater River; from riding horses over the Lolo Trail to sleeping at Fort Clatsop. With the Lewis and Clark bicentennial only a few years in the future, both of us assumed we had many more memories to make.

Steve's books had by now made him famous and wealthy (both unusual developments for a history professor), but what impressed and inspired me was the way he channeled his newfound fame and fortune into his passion for sharing and preserving the story of American history. He had founded the National D-Day Museum in New Orleans. He had joined the board of American Rivers, a conservation group, and was spearheading their drive to restore portions of the Missouri to something a little closer to the river the Corps of Discovery had traveled. He had helped keep the National Council for the Lewis and Clark Bicentennial financially afloat. With his son Hugh he was leading a trail stewardship project for the Lewis and Clark Trail Heritage Foundation, an attempt to educate tourists retracing the expedition's route not to damage sensitive sites. And all along the Lewis and Clark trail he had made guest appearances and given generous donations to small, local organizations struggling to build interpretative centers or preserve a small parcel of land.

The mission that had brought us back to the White Cliffs was to accompany then–Secretary of the Interior Bruce Babbitt on a brief tour. The BLM had decided (wisely) not to restore the Eye of the Needle, but the vandalism and a number of other issues had prompted Babbitt to consider new measures to provide the White Cliffs with greater protection. Steve and I were happy to extol their rare combination of scenic beauty and historical significance as Babbitt and his entourage of aides and reporters gathered at the canoe ramp. We described how fortunate we considered ourselves to have been able, on this one section of the trail, to see the same things Lewis and Clark had seen nearly two hundred years earlier; how even more fortunate we were to have been able to pass on that experience to our children (and Steve to his grandchildren); and how we hoped that they, in turn, would be able to pass it along to their children and grandchildren. We read aloud from the expedition's journals with particular gusto. In our enthusiasm, we even suggested that the government declare a White Cliffs National Park (an idea that proved to be wildly unpopular in that immediate area of Montana). Then we paddled our canoes downstream, saw a pair of bald eagles, helped Babbitt put up a section of fence to shield some cottonwood saplings from grazing cattle, and showed him the Stonewall Creek section before a BLM boat shuttled us all back upstream.

A year later, we met again in the East Room of the White House—the very room Lewis had occupied for two and a half years while serving as President Jefferson's private secretary—for the last official event of the outgoing Clinton administration. At that ceremony, President Clinton posthumously promoted William Clark to the true rank of captain and declared York and Sacagawea as honorary sergeants of the Corps of Discovery. And using the Antiquities Act in the same way Theodore Roosevelt had first used it to save the Grand Canyon, he set aside the White Cliffs as a national monument.

Steve had the honor of speaking at the ceremony and received the pen with which President Clinton signed Clark's promotion to the same rank as Lewis. I had the honor of being there to hear Steve quote from Lewis's journal one more time (and received the pen that created the new national monument). We reminisced about our first trip through the White Cliffs so many years ago, the sheer happenstance that had brought us together, the long and winding trail each of us had traveled since that time, and how lucky we felt that those trails had somehow managed to keep crossing. We discussed the possibility of a big, two-family, multigenerational trip through the White Cliffs to properly celebrate the bicentennial amidst never-ending scenes of visionary enchantment.

I hold the memory of that moment, far as it was from Montana, in the same safe place where I keep my other memories of the White Cliffs—because it was the last time I saw Steve in person, before cancer took him away at too young an age. I like to think that someday, maybe our distant descendants will meet on the upper Missouri—by chance or by design—and camp at Stonewall Creek and look out at the river while one of them reads aloud from the Lewis and Clark journals with great passion and feeling. Neither Steve nor I will be there, but I now feel more confident that the White Cliffs will be.

9

Meriwether Lewis's "Curious Adventure"

This essay comes from a speech I gave on July 2, 1998, in Great Falls, Montana, at the annual meeting of the Lewis and Clark Trail Heritage Foundation. The crowd gathered on the shore of the Missouri River at the same spot where Lewis had jumped in to escape the grizzly bear. My family—Dianne and our children, Emmy and Will—remembers the moment because the mosquitoes, as Clark would have put it, were "extremely numerous and troublesome."

On the Lewis and Clark "calendar of events" a handful of dates automatically stand out—dates like May 14, 1804, when the expedition first set off from Camp Dubois on their epic journey; or August 12, 1805, when Lewis reached the summit of Lemhi Pass and saw the great dream of a Northwest Passage vanish before him in the jumbled peaks of endless mountains stretching westward. Students of the expedition remember November 7, 1805, for Clark's famous journal entry, "Ocian in view! O! the joy"—remember it not only for his inventive spelling and his uncharacteristic use of double exclamation points to punctuate the almost unspeakable emotion of the moment, but also because, as Clark soon discovered, the ocean *really wasn't in view.* And no one forgets September 23, 1806, the day the startled residents of St. Louis looked up to see the expedition's white pirogue and flotilla of dugout canoes swinging into view and then heard a volley of three rounds from the grizzled explorers, whom everyone assumed had long since been swallowed up by the vastness of the West.

In central Montana the two most notable dates are June 13, 1805, when a jubilant and enraptured Lewis first came across the Great Falls, the "sublimely grand spectacle," he said, that "formes the grandest sight I ever beheld"; and July 4, 1805—the day the expedition's exhausting portage around the falls was finally complete; the twenty-ninth birthday of the nation whose flag and future the Corps of Discovery was carrying toward the continent's farthest shore; the holiday they celebrated well into the night by draining the last of their whiskey.

But for me, sometimes it's the less obvious moments of the expedition that offer up the most interest. One of those is June 14, 1805—the day *after* Lewis first made his discovery of the Great Falls. Though perhaps not as historically significant as the day preceding it, June 14 would have its own share of discoveries. It, too, would have its moments of excitement and high drama—as well as its insights into the complex mind of the expedition's intriguing commander.

I think of the day in the way that Lewis himself referred to it, not once but twice in his recounting of June 14, 1805. Call it Meriwether Lewis's "Curious Adventure."

He awoke that morning before dawn—which at that latitude in mid-June would be around 4:30 A.M.—with the newly discovered falls thundering next to his campsite. The steady roar of those falls must have been music to his ears, because without doubt this was the best morning of the entire expedition up to this point for Meriwether Lewis.

Only a few days earlier, back with the rest of the Corps at the Missouri's junction with the unexpected Marias River, he had been listening to all the reasons why the men believed the *Marias* was the true Missouri, why *it* was the fork that would lead them to the waterfall described by the Hidatsas the previous winter at Fort Mandan, and therefore why *it* was river that would lead them to the Northwest Passage. This northern fork was muddy, just as the river had been all the way from St. Louis, they argued, and thus must be the true Missouri.

Lewis and Clark had thought otherwise—that the Missouri should be getting clearer, like a mountain river, if it was to lead them to the short portage everyone expected between the Atlantic and Pacific watersheds. But given the gravity of the situation, the captains had decided to delay for a week while they reconnoitered the two forks. "To ascend [the wrong] stream," Lewis had confided to his journal, "would not only loose us the whole of this season, but would probably so dishearten the party that it might defeat the expedition altogether." The reconnoitering, however, had solved nothing. When it was over, Lewis and Clark still wanted to take the southern fork; the men, following the lead of their best boatman, Pierre Cruzatte, still wanted to take the northern one, though they admitted the choice was up to the captains. The captains had pointed up the southern fork, with Lewis and a small scouting party pushing ahead of the others.

Think, therefore, what it meant to Lewis on June 13 when he had finally come upon the Great Falls, roaring just as the Hidatsas had described it. It meant they were on the correct fork of the Missouri. It meant they would not have to retrace their steps, go back to the Marias, and head up that river— with all the maddening, additional delays associated with such a "retrograde march," as Lewis would have grudgingly called it. On a more personal level, it meant something more. It meant that Lewis and Clark, not the men, *had been right.*

Think also about the consequences if it had been the other way around; think about it for at least a moment, because it most assuredly must have been running through Lewis's mind for days on end. If the captains had been wrong there would have been more delays—and more discouragement—at a crucial time, when the expedition desperately needed the reassurance that this far out in the unmapped and incredible, yawning distances of the West they could rely on their leaders to at least head them in the right direction. So an even more critical consequence would have been an unmistakable undermining of the captains' authority. Every decision, every order from that moment on would have been subjected to inevitable second-guessing, murmuring, and backbiting. (If you want to know how well a group full of second-guessers, murmurers, and backbiters crosses the continent, study the journals of the Donner Party.)

Consider this a few seconds more from Lewis's point of view. No one enjoys being proven wrong—losing face—in front of other people. Officers particularly want to avoid it in front of their subordinates (even more than parents in front of their own children). And if we know anything about the character of Meriwether Lewis, we know he was especially sensitive about not losing face in front of anyone. So on June 13, when he stood at the base of the Great Falls and struggled again and again to describe their power and their beauty and his sense of absolute elation at being the first American citizen to behold them, mixed in with his ecstasy was the knowledge that he would not lose face with his men—and that made the beauty of the falls that much more beautiful.

He had been sick for days, unable to keep anything down, but his dinner that night, of buffalo hump and tongue and marrowbone, parched meal, salt and pepper, was heartily consumed—along with the first cutthroat trout ever described for science, which Silas Goodrich had caught at the base of the falls and gladly presented to the captain. The trout only added to the sense of excited bliss that had overtaken him.

When Lewis awoke on June 14, he was still under its spell. At the crack of dawn he sent Joseph Field downriver to give Clark and the rest of the expedition the encouraging news about the falls. George Drouillard, George Gibson, and Goodrich were dispatched to bring in the meat from a buffalo they had shot the day before and to prepare it for drying. Meanwhile, Meriwether Lewis . . . waited. Was he writing his effusive account of the Great Falls while the early morning sun illuminated the roiling waters and produced the beautiful rainbow he so vividly described? Did he have a second helping of the cutthroat trout? Was he simply relaxing, basking in the serene knowledge that during the great test of leadership and geographical deduction that had confronted them at the Marias, he and Clark had passed with flying colors—a fact that the others would learn just as soon as Field reached them, but something he could momentarily savor by himself? We don't know. We do know it wasn't until nearly six hours after sunrise— around 10 A.M.—that Lewis decided to take a solitary stroll upriver.

He anticipated going only a few miles and returning before dinner. The Hidatsas, after all, had mentioned only one waterfall, and Lewis assumed a short hike would take him past the rapids above the falls and allow him to begin planning the short portage still firmly in his mind. If he thought otherwise, he wouldn't have waited until 10 A.M. to set off. He brought along his rifle and his espontoon (a long staff with a metal point). The weather was clear, wind from the southwest, and warm enough—headed toward the mid-seventies—for him to decide to wear his yellow flannel shirt without his leather overshirt. Walking over the rough ground on the river's north side, he saw continuous rapids and a few small cascades for a distance of roughly five miles.

That's when he received his first surprise of the day: a nineteen-foot waterfall angling across the river. He named it Crooked Falls (a name it still retains) and considered returning to camp with this new information. But a constant, loud noise just upstream, around a sharp bend in the Missouri, drew him farther upriver. Surprise number two: just around the bend . . . was *another* waterfall. This one (now called Rainbow Falls) was fifty feet high, intersected the river at a right angle, and had an edge, Lewis writes, "as regular and as straight as if formed by art, without a niche or a brake in it."

If Lewis was disappointed or unnerved by this revelation of two more major obstacles in the expedition's way, he doesn't exhibit it in his journal. Instead, he rhapsodizes about Rainbow Falls in much the same manner—though not at the same length—as he had about the Great Falls the day before. He even weighs the two on the scales of beauty, concluding that "at length I determined between these two great rivals for glory that this (Rainbow Falls) was *pleasingly beautifull*, while the other (the Great Falls) was *sublimely grand*." I believe that still "bestows the palm," as Lewis would have phrased it, on the Great Falls—"sublimely grand" trumping "pleasingly beautiful" in my own mind—but Lewis himself diplomatically avoids ranking them, leaving the judgment for each of us to make on our own.

Looking upriver from Rainbow Falls, he got surprise number three: yet another falls at the distance of half a mile. "Thus invited," he writes, "I did not once think of returning but hurried thither to amuse myself with this newly discovered object." Ponder those words—"*amuse myself* with this newly discovered object." This was the third unexpected waterfall he had come across in what started out as a little walk to peruse a short stretch of rapids; the plans for a half-day portage are already in rubble; and Lewis is using terms like "amuse myself"? He was either deep in self-denial at this point, or perhaps that state of bliss from the previous day's discovery was even stronger than originally imagined.

This next surprise was what became known as Colter Falls, now entombed in the waters behind Rainbow Dam. It was a cascade, Lewis writes, that "in any other neighborhood but this . . . would probably be extolled for its beauty and magnificence." But up against Rainbow Falls and the Great Falls, he decided, it was not worth tarrying over. Besides, as he pressed forward another two and a half miles Lewis was now running short of waterfall adjectives and he probably wanted to save whatever ones he had left, in case there were any more surprises lurking around the next bend of the Missouri.

And there was: surprise number four (or waterfall number five when you count the unsurprising Great Falls), a cataract of twenty-six feet, showering a fine mist into the air and sending torrents of water around a small island, where an eagle had placed her nest in the crown of a lone cottonwood—Black Eagle Falls. In Lewis's estimation, these falls were not quite up to the incredibly high standards set by Rainbow Falls and Great Falls, but they were certainly, he writes, "a more noble, interesting object than the celibrated falls of [the] Potomac or [Schuylkill]" Rivers back in the East.

If you're following this ranking system—with its "sublimely grand" and "pleasingly beautifull" and "noble" objects—what it means is that, with the notable exception of Niagara Falls, Lewis is claiming that he has just discovered the second-, third-, and fourth-most majestic waterfalls in North America, all in the space of twenty-four hours. No wonder that his journal writings still seem infused with rapture and wonder, even a little cockiness, rather than focusing on the fact that by now he's hiked more than ten miles and he still isn't sure whether even more cascades await him just upstream.

He decided to climb the large hill just north of Black Eagle Falls (the hill where the Anaconda copper company would later erect its giant smelter smokestack, the most commanding prospect in the city of Great Falls) for a better view upriver. What a view it was. A "beautifull and extensive plain" stretched from the river all the way to the base of snowclad mountains to the south and southwest. In the fertile valley at his feet, Lewis saw a herd of a thousand buffalo grazing peacefully, and vast flocks of geese feeding along the river's shore. Even more pleasing, for as far as he could see the Missouri was now a "smooth, even and unruffled sheet of water" nearly a mile wide, apparently done with its succession of rapids and waterfalls. And four miles away a large river flowed into the Missouri from the distant mountains—another landmark the Hidatsas had described to the captains, the river they called the Medicine (now called the Sun)—further proof that the decision Lewis and Clark had made at the Marias had kept them on track toward the headwaters of the Missouri and the Northwest Passage.

Taken in one sweeping panorama, it was, Lewis writes, "a ravishing prospect," and he rested a few minutes to drink it all in. He could have decided now to return to his camp. He had hiked more than ten miles at this point. It must have been midafternoon, and he was much farther from his campsite back at the Great Falls than he originally planned. With a placid, smooth Missouri stretching to the south, his reconnaissance was completed, and he had learned much more from his ramble than he had initially bargained for. Most explorers in most circumstances would have called it a day. Not Meriwether Lewis on June 14, 1805. Instead he determined to push forward to the mouth of the Medicine River.

Now things got even stranger, and his "curious adventure" took some new twists. After descending to the valley, he decided to shoot one of the buffalo in the teeming herd—for supper in case he needed to spend the night before returning to the other men. He selected a nice, fat one, shot it through the lungs, and was, he writes, "gazing attentively on the poor animal discharging blood in streams from his mouth and nostrils, expecting him to fall every instant."

Lost in this vivid reverie, Lewis suddenly noticed something only twenty paces away. It was a grizzly—one of those huge, fearless monsters that had been thoroughly intimidating the Corps of Discovery with their ferocity and near-invulnerability for nearly two months, ever since the expedition passed the mouth of the Yellowstone. The explorers had encountered more than thirty grizzlies in that time, killing fourteen and wounding five others. Who knows where this bear came from so suddenly, or how it had managed to get so close to Lewis undetected on the open plains, with not a single tree or bush within three hundred yards by the captain's estimates. Lewis instantly raised his gun to fire—and just as instantly realized that he had been watching that buffalo bleed to death instead of reloading his rifle.

Although they can weigh more than five hundred pounds, grizzlies can easily reach speeds of more than thirty miles per hour over short distances, which makes twenty paces not much of a head start, especially over open ground. If ever there was a chance for the grizzly bears of Montana to even the score with the Corps of Discovery for all their fallen comrades, this was it.

Lewis began retreating at a brisk walk, hoping the bear wouldn't pursue him. No such luck. "I had no sooner terned myself," Lewis writes, "but he pitched at me, open mouthed and full speed." Lewis sprinted for eighty yards, but quickly learned what all westerners are taught from childhood: in a hundred-yard dash, bet on the grizzly. With the bear gaining on him, Lewis reached the Missouri, jumped off the shallow riverbank, splashed into waist-deep water, and in desperation wheeled around with his espontoon, pointing it as firmly as he could while still clutching his unloaded rifle. At the same time, the grizzly reached the edge of the water, snarling less than twenty feet away.

In the expedition's scrapes with grizzlies up to this moment, the unifying characteristic had been the bears' aggressive fearlessness, as if they were intent on proving—guns or no guns—which mammal deserved to sit atop the food chain of the Great Plains. Time and time again it had required multiple rounds of musket fire (a dozen in one instance) to bring down an enraged grizzly and save the life of one or another of the men. One-shot kills were unheard of, and in this instance Lewis didn't even have one shot between himself and the grizzly twenty feet away.

But this particular grizzly apparently was not closely related to the others, or perhaps it was to its brethren what the Cowardly Lion was to the real kings of the jungle: more bluster than bravery. Rather than swiping the espontoon from Lewis's hands like a matchstick and making a brief appetizer out of the captain before turning to the dead buffalo for a main course, *this* grizzly inexplicably turned tail and ran off. It ran away as fast as it had pursued

Lewis; ran at full speed, occasionally looking over its shoulder; ran for three miles until it disappeared into the woods along the Medicine River.

Now consider what Meriwether Lewis did next. Did he count his blessings and head in the opposite direction toward safety and his camp? Let him answer in his own words: "As soon as I saw him run of[f] in that manner I returned to the shore and charged my gun, which I had still retained in my hand throughout this curious adventure. . . . My gun reloaded I felt confidence once more in my strength; and determined not to be thwarted in my design of visiting medicine river. . . . I passed through the plain nearly in the direction which the bear had run." In other words, he followed the grizzly. A "curious adventure" indeed.

Upon reaching the Medicine River (a "handsome stream" in his words, where the grizzly fortunately made no second appearance), Lewis's watch told him it was now 6:30 P.M., eight and a half hours since his departure from the camp he thought was twelve miles away (but which I would estimate is closer to fifteen miles downstream). Time—finally—to turn back. But his gaze soon fell upon a strange animal: a "tyger cat" he calls it, brownish yellow, standing near its burrow, probably a wolverine. It made signs that it might spring at him but disappeared into its hole when he shot at it. This time he immediately reloaded.

"It now seemed to me that all the beasts of the neighbourhood had made a league to distroy me," he writes, "or that some fortune was disposed to amuse herself at my expence, for I had not proceded more than three hundred yards from the burrow of the tyger cat, before three bull buffaloe, which wer feeding with a large herd about half a mile from me on my left, seperated from the herd and ran full speed towards me." On a "curious" day like this, it probably comes as no surprise to learn that running for his life from three stampeding buffalo bulls, or at least dropping the lead bull with a shot from his rifle, simply wasn't considered an option by Meriwether Lewis. No, instead, he writes, "I thought at least to give them some amusement and altered my direction to meet them." And of course, rather than stomping him to dust on the plains for his foolishness, the bulls suddenly stopped about a hundred yards away and then they, too, turned around and hastily ran off.

It's at this point that Lewis's state of mind warrants revisiting—that sense of undiluted euphoria he had first experienced at the Great Falls the day before but which was still with him when he awoke that morning; that incredible rush of excitement and wonder that had allowed him to view four more waterfalls not as extra obstacles to be overcome but as sublime works of nature; feeling alive with such incredible intensity that even moments of extreme danger can be viewed with detached bemusement. Perhaps such a state of mind somehow magically cloaks a man with temporary invulnerability (unless it was the yellow flannel shirt, acting as some sort of superpowerful animal repellant).

Lewis himself seems to have perceived some magic in the day—a magic he was unsure would last much longer. Despite the late hour and the long distance to camp, he writes, "I then continued my rout homewards passed the buffaloe which I had killed, but did not think it prudent to remain all night at this place which really from the succession of curious adventures wore the impression on my mind of inchantment; at sometimes for a moment I thought it might be a dream, but the prickley pears which pierced my feet very severely once in a while, particularly after it grew dark, convinced me that I was really awake."

Late that night—the journals don't reveal what time—after his thirty-mile day on foot, Lewis arrived back in camp at the Great Falls, where Drouillard, Gibson, and Goodrich had been worried sick for his safety. Having expected him back hours earlier, the captain explains, "they had formed a thousand conjectures, all of which equally forboding my death," and were making plans to search for his corpse the next morning.

But fate had other plans for Meriwether Lewis—a fate that would not allow mere grizzly bears, or tyger cats, or stampeding buffalo, or a succession of waterfalls to stand between him and the end of his journey. There would be plenty of days ahead when he would see danger and disappointment for what it was. And there would be plenty of other times when he would be unable to greet triumph and success and good fortune without a sense of inadequacy, sorrow, and his own deep forebodings.

As history would prove, Meriwether Lewis was perfectly capable of seeing even the sunniest of days as situations when the glass of life was half-empty. But not this day. Mark down June 14, 1805, as a special day on the Corps of Discovery's calendar and in Lewis's all-too-abbreviated life—not because it was a turning point for the expedition, or because something particularly historic occurred. Mark it down because on June 14, 1805, everywhere Meriwether Lewis turned, everything he saw, everything he did, convinced him that the glass of life was instead half-full—half-full and brimming over.

10

"Toilsome Days and Wristless Nights"

I gave the speech upon which this essay was based while standing on a flatbed trailer parked next to the Clark Canyon Reservoir, whose waters now entomb the original site of Camp Fortunate. It was for the annual meeting of the Lewis and Clark Trail Heritage Foundation in August 2000, during a time of intense forest fires in Montana and Idaho. Not only couldn't we see Camp Fortunate because of the reservoir, but when we later ascended Lemhi Pass we couldn't see any mountains in the distance because of the smoke.

On July 27, 1805, the Corps of Discovery reached what Meriwether Lewis called "an essential point in the geography of this western part of the continent"—the place, in what is now southwestern Montana, where the Gallatin, Madison, and Jefferson Rivers meet to form the Missouri, the mighty river the expedition had been slowly but steadily ascending for more than a year. In their quest to find a water route across the continent they had finally entered the Rocky Mountains, and everyone on the expedition recognized that the next few weeks would be fateful to their success or failure.

No one was more acutely aware of this than Meriwether Lewis, whose journals for this period are, I believe, the most revealing of the entire journey. Through them it is possible to walk in Lewis's footsteps from the Three Forks to the Continental Divide—a crucial section of the trail that would prove to be "an essential point" not only in the geography of the West but in understanding the geography of his character.

"We are now several hundred miles within the bosom of this wild and mountainous country," Lewis wrote upon reaching the Three Forks, "where game may rationally be expected shortly to become scarce and subsistence precarious without any information with rispect to the country not knowing how far these mountains continue, or wher to direct our course to pass them to advantage or intersept a navigable branch of the Columbia, or even were we on such an one the probability is that we should not find any timber within these mountains large enough for canoes if we judge from the portion of them through which we have passed."

What he's admitting—to his journal at least—is this: these western mountains are slowly revealing themselves to be more formidable than he and President Jefferson had anticipated back in Washington (more formidable even than he and Clark had imagined at Fort Mandan); they've reached the edge of the geographical information they had gleaned from the Hidatsas the previous winter and are now more unsure about the route ahead than at any point in the journey so far; and even if they *can* find the Northwest Passage and a navigable stream to the Pacific, they should not expect to find trees suitable for making more canoes. Nearly three thousand miles from their starting point at the Missouri's mouth, that's a sobering admission to make.

Understandably then, Lewis wrote, "We begin to feel considerable anxiety with rispect to the Snake (Shoshone) Indians. If we do not find them or some other nation who have horses I fear the successfull issue of our voyage will be very doubtfull." What Jefferson so explicitly called "the object of your mission" had not changed for Lewis: to follow the Missouri to its source, find the Northwest Passage to a tributary of the Columbia, and take that river to the Pacific. But now a more immediate, more crucial objective had crowded in: finding the Shoshones and their horses. In the captains' minds, a simple equation had emerged. No Shoshones, no horses. No horses, no success. And there's nothing like the prospect of impending failure to concentrate the mind.

For several days, they had been seeing signs of Indians—smoke signals in the distance and occasional abandoned campsites, some of them only a few days old. *Signs* of Indians, but no Indians. Just beyond the Three Forks, as the expedition pushed up the Jefferson, Sacagawea provided a spark of hope when she showed the explorers the exact spot where the Hidatsas had kidnapped her five years earlier and told the captains they were at last nearing the land of her people. On August 8 she pointed south at a rocky bluff projecting over the river. The Shoshones called it Beaverhead Rock, she told them; their summering grounds were just beyond it, on a river flowing west.

"As it is now all important with us to meet with those people as soon as possible, I determined to proceed [ahead] tomorrow with a small party to the source of . . . this river and pass the mountains to the Columbia; and down that river until I find the Indians," Lewis wrote after hearing this tantalizing news. "In short," he added, "it is my resolusion to find them, or some others who have horses, if it should cause me a trip of a month."

Note the urgency in his words. It's finding Indians with horses that is "now all important"; all-important enough for an unprecedented one-month reconnaissance. The fact that he would also be crossing the Continental Divide—and presumably discovering the Northwest Passage—seems to have taken a back seat to discovering Indians with horses.

The seriousness of the situation was further highlighted the next morning, when Lewis wrote out some instructions for Clark, "lest," he says, "any accedent should befall me on the long and reather hazardous rout I was now about to take." Then, immediately after breakfast, he slung his pack on his back and set off on foot with George Drouillard, John Shields, and Hugh McNeal. In his weather journal, Lewis called this small band of four his "party of discovery." They made sixteen miles that first day, camping northeast of modern-day Dillon and dining on the meat of two antelope they had killed on their way.

On August 10 the four men set out "very early" in the morning along the Beaverhead River. After passing a large creek that Lewis named for McNeal (today's Blacktail Deer Creek), they followed an Indian trail south to Rattlesnake Cliffs, a name applied by Lewis that has survived to this day (as have the descendants of the rattlesnakes he described there). They saw some bald eagles and two osprey, ate a hasty lunch of freshly killed deer, and sometime in the afternoon arrived at the spot now dominated by the Clark Canyon Dam and Reservoir—in my estimation one of the most significant spots on the entire Lewis and Clark trail.

Lewis described it as "a hadsome open and leavel vally where the river divided itself nearly into two equal branches." (Given the dam and the reservoir that now inundates this area with acres upon acres of water, modern explorers have to use their imaginations or simply take Lewis's word for it: this *was* a handsome, open, and level valley on August 10, 1805.) "Immediately in the level plain between the forks and about 1/2 a mile distance from them," Lewis continued, "stands a high rocky mountain, the base of which is surrounded by the level plain; it has a singular appearance." The top of the small mountain is still visible, poking out of the reservoir—singular today in the fact that it's the only landmark not under water.

Because of the shallowness of the two streams converging here, Lewis concluded that this place was as far as the expedition's canoes could go. Seeing snow on some nearby mountaintops, he was amazed, he said, that the Missouri had provided such a gentle ascent to so high an elevation. "If the Columbia furnishes us such another example," he wrote, "a communication across the continent by water will be practicable and safe"—though already he had some misgivings about that prospect.

His more immediate concern was horses, so he needed to keep moving. Lewis scratched out a note to Clark, saying to wait here for his return, attached it to a dry willow pole he placed at the forks of the two creeks, and, after a brief confusion over which stream to follow, set out along the one leading west—what is now called Horse Prairie Creek. He and his three companions covered another five miles before setting up camp for the night in a valley Lewis called Shoshone Cove, "one of the handsomest coves I ever saw." They killed a deer for supper and cooked it over a fire of willow brush, there being only four cottonwoods in the entire valley, according to Lewis's count. After covering thirty hard miles since morning, they must have eaten heartily and slept soundly.

The next day, August 11, began an extraordinary week for Meriwether Lewis. It would become an uninterrupted emotional roller coaster for him— a week in which his literal crossing and recrossing of the Continental Divide would be mirrored by the peaks and valleys within his own inner landscape; moments of great anticipation followed quickly by profound disappointment; brief satisfactions crowded out by constant worries; soaring heights of supreme achievement plunging into darkest despair. His journey over and back would be, perhaps, the young captain's most mentally fatiguing and challenging week of the entire expedition. It would demand his utmost in concentration and quick thinking. It would repeatedly test his personal courage. It would challenge his inner fortitude, his ability to move forward in the face of repeated discouragement. It would rub his nerve endings raw. And in the end, this psychological crucible would strip everything away to reveal his soul.

The emotional roller-coaster ride began on the morning of August 11, five miles up Horse Prairie Creek, when, off in the distance, about two miles away, Lewis saw something that made him "overjoyed at the sight." It was an Indian—the first Indian the explorers had seen since leaving North Dakota. Taking a closer look through his spyglass, Lewis discovered even better news: by his clothes this Indian appeared to be a Shoshone, and he was mounted on "an eligant horse."

The captain could hardly believe his luck. Only two days out on a reconnaissance he had been prepared to last a month, and here was a Shoshone on an elegant horse. "I . . . had no doubt of obtaining a friendly introduction to his nation," Lewis wrote, "provided I could get near enough to him to convince him of our being whitemen."

He marched forward. The Indian slowly approached. So far, so good. But with a mile still separating them, the Indian stopped, and so did Lewis, who unrolled his blanket and waved it up and down three times in a signal of friendship. The Shoshone didn't move. Lewis put down his gun, took some trinkets from his pack, and advanced slowly. You can almost hear his heart beating like a drum as he tried to walk as calmly as possible.

At two hundred paces, the Indian became wary and turned his horse. Lewis called out "tab-ba-bone," which he understood from Sacagawea to be the Shoshone word for "white man," but the Indian seemed more concerned about Drouillard and Shields, both advancing on the flanks. Lewis signaled them to halt, but only Drouillard saw it and obeyed. At 150 yards the captain called out "tab-ba-bone" again, held up the trinkets he was offering, and rolled up his shirtsleeve to prove he was a white man. The Indian hesitated and Lewis moved forward some more, as leisurely as he could. But when the separation was reduced to a hundred paces, the Shoshone "suddonly turned his hose about, gave him the whip leaped the creek and disapeared in the willow brush in an instant."

It may have been Shields, advancing on the flank, who frightened the Indian off; it may have been Lewis's shouts of "tab-ba-bone," which instead of "white man" more precisely means "stranger." Regardless of the cause, the Shoshone was gone—"and with him," a crestfallen Lewis wrote, "vanished all my hopes of obtaining horses for the present. I now felt quite as much mortification and disappointment," he added, "as I had pleasure and expectation at the first sight of this indian." The true measure of his disappointment came out in his uncharacteristic response. Lewis bitterly upbraided his men, particularly Shields, blaming them not only for the Indian's flight but also for leaving behind the spyglass which, in truth, *he* had forgotten a mile back in his excitement.

The foursome tried to follow the Shoshone's trail, but a heavy rain, mixed with a little hail, quickly made tracking impossible. Wet, miserable, and having covered twenty miles, they made camp under the small American flag Lewis had attached to a pole. That night, I imagine, the men gave their captain a little wider berth around the campfire.

Monday, August 12, provided an even greater expectation and an even greater disappointment. After some searching, Lewis and his party came upon a well-worn Indian trail. It led them past some recently abandoned wickiups—a hopeful sign—and then turned abruptly west toward a low saddle in the mountains (today's Lemhi Pass). Lewis's spirits picked up. "I therefore did not dispair of shortly finding a passage over the mountains and of taisting the waters of the great Columbia this evening," he wrote. At the base of the ridge, McNeal straddled Trail Creek and "thanked his god that he had lived to bestride the mighty & heretofore deemed endless Missouri."

They hurried forward to the source of the creek, a small spring bubbling up just a few hundred yards from the crest of the ridge—"the most distant fountain," according to Lewis, "of the waters of the mighty Missouri in surch of which we have spent so many toilsome days and wristless nights." *Toilsome days and wristless nights.* From St. Louis to Lemhi Pass there had been too many of both to count. Lewis needed only to think back twenty-four hours to refresh his memory: the disappearing Shoshone and the dreary camp after a mountain rainstorm had surely made for an unforgettable "toilsome day and wristless night." But those were now behind him.

"Thus far," he wrote, "I had accomplished one of those great objects on which my mind has been unalterably fixed for many years, judge then of the pleasure I felt in allying my thirst with this pure and ice cold water." This was the moment Lewis had been dreaming of for more than twelve years—dreaming of from the time in 1793 when he was only eighteen years old and had brashly approached Jefferson (unsuccessfully) about leading what became instead the Michaux expedition; dreaming of throughout his two and a half years at Jefferson's side in the White House, where for who knows how many evenings the president and his young protégé had excitedly discussed a Northwest Passage beckoning at the Missouri's farthest reach; dreaming of every "toilsome day and wristless night" since leaving Washington in 1803.

Finding the Missouri's headwaters and—just beyond it—the Northwest Passage was the "object of your mission." It was the expedition's North Star upon which Lewis's mind had been "unalterably fixed." And now, with the taste of pure, cold water from those headwaters still in his mouth, as he climbed the last few remaining steps toward the long-dreamed-for Passage, it's hard to imagine Meriwether Lewis thinking about Shoshones and horses.

With each step he must have been anticipating the transcendent accomplishment of discovering the great prize that had eluded every explorer since Christopher Columbus. Only thirty years old and burning with the same ambitions that had prompted him to volunteer for this quest as a teenager, he had to be thinking about fame and his place in history. He would have been thinking about . . . himself. But what he saw from the crest of Lemhi Pass gave him something much different to ponder, because spread out before him was not a Northwest Passage, the fabled water route across North America, but, in his words, "immence ranges of high mountains still to the West of us with their tops partially covered with snow."

If Lewis paused to absorb that deflating vista and to contemplate its profound consequences, he doesn't mention it in his journals. He doesn't tell us what was running through his mind as the great dream literally vanished before his eyes. Maybe the surprise left him speechless. Perhaps the disappointment was simply too great for words. Or maybe—and I think this is more likely the case—the forbidding panorama from Lemhi Pass not only snapped Lewis out of any reverie about fame and history and personal achievement but instantly refocused his mind on the fate of his men and his expedition.

Within the officer corps of the military are three words that remind every commander of his responsibilities. In order of importance, those three words are: "Mission, men, self." The "self" comes last, behind the mission and the men. At Lemhi Pass, with those immense and snow-clad mountains stretching out endlessly before him, threatening not just the success of his expedition but the survival of his men, Meriwether Lewis quickly had to put his priorities back in proper order. Which is to say, he had to put his personal feelings aside and direct his energies once more to finding Shoshones and horses. If they had been "all important" before, they were immeasurably more essential now.

To judge from the journals, Lewis paused only briefly on the ridgeline before descending its western slope. In passing, and without exultation or elaboration, he mentions tasting "the waters of the great Columbia river," hiking several more miles down the mountain, and stopping to make camp near a spring. This was their first campsite beyond the recently expanded boundaries of the United States, on the Pacific side of the continent, but Lewis made no note of it that night. Instead, he recorded the lack of fresh meat to

eat and coming across a "deep perple currant"—the Hudson gooseberry—
that seemed to him a new species. Its flavor, he wrote, was "ascid & very
inferior." Those words probably also described his mood.

Back on the Indian trail the next morning, August 13, Lewis's party saw
some Shoshones a mile away, but the Indians fled at the strangers' approach.
Hopes raised and dashed once more—and then raised again when the explorers rounded a corner and surprised three Shoshone women who didn't
have time to flee. Lewis gave them presents and had no sooner persuaded
them of his peaceful intentions when sixty mounted warriors galloped up
"at nearly full speed," armed head to foot and ready to fight off what they
presumed was an enemy attack. In a moment fraught with peril, when his
heart must have been pumping pure adrenaline and his mind must have been
racing through every conceivable possibility, Lewis did a remarkable thing,
proving both his quick thinking and, most of all, his undeniable courage.
He dropped his gun, picked up the American flag, and approached alone.

That—and the excited talk of the women showing off their new presents—
persuaded the chief, Cameahwait, to receive the strangers as friends. He led
them to his village on the Lemhi River, put them up in the only leather tepee
that had survived a raid by the Atsinas that spring, and shared what meager
food the Shoshones had to offer: cakes of chokecherries and service berries,
and a bit of roasted salmon which confirmed to Lewis that he was, indeed,
on a tributary of the Columbia.

The bad news of August 14—"unwelcome information," in the captain's
words—was that Cameahwait said the nearby rivers were unnavigable, even
though they did eventually lead to what he called the "stinking lake" of "illy-
taisted waters" far to the west. The good news was that the Shoshones had
a magnificent herd of four hundred horses, some of them as fine as the best
in Virginia, and Lewis went to bed that night assured that his expedition
would have the use of some of them.

On August 15 that assurance was punctured. The Shoshones were reluctant
to leave with Lewis for the forks of the Beaverhead, where he promised that
Clark and other white men would be waiting. They feared he was in league
with their enemies and was planning to lead them into a deadly ambush. "I
told Cameahwait that I was sorry to find that they had put so little confidence
in us, that I knew they were not acquainted with whitemen and therefore
could forgive them," Lewis wrote. "That among whitemen it was considered
disgracefull to lye or entrap an enimy by falsehood."

It's worth noting that, even though the Shoshones had never met white
people before, they didn't buy the white-men-never-lie argument for a sec-

ond. But when Lewis tried a different approach—questioning the Indians' bravery—Cameahwait and a dozen more agreed to accompany him, and they all set off. (As they departed, the women of the village wailed a death song in their honor.) Together, the entourage crossed Lemhi Pass and reached Shoshone cove by sunset.

Near evening of the next day, August 16, they finally arrived back at the spot where Lewis had left his note—but to his great "mortification," Clark and the rest of the expedition were nowhere to be found. The Shoshones grew nervous and increasingly suspicious that their fears of betrayal had been correct. Some of them complained to Cameahwait that he had unnecessarily endangered the tribe by trusting the word of this white man.

Reading the journals two centuries later, it's still possible to feel the young captain's mind kick into overdrive. "I knew that if these people left me," he wrote, "that they would immediately disperse and secrete themselves in the mountains where it would be impossible to find them . . . and that they would spread the allarm to all other bands within our reach & of course we should be disappointed in obtaining horses, which would vastly retard and increase the labour of our voyage and I feared might so discourage the men as to defeat the expedition altogether."

Earlier, Lewis had given the chief his cocked hat and feather in return for a Shoshone tippet—an exchange which they both understood to mean that if this *was* a trap, the attackers would have trouble discerning friend from foe. Lewis's men did likewise. Now he handed Cameahwait his gun, declaring that if an ambush occurred the chief could shoot him. Once more his men followed his courageous and quick-witted example. Then he did the very thing he had promised Cameahwait that white men never do: he told a bald-faced lie. Retrieving the note he had written, he claimed instead that it was a message from *Clark* saying that the expedition would arrive soon.

Whether it was this deception or the act of considerable bravery in handing over the guns that impressed the Shoshones, they agreed to wait another day. But they were still wary. "My mind was in reallity quite as gloomy as the most affrighted indian," Lewis admitted, "but I affected cheerfullness to keep the Indians so who were about me." To pique their curiosity, he told them a woman of their nation was with the expedition, as well as a man whose skin was black. But as darkness fell, Cameahwait lay down as close to Lewis as possible, and most of his tribe hid themselves in the willows in case of a surprise attack.

Of all Lewis's nights on the long trail, this was his most "wristless." "I slept but little as might be well expected," he wrote, "my mind dwelling on the state of the expedition which I have ever held in equal estimation with my own existence, and the fait of which appeared at this moment to depend in a great measure upon the caprice of a few savages who are ever as fickle as the wind."

He's not being entirely fair to the Shoshones in that passage. Thus far in their existence, every armed stranger from the east had been an enemy bringing death and destruction. They were as legitimately concerned as Lewis about what the morning would bring. But his words convey how agitated his mind must have been throughout the night. The Indians had *his* guns as well as *their* horses—and if Clark didn't show up soon, he was running out of tricks to keep them pacified. It's hardly surprising that he couldn't sleep.

At dawn on August 17, Lewis dispatched Drouillard and an Indian escort downriver to find Clark as quickly as possible. Meanwhile, Lewis, Cameahwait, and the others waited nervously at camp. One hour went by, each minute seemingly an eternity. Another hour passed. Then an Indian galloped up with jubilant news: white men were on the way! Minutes later, Clark himself appeared, with Charbonneau and Sacagawea. And finally the rest of the expedition heaved into view, pulling their canoes.

Imagine the scene—the shouts and the laughter and the buzz of activity as the tensions on all sides suddenly let loose. The Shoshones, according to Lewis, were "transported with joy" and sang as they accompanied Clark into camp, where Cameahwait tied pieces of shell into his hair. "Every article about us appeared to excite astonishment in ther minds," he wrote: knives and beads and mirrors, and the first lyed corn they had ever tasted. York and Seaman elicited the Indians' admiration; Lewis's air gun was "so perfectly incomprehensible," he said, "that they immediately denominated it the great medicine."

The men of the expedition were, in Lewis's words, "much elated" too. For several days they had been complaining to Clark about dragging their canoes against the swift and shallow waters of the Beaverhead, and no doubt worrying about when—or if—they'd see Lewis again. Now here he was, surrounded with horses and a band of friendly Indians. For the first time in four months they would have someone other than themselves with whom to share a campfire.

Sacagawea was particularly joyful. Upon arrival she had been reunited with Jumping Fish, a girl who had escaped the same Hidatsa raid five years earlier that had ripped Sacagawea from her people. And then, when she was brought in to translate for the captains as they began negotiations for the

Shoshone horses, she slowly realized that the chief was none other than her brother. The emotional reunion had a powerful effect on both captains. "She instantly jumped up," Clark wrote, "and ran and embraced him, throwing over him her blanket, and weeping profusely."

Clark himself must have been greatly relieved, not just at the incredible luck of having returned the chief's sister, but at his own reunion with his good friend and fellow commander after what had been their longest separation since leaving St. Louis. And Lewis? He would have been the most relieved of all. All the anxieties of a week's worth of "toilsome days and wristless nights"; all the constant worries about finding the Shoshones and then struggling to keep them and their horses from disappearing; all the daily up-and-down emotions he had gone through as each expectation had been dashed to pieces; all the adrenaline that had been sustaining him through every danger; and all the inner reserves he had called upon to get beyond each new, unexpected obstacle—all that would have drained through his mind and body like a spring flood.

To cap the day, the hunters brought in four deer and an antelope for a proper feast. Is it any wonder that the captains named this spot Camp Fortunate?

The rejoicing couldn't go on forever. There was still much to do. The next day, Sunday, August 18, the men were ordered to open and air out their baggage and begin separating what would be cached at Camp Fortunate and what would be taken by horseback across the mountains.

At ten o'clock, Clark, eleven men, the Charbonneaus, and all the Indians except four departed—Clark to scout the Salmon River to see if it was as impassable as the Shoshones claimed, and Cameahwait to his village to bring back more horses. The bargaining was already going well. For an old uniform coat, a pair of leggings, a few handkerchiefs, and three knives—articles worth less than twenty dollars back in the States—Lewis purchased three "very good" horses and sent Clark off with two of them.

The evening scene at Camp Fortunate would have been much quieter than the festive night before. The Indians and more than a third of the expedition were now miles away. A wind swept in from the southwest. A cold rain began to fall. I imagine the remaining men huddling near their fires to ward off the chill, perhaps talking quietly among themselves after their meal of venison and beaver tail.

With his usual mess partners gone (Clark, York, Charbonneau, Sacagawea, and baby Baptiste), Lewis would have been alone once more, with just his thoughts to keep him company. But on this night, the immediate concerns that had occupied his mind throughout the previous tumultuous and exhausting week no longer pressed in upon him. The faint murmur of his men or the low snort and pawing hoof of a Shoshone horse would have reminded him that he could rest—at least briefly—from worrying about the expedition's survival.

It was Lewis's thirty-first birthday, and now, in quiet solitude, he finally had time to reflect—on his life, and on the week just past, especially, I think, that daunting, dream-busting view from Lemhi Pass. All those mountains. . . . At the time he first saw them, he had no choice but to shunt their meaning aside in his single-minded pursuit of horses. Now there was nothing to keep him from dwelling on their significance—to geography, to Jefferson's hopes, and to his own place in history. He had not been sent merely to merely cross the Continental Divide but to find the Northwest Passage. Instead, he had found . . . all those mountains.

And so, with his good friend Clark absent (and approaching the discouraging vista himself), an older companion of Meriwether Lewis's silently slipped in and joined him at the campfire: self-doubt. This companion could usually be counted on to make an appearance at solitary moments like these. It's as if he guided Lewis's hand for the concluding passages of that day's journal:

This day I completed my thirty first year, and conceived that I had in all human probability now existed about half the period which I am to remain in this Sublunary world. I reflected that I had as yet done but little, very little, indeed, to further the hapiness of the human race, or to advance the information of the succeeding generation. I viewed with regret the many hours I have spent in indolence, and now soarly feel the want of that information which those hours would have given me had they been judiciously expended. but since they are past and cannot be recalled, I dash from me the gloomy thought, and resolved in future, to redouble my exertions and at least indeavour to promote those two primary objects of human existence, by giving them the aid of that portion of talents which nature and fortune have bestoed on me; or in future, to live *for mankind*, as I have heretofore lived *for myself.*

There's a poignant sadness in that final self-exhortation, knowing what we know of Lewis's ultimate fate: to commit suicide on a lonely trail in Tennessee. I don't think he was ever able to dash gloomy thoughts completely. And while no one should doubt his resolve to redouble his exertions to live for mankind instead of for himself, I also suspect he somehow never considered himself successful enough at it.

In Clark's absence, we'd like to reach across time and place a gentle, brotherly hand on his shoulder and try to ease his mind on this most restless of nights. We ache to tell him not to judge himself so harshly and to assure him that, regardless of how much longer he might live in this "Sublunary world," he had already done much, very much indeed, to further the happiness of the human race and advance the information of succeeding generations. We yearn to tell him that he and his expedition would leave behind many lessons for succeeding generations—about courage and leadership and perseverance in the face of adversity. And in particular we wish to tell him that, even though he failed to find a Northwest Passage, the overriding lesson of his Corps of Discovery is the discovery that "you can't do it alone"—it takes friends and teamwork and a sense of community to succeed. But it's too far a distance for us to reach. We have to surrender to history and leave him, alone at his campfire, struggling with his own demons, failing to learn the very lesson he so eloquently taught us.

Eighty years later, when he, too, was a young man, Teddy Roosevelt came west in 1884, in part to deal with his depression and grief over the death of his mother and wife on the same day. In the measureless expanses of the West, Roosevelt found both exhilaration and a personal peace—and eventually returned to the East refreshed and ready to embark on a brilliant career. "Black care," he wrote, "rarely sits behind a rider whose pace is fast enough." But for Lewis, the West simply was not big enough for such an escape. At a place he had ironically named Camp Fortunate, after an emotionally frenetic week, Meriwether Lewis slackened his pace for a well-earned rest on his birthday. He rested, but he could not find peace. I don't think he ever did.

II

"The Most Hospitable, Honest and Sincere People"

This essay grew from informal remarks given at the collection of earth lodges at On a Slant Village in Mandan, North Dakota, in June 1999, when the design mold of the Sacagawea golden dollar coin was officially presented to representatives of Indian tribes along Lewis and Clark's route. Later that same year, on a tour with Steve Ambrose, I developed them a little further in a talk I gave at Lolo Pass. If the bicentennial of the Corps of Discovery comes and goes without the many voices of native people being recognized and their stories being heard, it will be a hollow commemoration.

The most widely held and deeply ingrained popular image of Lewis and Clark also happens to be the most serious misconception of their expedition. In that image they cross the continent on their own, somehow finding their way through an uninhabited wilderness and blazing a trail where no one had ever gone before. The truth is quite different. The West they crossed was hardly an uninhabited space at the start of nineteenth century. Indians were not only already inhabiting it, they had been living on it and traveling back and forth across it for hundreds of generations.

And the even harder truth is this: without those Indians, Lewis and Clark would never have made it to the Pacific Ocean and back. That central but often forgotten fact is worth restating, perhaps slightly rephrased to drive it home: if the West *had* been uninhabited, the Corps of Discovery simply would not have succeeded.

Make no mistake: to a man, the members of the expedition were uncommonly tough, amazingly resourceful, doggedly determined, and supremely courageous. William Clark was as good at intuiting and then mapping an unfamiliar landscape as any explorer this country has ever produced. And no one should ever doubt Meriwether Lewis's single-minded devotion to his mission, a sense of purpose that drove him each day toward his goal in spite of any obstacle. Nonetheless, time and time again, it was Indians who made the difference between success and failure.

The Mandans gave them buffalo meat and corn to survive the fierce North Dakota winter. The Hidatsas gave them information about the uncertain, unmapped route that still awaited them along the upper Missouri—describing mileposts to anticipate, down to the details of the sound of the Great Falls and a solitary eagle's nest in a cottonwood tree that would assure the explorers they were on the right track. Without Shoshone and Salish horses, Lewis and Clark could not have crossed the Bitterroot Mountains. Without salmon and camas roots offered freely by the Nez Percés, they would not have recovered from near-starvation after emerging from the mountains, and they would have been delayed for weeks trying to carve out dugout canoes if the Nez Percés hadn't given them instructions on a quicker method. The tribes of the arid Columbia Plateau provided them with much-needed food (dogs mostly) on the expedition's way out and back, when game was impossible to find and the men, despite their hunger, disdained the salmon teeming in the river. More food—and essential information—came from the Chinooks and the Clatsops along the Pacific Coast.

The help of Native Americans—help at almost every turn—made it possible for Lewis and Clark to survive, succeed, and become national heroes. If that fact seems at all surprising to us today, it is the fault of our national memory, not Lewis and Clark. From start to finish, *they* understood how crucial Indians were to their journey.

Lewis knew it even before setting off. He considered Indians so important to the prospects of what he called his "darling project" that in Philadelphia he spent $669.50—nearly one quarter of the expedition's entire congressional appropriation—on Indian presents: 8 brass kettles, 130 rolls of tobacco, 500 brooches, 12 dozen pocket mirrors, 4,600 sewing needles, 33 pounds of tiny colored beads, silk ribbons and yards of bright-colored cloth, tomahawks that doubled as pipes, and much more. This doesn't even count the boxes of Jefferson peace medals provided at no charge by the government's mint.

Clark certainly understood this point every time he sat down around a campfire with an interpreter and an Indian chief and asked questions about the tributaries of the Missouri and Columbia—about far-flung lands he would not see with his own eyes. Then, as the chief scratched lines in the dirt, with humps of clay to mark mountains, Clark would add that information to the new map of the West he was compiling for President Jefferson.

Sacagawea, the one full-blood Indian on the expedition, admittedly has become nearly as famous as the two captains who give the expedition its name, and although her role often tends to be over-romanticized, her contribution to the Corps of Discovery's achievements is indisputable. She was a mere teenager (and pregnant) when the captains met her at Fort Mandan in the late fall of 1804, but their journals show they immediately sensed that she could be the key to getting Shoshone horses once they reached her homeland in the western mountains. Technically, they may have hired (and later paid) her French-Canadian husband, Charbonneau; but in truth, it was Sacagawea they knew they needed, and so they hired him, on the condition that she come along. When her childbirth proved difficult, Lewis stepped in as midwife to make sure she pulled through. When she was in even graver medical danger near the Great Falls, an alarmed "Doctor" Lewis went to work again—partly out of humane concern for the young mother, to be sure, but also, he admitted in his journal, because without her he feared they would never be able to negotiate with her people for horses and the whole enterprise would fail.

Even after she helped them obtain Shoshone horses, Clark noted another vital role Sacagawea performed. "The sight of This Indian woman," he wrote as they met tribe after tribe on the Columbia, "confirmed those people of our friendly intentions, as no woman ever accompanies a war party of Indians in this quarter." And later, on the return journey, he duly credited her with pointing out the best route to the Yellowstone River, across what is now called Bozeman Pass, named in honor of a man who "blazed" his trail more than half a century after Sacagawea calmly piloted the Corps of Discovery over it.

Sacagawea now has more statues in her honor than any other woman in American history, and she and her baby now grace a new dollar coin, so it can hardly be said that she's been forgotten or overlooked. But the attention given to her, as a traveling member of the principal cast of characters, has tended to overshadow the fact that the explorers met—and relied just as heavily upon—many other Indians along the way. Once again, if they seem to have disappeared from the public's appreciation of the expedition's story, don't blame Lewis and Clark. In the captains' journals they appear again and again—and not as abstractions but as real, living, breathing people with real personalities and real names.

A chief named Shake Hand of the Yankton Sioux politely accepted his Jefferson peace medal from the captains, noting—and who knows if he meant this ironically, or even if they would have understood it if he did—that he intended to put it with the peace medals he had already been given by the Spanish and British on behalf of the other "Great Fathers" who during the last quarter century seemed to have been sending representatives up the lower Missouri like so many Fuller brush salesmen. Arcawecharchi, another Yankton chief, struck a similar tone when the captains presented him with a fifteen-star flag. "I am a man and a chief of some note," he told them with dignity on a hot summer day, after listening to their lengthy and occasionally condescending speech, each paragraph of which began with the word *Children*. "I am glad my grandfather has sent you to the people on this river," he added, "and that he has given us a flag large and handsome, the shade of which we can sit under."

The equally proud Black Buffalo of the Teton Sioux, or Lakota, demonstrated remarkable diplomacy when he prevented a bloody battle that most likely would have resulted in the deaths of many of his tribe as well as the effective destruction of the expedition. Farther upriver, chiefs named Kakawissassa, Piahito, and Pocasse of the Arikaras patiently explained that they did not want any alcohol because it turned people into fools, and during the flogging of the mutinous John Newman they told the captains that they considered it uncivilized to whip a man in public.

Just before the onset of the murderously harsh winter in North Dakota, the generous Sheheke of the Mandans told Lewis and Clark, "If we eat, you shall eat; if we starve, you must starve also." Cameahwait of the Shoshones, whose people *were* starving, decided nevertheless to delay his tribe's annual buffalo hunt in order to help the first white men his tribe had ever encountered. And on the far side of the Bitterroots, the expedition was fortunate to encounter Twisted Hair of the Nez Percés, whom Clark described as "a cheerful, sincere man," and an old woman the journals only barely mention but who, according to tribal history, is the one who persuaded her people to befriend rather than kill the weak and starving strangers from the East: Watkuweis, who told the Nez Percés, "do them no hurt."

There was Yelleppit of the Walulas, who presented Clark with "a very eligant white horse," Coboway of the Clatsops, Comcomly of the Chinooks, and so many more—men and women from nearly four dozen different tribes who admittedly were not members of the Corps of Discovery but whose names deserve mentioning and remembering because without them men with names like George Drouillard, John Ordway, Joseph Whitehouse, and all the way through the roster to Meriwether Lewis and William Clark—and Sacagawea—could not have accomplished something so worthy of commemorating two hundred years later.

There is always some risk of overpainting this into a soft pastel portrait of one big happy family, everyone getting along with one another for the purest of reasons. But Lewis and Clark had edges. So did every Indian they met. They were all human, after all, bringing to every encounter their own biases, their own self-interests, and the weight of their own cultures.

In Lewis and Clark's (and Jefferson's) vocabulary, all Indians were "savages." This applied to tribes the captains considered hostile, such as the Teton Sioux ("the vilest miscreants of the savage race," according to Clark), as well as those they considered helpful, such as the Mandans ("the most friendly and well disposed savages that we have yet met with," according to Lewis). They were "savages" by definition, because to the captains and the president who sent them west, Native Americans simply were not as culturally advanced as those brought up in the "civilized world." (Part of Jefferson's dream was to use the Louisiana Territory as a safe haven for Indians—including those he proposed to remove from the East—where they could live separately from whites until, with help and the advance of several generations, the two races were ready to intermingle seamlessly.)

From that point of view, addressing each tribe the expedition met as "children" did not seem unusual, nor did the paternal and occasionally scolding tone of the captains' message. "The great chief of the Seventeen great nations of America, has become your only father," the captains would announce, in a long-winded speech Lewis wrote for their first Indian parley in August 1804. "He is the only friend to whom you can now look for protection, or from whom you can ask favours . . . he will serve you, & not deceive you." Then they would enjoin the "children" to do business only with American traders, who, the captains promised, would soon be providing "a regular and plentifull supply of goods" and "on much better terms than you have ever received" from the French or the Spanish or the British. Further, the Indians were instructed to live in peace with all white men and, equally important, to stop their incessant intertribal warfare (which was considered bad for the fur trade).

If they disobeyed, it would "bring upon your nation the displeasure of your great father . . . who could consume you as the fire consumes the grass of the plains." (As a lesser punishment, he might shut off the supply of trade goods.) But if "the great Spirit will open your ears to our councils," the captains promised, "you will have nothing to fear, because the great Spirit will smile upon your nation, and in future ages will make you to outnumber the trees of the forest."

Over on the Indian side of the council fire, where chiefs had been listening to orations about distant "great fathers" for upward of a century in some cases, such speeches were merely a routine ritual that preceded the real business: getting the white man's trade goods that made their people's lives easier (manufactured awls and fish hooks), more pleasurable (tobacco, beads, mirrors), and, in their view, safer (guns to use against enemy tribes). But why should they worry that this "new father," who lived "where the land ends and the Sun rises from the face of the great waters," would present any greater threat to their sovereignty and survival than the "old fathers," who, Lewis and Clark said, had now returned to their homes across the sea? The *real* threats seemed to be more familiar and long-standing: enemy tribes—attested to most graphically by the Omaha scalps proudly displayed by the Lakotas, the Mandan buffalo robe painted with gruesome battle scenes, and all the other war trophies and tales of valor every tribe made sure to show and tell to the captains upon their arrival.

These new white men may have had a bigger boat and a larger contingent of soldiers than the Indians had seen before, but none of the tribes seemed to feel intimidated by the expedition's immediate presence—or particularly worried about the "seventeen great nations of America" on the far side of the Mississippi, even if they included "cities . . . as numerous as the stars of the heavens."

Quite the contrary, it was more often the Corps of Discovery that felt outnumbered and in need of being on military alert. One-Eye of the Hidatsas (also known as Le Borgne) scoffed that, if he wished, his warriors would have no more trouble handling Lewis and Clark's soldiers than "so many wolves." In early 1805, John Ordway recorded that a trader among the Lakotas "heared the Souix Say that they Should come to war in the Spring against us and the Mandans." The weight of personal experience and tribal history inclined the chiefs listening to Lewis and Clark to focus more on the part of the speech about the wonderful trade opportunities being offered by the new "great father," and pretty much dismiss the section about being consumed by a great grass fire.

From the vantage point of today, with the luxury of hindsight, it seems easy enough to see where this was heading: a nineteenth century that for

Indian peoples of the West would be the most chaotic and traumatic in their history. But Lewis and Clark and the Indians they met didn't have that luxury. Products of their time, they were simply trying to manage the best they could, according to their own best judgments.

A Lakota chief named the Partisan tried to prevent the expedition from proceeding upriver, not because he foresaw American westward expansion as the beginning of the end for his people, but because he wanted the Lakotas to control the American trade on the middle Missouri—and he perceived a rise in his own status if he could force concessions from the strangers in the big boat. One-Eye of the Hidatsas heard the captains' exhortations about intertribal peace during the winter—and in the spring sent a war party out against the Shoshones, just as his people had always done. The Shoshones were happy to provide the expedition with horses not simply out of generosity or gratitude that Sacagawea had been returned to her homeland, but because they were desperate to open a trade network with whites that would provide them with guns—deadly weapons they lacked, which was why the Hidatsas and Blackfeet and Atsinas (who had plenty of guns) had been able to so easily dispossess them on the plains. "If we had guns," the Shoshone chief Cameahwait explained to Lewis, referring to his half-starved people, "we could live in the country of the buffaloe and eat as our enimies do, and not be compelled to hide ourselves in these mountains and live on roots and berries as the bear do."

Lewis and Clark endeavored to obey Jefferson's instruction that "in all your intercourse with the natives, treat them in the most friendly & conciliatory manner which their own conduct will admit," but they stole a canoe from the amiable Clatsop chief Coboway when it served their purpose. When Lewis's dog Seaman was abducted, however, Lewis was prepared to burn a village on the lower Columbia to the ground if they didn't immediately release him. After a Walula man made fun of Lewis for having roasted dog for dinner, the captain "struck him in the breast and face, siezed my tomahawk and shewed him by signs if he repeated his insolence I would tommahawk him." And on the Two Medicine River in northwestern Montana, two young Blackfeet were killed as they attempted to steal horses from Lewis and a small scouting party. In the heat of the moment, Lewis even left a Jefferson peace medal on one of the corpses so that the Blackfeet "might be informed who we were."

During a journey of two and a half years, the expedition's relations with Indians had its full share of suspicions, disagreements, tensions, and misunderstandings on both sides. There's nothing remarkable about that. What is remarkable—particularly considering the blood-soaked annals of white exploration in the New World—is that the fight with the Blackfeet turned out to be the only incident of deadly violence between the Corps of Discovery and the thousands of Indians they met.

What stands out is how multidimensional and richly human the encounters were, how earnestly both sides often strove to understand one another even in the midst of the most trying circumstances, and finally, just how many friendships were actually forged across the great cultural divide.

A perfect place to contemplate the crucial—and almost omnipresent—role that Native Americans played in this story is the Lolo Trail, the portion of the expedition's route from the western border of Montana across the Bitterroot Mountains of Idaho to the Clearwater River. It's also a perfect spot to be reminded that Lewis and Clark's moccasins weren't the first to strike the ground they traveled, that they didn't really blaze a trail; nearly always they followed trails already well worn from generations of use.

On September 9, 1805, traveling with horses provided to them by the Shoshones and the Salish, the expedition reached the juncture of what is now Lolo Creek and the Bitterroot River and named their camp Travelers' Rest. Here their guide, an aging Shoshone they called Old Toby, gave them some startling information. The Missouri River was only four days' journey on horseback due east! Way back in North Dakota, the Hidatsas had mentioned this shortcut, but in obedience to Jefferson's orders to follow the winding Missouri to its source, the captains hadn't taken it. As a result, the expedition had used up fifty-three days instead of four to reach the same spot.

Three Nez Percés showed up at Travelers' Rest the next evening (they were chasing two Shoshones who, they said, had stolen twenty-one of their horses). Their tribe had been going back and forth over the Bitterroots for centuries, and they told the captains it should take only six days to cross the mountains and reach a river that was navigable to the Pacific. One of them even agreed to show them the way. But on September 11 there were delays in getting everyone started, and by 3 P.M. the Nez Percé guide had gotten restless and proceeded on alone.

No one seemed worried about his departure: they still had Old Toby, who had crossed the mountains once as a youngster, and as they came up Lolo Creek, the trail worn by so much Indian travel seemed clear enough to follow easily. They saw a tree decorated with Indian paint and adorned with ribbons and a grizzly bearskin—a place of Indian worship, Joseph Whitehouse speculated, a "medicine tree." They camped that night next to some old Indian lodges.

The next day, September 12, the going got a little harder. They were on the march, some of them, from 7 A.M. to 10 P.M., covering twenty-three miles over hilly terrain on trails choked by fallen timber. "Party and horses much fatigued," Clark wrote when they finally camped, adding that over the years Indians had peeled the bark from some of the pine trees, apparently out of hunger.

On September 13 they came past what is now called Lolo hot springs, a small roadside resort. It was something of a resort back in 1805, too. All of the journals note that near this series of springs Indians had moved rocks and gravel to form pools, trapping the hot water as places to bathe and relax. Some of the men washed their faces in the water, which Whitehouse says was "considerable above blood heat." Others drank a little of it; Clark says he "found it hot & not bad tasted." Then they moved on.

The problem now wasn't finding a trail but deciding *which* trail to take— there were so many radiating in and out of the little wilderness spa. Old Toby took one that turned out to be a three-mile detour—an "intolerable rout" according to Clark—before getting back on track and returning them, at the headwaters of Lolo Creek, to what the captain called a "verry fine leavel open & firm" trail that eventually led them to Packers Meadow and camp for the night.

From there, things got worse. Old Toby's memory proved faulty, and he mistakenly left the main trail (which followed the ridgelines) to lead them down a steep descent to the Lochsa River. Clark's journal summarizes the situation in four words: "Take the wrong road."

Now began the severest test of the expedition. They spent a hard day ("the road as bad as it can possibly be to pass," Clark wrote) climbing back up to the ridgeline, their horses slipping and falling, the men growing more and more exhausted. The going wasn't much easier back on the main trail. They had run out of food, and with no game to be found the men butchered a few colts for meals. More horses tumbled down rocky slopes. The men—cold, wet, and hungry—camped some nights without even any water available. Then it snowed. "Some of the men without Socks, wrapped rags on their feet, and loaded up our horses and Set out without anything to eat, and proceeded on," Joseph Whitehouse recorded on September 16, "Could hardly See the old trail for the Snow." Clark, too, complained of "great dificulty in finding the road" because of the snow. Equally discouraging was the view that awaited them at every turn: "high rugged mountains in every direction, as far as I could see."

The six-day mountain crossing turned into an eleven-day ordeal in which the Corps of Discovery teetered on the brink of starvation and came its closest to complete failure. "Suffice it say," Lewis would later write, "that we suffered everything Cold, Hunger & Fatigue could impart, or the Keenest Anxiety for the fate of [the] Expedition in which our whole Souls were embarked." On September 22 they finally staggered out of the mountains and into a Nez Percé village.

The point of this is not to blame Old Toby for a mistake in pathfinding—this wasn't his home territory, he'd only traveled the trail once many years earlier, and the mid-September storm complicated matters even more. What the story of the Bitterroot crossing demonstrates is that, even though the old Indian was not the best possible guide, he was still better than having none at all; that even within this remote wilderness jumble of fallen trees, precipitous slopes, and mountain peaks as far as the eye could reach, there was still an Indian trail; and that, with all their references to "the old trail" and "road," our intrepid white explorers realized every step of the way that they were not so much trying to *discover* an untrodden route as they were hoping to *follow* the best path that Indians used habitually.

As Lewis himself would admit on the return trip, crossing the Bitterroots in either direction would have been impossible for the explorers, left to their own devices. "We conceived it madness," he wrote in 1806, "to proceed without a guide." So on the way back east they hired five Nez Percé teenagers, who got them across in the promised six days. At Travelers' Rest they said the captains didn't need their services to lead the expedition over the shortcut to the Great Falls—the Indian trail was so hard to miss that even white men could follow it.

On June 29, 1806, when they all emerged from the mountains for the last time, they arrived at the Lolo hot springs in time to make camp. "Both the men and indians amused themselves with the use of a bath this evening," Lewis tells us. "I observed," he adds, "that the indians after remaining in the hot bath as long as they could bear it ran and plunged themselves into the creek, the water of which is now as cold as ice can make it."

Lewis himself stayed put in the hot springs, remaining nineteen minutes, he says, though "it was with dificulty I could remain thus long and it caused a profuse sweat." John Ordway took to the springs, too, "but the water [i]s so hot," he writes, "that it makes the Skin Smart when I first entered it."

Getting in once was enough for him. Like his captain, he was content to watch the Nez Percé boys frolic back and forth from hot springs to cold creek. The Indian guides, Lewis concluded, were "a race of hardy strong athletic young men," from a tribe he called "the most hospitable, honest and sincere people that we have met with on our voyage."

It's tempting to drop this entire subject here, with the image of white explorers and Indian guides peacefully enjoying each other's company and of an American officer and hero gratefully acknowledging his expedition's debt to the Native Americans who helped make his mission a success. To a great extent—with some notable exceptions—that image pretty well summarizes Lewis and Clark's relations with the Indians they encountered: peaceful, not hostile; full of mutual respect and a clear understanding on the Corps of Discovery's part of their reliance on the people whose homelands they were traversing.

But to stop the story there would be to totally ignore what happened to those same native peoples *after* they befriended Lewis and Clark. And ignoring the Indians *after* Lewis and Clark's journey would be as bad a history as ignoring their role *during* the journey. It would also, I think, do an injustice to Lewis and Clark's memory and honor.

My friend the writer William Least Heat-Moon has said that "the sorrow behind the Corps of Discovery is that what they did so well, later people were not able to do half so well." In dealing with native peoples, he said, our nation "didn't learn what they taught themselves. Lewis and Clark went as students; they came back as teachers, and we failed to learn the lessons that they had learned."

How quickly those lessons were forgotten—and how totally—can also be demonstrated near the Lolo Trail. In 1876, during the centennial celebration of the nation's founding declaration of freedom and equality, the Salish were being forced to move from their homelands in the Bitterroot Valley. Only seventy years earlier, Lewis and Clark had been the first white men the Salish had ever seen, and yet, as Private Whitehouse had recorded, "they received us as friends" and provided the expedition with fresh horses to cross the mountains. But by 1876—within the living memory of the Corps of Discovery—all of that had been forgotten (or conveniently ignored) as Salish lands were being taken. The Salish, however, had not forgotten, and their chief, Charlot, put what had become a bitter memory into words:

Since our forefathers first beheld [Lewis and Clark], more than seven times ten winters have snowed and melted. . . . We were happy when [the white men] first came. We first thought he came from the light, but he comes like the dusk of the evening now, not like the dawn of the morning. He comes like a day that has passed, and night enters our future with him. . . .

. . . Had Heaven's Chief burned him with some mark to refuse him, we might have refused him. No; we did not refuse him in his weakness. In his poverty we fed, we cherished him—yes, befriended him and showed him the fords and defiles of our lands.

[But] he has filled graves with our bones. . . . His course is destruction; he spoils what the spirit who gave us this country made beautiful and clean. . . .

His laws never gave us a blade, nor a tree, nor a duck, nor a grouse, nor a trout. . . .

How often does he come? You know he comes as long as he lives, and takes more and more, and dirties what he leaves.

In a nutshell, what happened to the Salish also happened to all the other western tribes that Lewis and Clark had met, shaken hands with, given peace medals to, and then relied upon to complete their epic journey. In the wake of the Corps of Discovery, each tribe experienced its own perilous journey through the new terrain of the West created by the new nation that claimed it.

The Clatsops' village was destroyed by a coastal bombardment after a misunderstanding with fur traders. The Mandans and Hidatsas were ravaged by smallpox, removed from their homes to a reservation farther up the Missouri, then removed again when a federally built dam inundated their fertile cornfields and small villages. The Lakotas fought the United States, lost, and were consigned to what is now the poorest county in the nation. The Nez Percés signed treaties that were continually broken, finally resisted, and ultimately embarked on a quest to find sanctuary in Canada that ended in tragedy. And so on.

Uniting all the individual stories is a theme of betrayal and loss, an over-arching bitter sadness that it didn't work out differently—and, if we look closely and honestly enough, a saga of Indian survival against all odds far more heroic than the Corps of Discovery's.

We need to remember them all, because without including their story, Lewis and Clark's story is incomplete. And until we learn what Lewis and Clark can still teach us about the first people to occupy this land, our nation's journey will be incomplete as well.

I2

Hallowed Ground

On the Fourth of July, 2000, I gave the speech upon which this essay is based
at Fort Columbia in Chinook, Washington, near the original location of the
expedition's Station Camp. Despite the date on the calendar, it was a raw and
rainy day—just a slight taste of what the Corps of Discovery experienced.
Many of the people who were there that day hope that Station Camp itself
will become a more prominent site on the Lewis and Clark trail. I couldn't
agree more.

On November 2, 1805, the Corps of Discovery steeled itself to conquer what
the men considered the final obstacle between themselves and the Pacific
Ocean: the Cascades of the Columbia River Gorge, roughly four miles of
boiling rapids and falls that William Clark called "the Great Shute." This
was the last of the great cataracts of the powerful Columbia—a harrowing
series of waterfalls, gorges, and rapids that had begun with Celilo Falls on
October 23, followed in quick succession by the Short and Long Narrows
near the Dalles, and then the Cascades, a mere 150 miles from sea.

Early that morning, the expedition's dugout canoes were prepared for
the final mile and a half of rapids. Hollowed out from Ponderosa pines only
a month earlier back among the Nez Percés in what is now Idaho, these
dugouts were big and bulky, hardly designed for quick maneuvering in
whitewater. Nevertheless, the expedition's best boatmen put them onto the
current and then steered madly as these floating tree trunks shot through the

foaming chaos of water and rock. One of them, Clark noted in his journal, struck a rock and split a little; three others took in water during the wild ride.

All in all, however, this final hazard was surmounted safely. Earlier in the day Clark had taken the precaution to order most of the baggage removed from the canoes and portaged around the cascade. For this job, he says, he "dispatched all the men who could not Swim." That's a prudent commander for you—always getting the most out of his men, whatever their shortcomings. (But it does beg a question about their recruitment back on the far side of the Mississippi nearly two years earlier. If you were about to set off on an expedition across the continent to find the *all-water route* to the sea, wouldn't one of the top requirements be the ability to swim?)

It must have been a great relief for swimmers and non-swimmers alike to load up the canoes below that final set of rapids and ease onto the broad Columbia. Relief, followed by excitement—because each mile they traveled now gave them new evidence that they were at last nearing the ocean. They noticed a tidal rise of nine inches on the river's shore; and a day later, an eighteen-inch rise and fall. On November 3 they passed the point where Lieutenant William Broughton, sailing upriver from the sea in Vancouver's historic expedition of 1792, had turned his ship around and headed back to the Pacific. They had finally emerged from a blank on the map to reach previously explored territory.

Better yet was news from the people Clark called "our Indian friends." "Towards evening," Joseph Whitehouse wrote in his journal, "we met Several Indians in a canoe who were going up the River. They Signed to us that in two Sleeps we Should See the Ocean vessels and white people." According to Clark, that same day a large group of Indians in two canoes, coming upstream from the Columbia's mouth, "informed us they Saw 3 vestles below."

Imagine the talk in camp that night. Three ships with white people only "two sleeps" away! To fully understand how electrifying that news must have been, consider what they'd just been through. When they left Fort Mandan in North Dakota back in April, they had expected to find the fabled Northwest Passage, take it through the single line of mountains conjectured on their maps, reach the ocean in late summer, and then head back east, perhaps getting as far as Fort Mandan again before winter. That was the theory.

Instead they had encountered one unexpected obstacle after another, time-consuming delay after time-consuming delay. A week deciding whether the Marias River was actually the Missouri. Nearly a month (instead of half a day) portaging around the Great Falls, which had turned out to be *five* water-falls, not one. The agonizingly slow ascent of the Jefferson and Beaverhead Rivers, taking them parallel to the mountains instead of through them. And then, at Lemhi Pass, the unexpected obstacle to trump all others: mountains, where mountains were not supposed to exist. No Northwest Passage. No short portage, but rather weeks of stumbling through the Bitterroots—cold, wet, starving, and as close to lost as the Corps of Discovery ever found itself. Getting deathly sick on the Nez Percés' salmon; resorting to dog meat on the Columbia plateau. And let's not forget what emotional toll was exacted each time their canoes had picked up speed and headed toward the thunder of yet another Columbia River chute and cataract. Even the swimmers must have come to dread that sound.

But now came the promise of a reward for all that toil and trouble: three ships only "two sleeps" away. A ship that could replenish their increasingly short supply of trade goods. A ship that could provide them with news from home—and more importantly take back news of their great achievement. A ship that could provide them with the first whiskey they had tasted since they drained their last barrel at the Great Falls on the Fourth of July. All of that, only "two sleeps" away.

On November 4, at a large Indian village where the men feasted on wa-pato, Clark noted "uriopian" goods everywhere he looked: guns, powder flasks, copper and brass trinkets, some tailored clothes. Farther downriver, John Ordway says, they met an Indian who "could talk & Speak Some words of English Such as curseing and blackguard." On November 6, according to Clark, they met another English-speaking Indian, said a "Mr. Haley" traded regularly with them at the river's mouth not far away. That night, the men recorded a tidal rise and fall of three feet.

By the morning of November 7 they must have been bursting to put their paddles in the water. The anticipation was as palpable as the morning fog, which itself was so thick they couldn't see across the river. But on they went, piloted through the dense mist by an Indian wearing a sailor's jacket. They stopped at another village, and once again, according to Whitehouse, Indians "made signs to us that there were vessells lying at the Mouth of this River." "We proceeded on," Ordway wrote, and for the first time since the morning they had left Fort Mandan seven months earlier, that phrase has more expectancy than resigned perseverance embedded in it.

At last the fog lifted—and the Corps of Discovery was treated to a breath-taking, heart-pumping vista. For the first time in such a long time, the western horizon offered them something other than a discouraging surprise. "Ocian in view! O! the joy," Clark wrote in his notebook, cracking open exclamation points like champagne bottles. They encamped that evening opposite Pillar Rock, and although the journals make passing mention of dampness and difficulty finding a suitable place for the night, there's no mistaking the emotion of the day. "Great joy in camp," Clark wrote, "we are in View of the Ocian, this great Pacific Octean which we [have] been So long anxious to See."

As those familiar with the Lewis and Clark story already know—and as those who live in the area know even better—Pillar Rock is hardly on the Pacific shore. It wasn't the ocean that Clark was so excitedly describing; it was Gray's Bay. They were still a good fifteen miles upstream from the coast. I imagine that Clark himself quickly realized this. But after traveling more than four thousand hard and grueling miles up the entire length of the Missouri, across those tremendous mountains, and down the treacherous rapids of the Clearwater, Snake, and Columbia Rivers—and given the anticipation that had been building steadily for five days—he can be forgiven for jumping the gun by a few miles.

Permit him and the rest of the Corps of Discovery this moment of jubilation. "Ocian in view! O! the joy." Let them savor it. "We are in View of the Ocian, this great Pacific Octean which we [have] been So long anxious to See."

Let them bask in their joy. They had earned it.

There's another reason to excuse them that premature moment of satisfaction on November 7, because on November 8 they received their official early-winter welcome to the Pacific Northwest—and realized once more that nothing ever came easily for the Corps of Discovery. A typical November coastal storm engulfed them as they inched along the shore of Gray's Bay, restricting them to only eight miles that day. Some Indians bearing salmon for trade blithely passed them in their elegant canoes, but the swells rolling in from the ocean storm rocked the expedition's lumbering dugouts so badly that Peter Weiser, Hugh McNeal, and Reuben Field got seasick. So did Sacagawea, who had been longing like the rest of them to see what her people called "the Stinking Lake." (Those dugouts, crucial as they were to the Corps of Discovery, turned out to be even more poorly suited for the rough waters at the Columbia's mouth than they had been for the river's cascades.)

The words "wet and disagreeable" appear in several journals that day—

a phrase that would soon replace "we proceeded on" as the expedition's shorthand phrase for standard operating procedure. "We are all wet and disagreeable," Clark wrote, and "we are at a loss to . . . find out if any Settlement is near the mouth of the river." The waves forced them to stop near Gray's Point, where they camped in the margin between the high and ebb tides. In the night the high tide overwhelmed them, and they scrambled to save the canoes and their baggage from destruction.

Things only got worse during November 9. It rained hard all morning, and as the wind picked up with the afternoon floodtide, huge driftwood logs—some of them two hundred feet long and seven feet in diameter—were loosened from the shoreline and sent crashing and thrashing around the campsite, now inundated with water. With "every man as wet as water could make them," Clark reported, "every exertion and the Strictest attention by the party was Scercely sufficient to defend our Canoes from being Crushed to pieces." Making conditions even more unbearable, some of the men had been drinking the brackish water of the estuary, and it acted on them like a dose of Rush's Thunderbolts. Patrick Gass noted that the only fresh water to be had was found in the rainwater collecting in the bottoms of the canoes.

For obvious reasons, they did not "proceed on" that day; they camped again in the same spot, at a place Clark called Dismal Point. "Not withstanding the disagreeable time of the party for Several days past," Clark wrote that night of his crew, "they are all Chearfull and full of anxiety to See further into the ocian." They had been through violent storms before out on the Great Plains, and they must have assumed that this one would pass just as quickly as those had.

They couldn't have been more wrong. On the morning of November 10 the storm still raged, but during a morning lull they loaded their dugouts and left Dismal Point, hoping to round Point Ellice and reach the coast. As they approached the point, however, the wind and waves returned, forcing them to do the one thing the Corps of Discovery hated more than anything else: retreat and give back two hard-earned miles. They unloaded their canoes, waited for the low tide, loaded up again, and tried once more to round Point Ellice. Furious waves defeated them again and forced them into another begrudging retreat to find whatever spot they could to camp for the night.

This one was even worse than the previous campsite. They stowed their baggage on high rocks, but searched in vain for an adequate place to sleep. "Here we scarcely had room to lie between the rocks and water," Gass wrote, "but we made shift to do it among some drift wood that had been beat up by the tide." Whitehouse wrote that during the day they could watch porpoises, sea otters, ducks, and seagulls in great abundance, but all they had to eat that night was pounded fish purchased farther up the river.

Their hopes—like the tides—had risen and fallen twice during the day. Adding to the indignity, the point that had turned them back now blocked any view toward the ocean they had been "so long anxious to see." Today it goes by the name of Point Ellice; on Clark's map, it appears as Point Distress. The storm pinned them there for four days. Without tents, they tied blankets and mats to poles to try to protect themselves from the rain as they huddled on the driftwood. But each high tide forced them temporarily to abandon even this makeshift camp and cower in the rocky crevices until the water receded.

More misery. The steady rain saturated the soil on the steep slopes above them, and small stones began sliding off onto them. Even more misery. At 3 A.M. on November 12, the storm brought sheets of lightning, then hail onto the exposed crew. There was a short period of clearing light at dawn, then an ominous black cloud rolled in from the southwest and, as Clark wrote, "the heavens became darkened." The cloud brought even harder rain and wind, and waves that were the highest yet. In the midst of this helpless situation, some Cathlamets paddled up, stopped briefly to sell the hungry explorers thirteen sockeye salmon, and then, as if the huge swells were nothing out of the ordinary, paddled on downstream and out of sight. The dejected men watched them depart, envying both their seaworthy canoe and their nimble skill in such rough waters. "They are on their way to trade those fish with white people," Clark noted, "which they make Signs live below, round a point."

On November 12 the captains dispatched three men to attempt another passing of Point Distress—to see if they could find those white men, or at least a better bay for a decent campsite. The point defeated them once more. On November 13 they tried again. This time John Colter, Alexander Willard, and George Shannon made it around Point Distress and disappeared. Back at camp, there was nothing to eat again but pounded fish. Whitehouse wrote that his buffalo robes were falling apart. Ordway reported that the storm continued raging. Gass summarized it as "another disagreeable rainy day."

Something about this situation seems to have brought out the best in William Clark's journal writing. Meriwether Lewis was in the midst of one of his periodic long gaps in record keeping—more than three months in this case—but Clark rose to the literary occasion. From the moment he wrote "O! the joy," his journal entries seem more descriptive than usual, and filled with an empathy for the plight of his men that reflects what must have been going on in both captains' minds. "It would be distressing to a feeling person to See our Situation at this time," Clark wrote, "all wet and cold with our bedding &c. also wet, in a Cove Scercely large [e]nough to Contain us, our Baggage in a Small holler about 1/2 a mile from us, and Canoes at the mercy of the waves & drift wood. Our party has been wet for 8 days and is truly disagreeable, their robes & leather Clothes are rotten from being Continually wet, and they are not in a Situation to get others, and we are not in a Situation to restore them."

By November 14 his concern had deepened. The robes and half of the few clothes the men still had were now rotted away. He could see snow on the high mountaintops to the south. "If we have cold weather before we Can kill & Dress Skins for Clothing," he wrote, "the bulk of the party will Suffer verry much." Earlier he had called their situation "disagreebable." Now, he said, "our situation is dangerous."

On the afternoon of November 14, Colter arrived back in camp by land with his report from his scouting mission. It was discouraging: no sign of white men. But, he said, if they all could manage to get beyond Point Distress, there was a sandy beach for a better encampment. Lewis decided to set off overland with four men to scout farther up the coast for trading vessels. Clark was to lead the rest of the party on one more attempt to round the point.

That night, I think, was one of the low points for the Corps of Discovery. Patrick Gass wrote that this weather was "the most disagreeable I had ever seen." That's a telling statement from someone who had gone through a North Dakota winter of forty-five degrees below zero and howling winds; blistering hot days in Montana, filled with torturous mosquitoes and punctuated by hailstorms that had knocked men to the ground; and then snow squalls in the Bitterroot Mountains, where some of the men had walked with rags wrapped around their feet. But the storm at Point Distress, according to Gass, was worse than all that.

Anyone who's done any camping knows how miserable it can be during a rainstorm. Hot weather can be uncomfortable; cold weather and snow can be more uncomfortable, even dangerous. And yet there can be an exhilaration about meeting the challenge of those extremes. Rain, on the other hand, is dispiriting even with the best of camping equipment to keep you moderately dry. Imagine camping in the rain without tents. Imagine that rain going on day after day, night after night, for two weeks. Imagine your clothes rotting from the rain.

"Disagreeable" begins to describe more than the weather conditions. It tells us the expedition's state of mind. Clark's choice of words reveals even more. This was, he wrote, "the most disagreeable time I have experienced, Confined on a temp[estuous] Coast, wet, where I can neither get out to hunt, return to a better situation, or proceed on." Unable to "proceed on"— can you imagine a worse feeling for the Corps of Discovery?

On November 15, everyone was itching to move. The wind stopped them once more, but during a brief pause in the afternoon they all were finally able to round Point Distress and go past an empty Chinook village of thirty-six houses. George Shannon joined them from his scouting mission with five Indians. The only white men he had seen were Lewis and his party, heading on their own reconnaissance. The high tide and big waves convinced Clark to set up camp. There was no use in trying to go any further, he noted.

From here they could survey the entire mouth of the Columbia. He called this bay Haley's Bay, after the man they had heard so much about but never met. The camp itself would come to be called Station Camp—and it would be their home for ten days. "Here we . . . formed a comfortable camp," Gass wrote, "and remained in full view of the ocean, at this time more raging than pacific."

Their first full day at Station Camp, November 16, got off to a good start. The weather cleared enough for them to put articles out to dry, and the hunters were finally able to be dispatched. They returned with two deer, one crane, and two ducks. York, Clark's slave, added to the larder with two geese and eight brant he had shot. That night's meal must have seemed like a feast.

From the journals it seems clear that everyone assumed this was as far as they were going. They could hear the surf, according to Whitehouse, and Gass noted that in the distance they could see "waves, like small mountains"—waves, it's worth noting, that had just crossed the widest stretch of the Pacific between Asia and North America. Barring some discovery by Lewis (maybe he would return with news of a trading post or ship), there apparently was no talk of wintering on the coast. Whitehouse: "We are now of the opinion that we cannot go any further with our Canoes, & think that we are at an end of our Voyage to the Pacific Ocean, and as soon as discoveries necessary are made, that we shall return a short distance up the River & provide our Selves with Winter Quarters." Gass: "We are now at the end of our voyage, which has been completely accomplished according to the intention of the expedition, the object of which was to discover a passage by the way of the Missouri and Columbia rivers to the Pacifc ocean; notwithstanding the difficulties, privations and dangers, which we had to encounter, endure and surmount." This is a moment every parent who has traveled with his or her family immediately understands. It's that moment when "Are we there yet?" is replaced by a different question: "Can we *go* now?"

On November 17 the hunters brought in three deer, two ducks, and four brant. The men measured the rising tide at eight and a half feet. After conferring with the chief of the local tribe, Clark recorded that their name was Chinook and they numbered four hundred souls. And in the evening, Lewis and his scouting party returned after searching the coast for thirty miles, according to Whitehouse, who quickly summarized Lewis's answer to the question on everyone's mind: "they had seen," he wrote, "no white people or vessels." (A day later Whitehouse would write that the captains named the farthest point Cape Disappointment, "on account of not finding Vessells there." He was wrong. An English sea captain, John Meares, had given it that name in 1788, during his fruitless search for the mouth of the Columbia—and so it already appeared as Cape Disappointment on the maps the captains had brought along. But Whitehouse's misperception only further proves the explorers' state of mind: in an expedition that often gave descriptive and suggestive names to every landmark, Cape Disappointment made perfect sense.)

By now, it seems, all hopes of finding a trading settlement or a harbor full of boats or of meeting the renowned "Mr. Haley" had pretty much vanished, and it's easy to sense the men's minds turning back upriver. Their mission had been to *reach* the ocean, not remain there. And their original plan had been to touch the sea, turn around, and get as far back east as possible. On the way downriver Clark himself had noted in his journal that the mouth of the Sandy River would make a good wintering spot.

Now Clark asked if anyone else wanted to hike to the ocean shore with him—perhaps to make one last attempt at spotting a ship, perhaps merely to satisfy himself by reaching the continent's edge, where the horizon is filled only by water. Only eleven men said they wanted to come—and two of those, the Field brothers, had just returned from the coast with Lewis. Think about that: out of an expedition of thirty-three intrepid explorers, nearly half—sixteen, to be exact—didn't see any need to go the extra few miles. In their minds, they *had* reached the ocean. "All others," Clark wrote of them, were "well contented with what part of the ocean & its curiosities which could be seen from the vicinity of the our camp." (You can almost see them rolling their eyes in the universal sign language that says: "Can we *go* now?")

Clark and his eleven companions set off on November 18, and over the course of two and a half days they investigated the place the Indians told them the trading ships often anchored; shot down a California condor whose wingspan they measured at nine feet and whose head would eventually be displayed in Peale's museum in Philadelphia; climbed the headlands of Cape Disappointment; hiked along the sandy shore of Long Beach; and finally turned back to Station Camp. "The men appear much Satisfied with their trip beholding with estonishment the high waves dashing against the rocks & this emence ocian. . . . Men all chearfull," their captain wrote. Then, tellingly, he added that they "express a Desire to winter near the falls this winter." (This is a little different from the standard "can we *go* now" moment. But we can still recognize it. It may have been the first time—but certainly was not the last—that American male tourists, after racing over every possible obstacle to reach an historic and scenic spot in the West, looked out at the sweeping vista for a few minutes, then looked at their watch and said, "OK, let's get going.")

Back at Station Camp, both before and after Clark's return, a steady stream of Indians—Chinooks and occasional Clatsops from across the river—came to trade and visit. From the information gathered during those visits, several things were becoming clearer. First, if they wanted success in trading, the explorers needed more blue beads than they had brought along. Sacagawea had to sacrifice a belt of blue beads to purchase a robe of two sea otter pelts which the captains desired. By implication, they could not hope to purchase a winter's worth of food with what few trade goods they had left; they would need to hunt to survive.

Second, although the rain had let up a little, this was obviously a place where blue skies were the exception, not the rule. Several of the men noted the extraordinary hats the natives made of white cedar and bear grass— "very handsomely wrought and waterproof," according to Gass—and one explorer purchased one in exchange for an old razor. By implication, people don't make finely wrought waterproof hats in places where it doesn't rain a lot.

Third, the traffic of trading vessels was certainly both common and heavy here: in addition to all the previous evidence, one Indian woman was seen with the name J. Bowmon tattooed on her left arm; many Indians showed the ravages of venereal disease; and a Clatsop showed up with red hair, light skin, and freckles. But the main trading season seemed to be over.

All those delays that had brought the Corps of Discovery to this area in November instead of in the summer had probably cost them their most likely opportunity to contact a trading vessel. What seaworthy captain in his right mind would try to approach an already treacherous coast during November storms like these?

The men's journals suggest that the consensus to head back east had hardened even further. "The wind blew so violent to day," Gass wrote on November 21, "and the waves ran so high, that we could not set out on our return, which it is our intention to do as soon as the weather and water will permit." Whitehouse is more specific. "The Swell in the River," he wrote, "ran so high that it detain'd us at our Camp from going up the River again, to look out for Winter Quarters."

The storm worsened on November 22. The wind blew "with violence," according to Clark, throwing the river out of its bank in waves that once again overwhelmed the camp and split one of the canoes. The Chinooks, who were visiting, crowded with the explorers into the crude shelters the men had made. Gass thought the river was the roughest he had yet seen. Clark deployed another exclamation point to write, "O! how horriable is the day." (*Can we go now?*)

On November 23 the storm abated a little, but rain fell at intervals. Sometime during the day, Lewis got out his branding iron—a special one that said "U.S. Capt. M. Lewis"—and somewhere near Station Camp blazed his name and the date on the side of a tree. Clark pulled out a knife to carve his own name, the date, and "by land" on an alder tree. "The party," Clark added, "all Cut the first letters of their names on different trees in the bottom."

This was not part of the United States at the time. Jefferson's Louisiana Purchase had doubled the size of his country, but the legal boundary extended only to the crest of the Rocky Mountains, not to the Pacific. Because their vessels had entered the mouth of the Columbia in 1792, both the United States and Britain had staked claims to the Northwest, but both recognized those claims were weak ones. With each cut into each tree, the Corps of Discovery was strengthening the American claim. "We came by land," was their message. "And we came in numbers." They were planting the flag. They were marking new territory.

Some of them—the captains in particular—had carved their names into trees and landmarks at other places, but this is the only instance in which the entire Corps of Discovery participated. I sense a bit of ceremony, ritual, and solemn finality to it. They were consecrating this spot. And they were preparing to leave it. × × ×

That night the stars came out, and the morning of November 24 dawned clear and cold, with a white frost on the ground. The men were eager to push toward the rising sun. But the captains delayed them—first to send out hunters; then to air out their sodden clothes and bedding in the rare sunlight; then to take astronomical observations to fix this spot as precisely as they could on Clark's map. By evening, after some Chinooks stopped by for a smoke and some trading, the Corps of Discovery was still at Station Camp. Then occurred what to me was the most powerfully meaningful single moment of an expedition filled with powerful, meaningful moments. This moment was beyond meaningful. It was transcendent.

The captains gathered the party together and, in a move that broke with all the rules of military command and protocol, announced that everyone would participate in the decision of what to do next. Out on the continent's farthest shore, beyond what was then the boundaries of the United States, the nation's first citizens to travel from sea to sea would do the very thing that defines our democracy. They would conduct a vote.

There is much we simply don't know about this magnificent moment. Why, for instance, did the captains call for a vote in the first place? As military captains they simply could have issued an order. But in this case they didn't. Why? Personally, I believe that while the rest of the party was firmly set on moving upriver, Lewis and Clark had already begun to question whether that was the best option. Clark's vote tally of November 24 contains the first and only mention of the captains' reasoning, but it's fair to assume that the two of them had been talking it over in the few days since Clark's return to camp from his excursion to Long Beach.

If game could be found on the other side of the river—and everyone understood that without game to hunt, no place would support them for the winter—Lewis now wanted to stay as close to the ocean as possible. It held out the possibility of seeing a ship by springtime, he said, and it provided the opportunity to make salt for their food. Besides, he argued, going upriver and wintering closer to the Rocky Mountains would not speed their return home: they would still have to wait for the snows to melt on the Bitterroots before attempting any mountain crossing next year.

Salt was not a consideration for Clark; he was indifferent to its uses and considered saltwater, in his words, "evil in as much as it is not helthy." But he, too, now preferred wintering near the coast—if, as the Clatsops promised, enough elk could be found in the neighborhood. The chance of getting resupplied by a ship with trade goods was worth waiting for, he thought, but the other advantage in Clark's mind was the prospect of a milder climate closer to the sea. The Indians claimed that winters here brought little snow, he noted, and the unusually warm November had convinced him they might be right. "If this Should be the Case," he wrote, always concerned for the welfare of his men, "it will most Certainly be the best Situation of our naked party dressed as they are altogether in leather."

I believe the captains had not previously shared these thoughts with the others. The "can we *go* now" sense of the enlisted men's journals is too strong and too certain to suggest otherwise, and what's apparent in those journals must have been even more apparent to the captains: their men were fully expecting to evacuate the coast at the earliest chance. Imposing an order contrary to that expectation—even if it ultimately were the best option— would have done more damage to their morale than all the storms and waves of Point Distress and Cape Disappointment combined. So, perhaps more out of the tactics of leadership than pure democratic principles, the captains called for a vote.

This *was* a stunning—and surprising—act of leadership. I'm sure the captains had already decided what they hoped the outcome would be. But there was no guarantee. They were betting that, left to their own devices and allowed to hear the arguments, people can be entrusted to make the correct decision; and they knew that, regardless of the outcome, the very act of inclusion strengthens the result. That is the gamble—and the promise—of democracy.

But how was the vote taken? What was the scene around the campfire on the night of November 24, 1805? Were there speeches by the captains, questions and counter-arguments from the men? Was there a show of hands, a standing division, a ballot, a roll call answered in turn by each person's voiced opinion? When York's vote was solicited, did anyone grumble or sulk that a black man, a slave, had just been accorded as much authority as anyone else? Were any eyebrows raised when Sacagawea—an Indian *and* a woman—had her opinion recorded? Why wasn't her husband's? Was it an oversight or deliberate, some sort of decision that the Charbonneau family should have only one vote, and the one that should count was Sacagawea's?

Were York and Sacagawea and the men surprised to be asked their opinion in the first place? Or by this point in their long journey did it seem matter-of-fact, the natural climax of a process that had steadily bound them together with each mile and each surmounted obstacle, a process that most certainly had not stripped them of their individuality but had steadily forced them to see their survival and their success in terms of the group, not the individual?

We don't know. The journals don't tell us. What we do know is the result of the tally, dutifully set down in Clark's journal.

When the vote was concluded, only Joseph Shields still wanted to leave immediately and winter upstream at Sandy River. All the others were willing to cross the Columbia to what is now Oregon and investigate whether elk and a suitable site for a fort and a place to make salt could be found. If those conditions couldn't be met, *then* they would "proceed on" upriver. (In that case, seven of them—including Clark—were in favor of going all the way to the Dalles for the winter. Nine—including all three sergeants and Lewis—favored the Sandy River as the backup option. Thirteen had no preference, as long as it was upriver. Sacagawea's concern was that wherever they wintered there be plenty of wapato.)

The journals also tell us something else, something as important as the decision itself—perhaps more important. They tell us the enlisted men's perception of what had just happened. Pay careful attention to their words. Gass: "At night the party were consulted by the commanding officers, as to the place most proper for winter quarters." Joseph Whitehouse: "In the Evening our Officers had the whole party assembled in order to consult which place would be the best for us to take up our Winter Quarters at." John Ordway: "Our officers conclude with the oppinion of the party to cross the River and look out a place for winter quarters."

It's worth noting that each of them found the event important enough to mention—and therefore it's safe to say that they were speaking on behalf of all the others who weren't keeping journals. But also consider the words they chose. The captains had "consulted" with them and then "conclude[d] with their oppinion." The decision had been made by "us," not "them."

Whatever had prompted the captains to use this extraordinary method, it worked. The decision, I believe, was the one the captains themselves would have ordered. But the process itself had created an even stronger bond within the expedition; thirty-three individuals merging into a single Corps of Discovery.

That's leadership of the highest order. That's democracy at its best.

The Lewis and Clark expedition had been conceived and dispatched across the continent by Thomas Jefferson, who dreamed of an "empire of liberty" stretching from the Atlantic to the Pacific (even if, back at Monticello, he was never quite able to let liberty spread across his plantation). Lewis recognized the president's central role in the expedition by calling him "the author of our enterprize." But Jefferson was also the author of something even more important—the Declaration of Independence, the document that conceived our nation on a radical premise: "We hold these truths to be self-evident, that all men are created equal, that they are endowed by their Creator with certain unalienable Rights, that among these are Life, Liberty and the pursuit of Happiness."

Many of the members of the Corps of Discovery had been alive when that radical premise had first been proclaimed. All of them had considered Independence Day of such significance that they made sure to celebrate it each year, wherever they were on their extraordinary journey. But at Station Camp on November 24, 1805, they didn't say those words; they *lived* those words—and, if only momentarily, breathed new life into them. When York voted, they were pushing the promise that "all men are created equal" into new territory. When Sacagawea voted, they took those words and crossed yet another boundary.

A day earlier, when they had emblazoned their names and initials on the windswept trees near camp, they had stretched the literal boundaries of their nation. They had touched the future, because the nation itself would follow them toward this shore—and encompass it in less than fifty years. But on November 24, by making a decision through the full participation of every member of the expedition—men and woman; black and white; foreign-born and native-born and Native American—at that exquisite moment, they also touched the future, a future even farther over the horizon line in 1805, a future that would take our nation more than a hundred years to reach.

Two centuries later, as we remember the Corps of Discovery, let us also remember that the journey is never over. We must never stop pursuing that horizon. Because the moment we do not "proceed on" toward it is the moment that the vital, insistent heartbeat in Jefferson's words stops. And if that ever happens, we will become a nation defined only by geographic boundaries, not by an enduring promise. At Station Camp the Corps of Discovery stretched those boundaries and gave that enduring promise renewed life. It is hallowed ground.

13

Meditations on a Grave

In the documentary film Ken Burns and I made about the Corps of Discovery, for the scene surrounding the death and burial of Sergeant Charles Floyd we couldn't use the real Floyd's Bluff, which now has a tall obelisk at its top and an interstate highway at its base—hardly the way it appeared two hundred years ago. Luckily, I knew a Lewis and Clark buff named Strode Hinds of Sioux City, Iowa, who spent days scouting the area for us until he found a rounded hill, unobstructed by modernity, that was the perfect substitute.

Strode was with us when we filmed what eventually became a visually lovely, emotionally moving moment in the documentary, but then he died before the finished film was released and therefore never saw the fruits of his contribution. This essay is dedicated to him—and to a number of other "old guards" from the Lewis and Clark Trail Heritage Foundation who have passed over the divide—in thanks for all they did to keep the memory of the Corps of Discovery alive when most of the nation didn't care.

The final stretch of the Corps of Discovery's homeward journey began in earnest on September 4, 1806, when they left the Great Plains behind for good and reached what is now the Iowa-Nebraska border. A few days earlier they had passed the spot where, in September 1804, they had first encountered the plains, saw their first antelopes, jackrabbits, coyotes, and prairie dogs, and were confronted by vast, treeless horizons telling them in no uncertain terms that they had entered an entirely new world. Now, in the reverse image of that experience, Clark noted the comforting appearance of black walnut trees, the first he had seen in a long time and as good a signal as any that they had returned at last to more familiar terrain.

The Missouri River's powerful current had likewise been seemingly transformed. Once their daily scourge and mortal enemy, it was now their ally, bearing the expedition's dugout canoes downstream as if it were in the same rush to reach St. Louis. Logging fifty, sixty, even seventy miles a day had become so commonplace that Clark recorded anything less in his journals with an "only"—as in, "incamped haveing Come 45 Miles only to day." What a difference from two years earlier, when a twenty-mile day fighting the river would have been cause for a victory celebration.

Despite their hurry, however, on this cloudy September day they would be content to cover thirty-six miles. A little before noon the men halted their canoes on the Iowa shore near the entrance of the stream they called Floyd's River, at the base of a steep hill they had named Floyd's Bluff. Then they climbed the bluff to pay their respects to the man who had given those landmarks his name: Sergeant Charles Floyd. Early on the outbound journey, on August 20, 1804, Floyd had died from "bilious cholic" (perhaps a burst appendix), becoming the first United States soldier to perish in the line of duty west of the Mississippi. "This Man at all times gave us proofs of his firmness and Determined resolution to doe Service to his Countery and honor to himself," Clark wrote at the time, referring to Floyd as "our Deceased Brother." The men had selected the most prominent hilltop in the immediate vicinity for his final resting place, branded a cedar post with Floyd's name and the date of his death, and "he was buried with the Honors of War much lamented."

Two years later, the graveside ceremony was equally somber. They found Floyd's burial plot disturbed and half covered, and the captains ordered the men to fill it properly with fresh soil before they proceeded on. The same pangs of loss for a fallen friend must have accompanied this solemn duty of reburial. But as they said farewell to his remains once more, I would imagine that Floyd's comrades were also experiencing some emotions much different from those that had flooded over them at the same spot on the westward journey.

In August 1804, every member of the expedition had been acutely aware that Floyd was the Corps of Discovery's first casualty. But the first of how many? The occasion of his death would have only heightened the two great uncertainties that surely haunted each expedition member's private thoughts: *Will this expedition succeed? And will I survive?*

By September 1806, both questions had been answered. The last potential physical threat—the Teton Sioux, still viewed by the captains with great suspicion—had been avoided at the end of August simply by the expedition's refusal to stop the canoes while the men traded insults with the warriors standing onshore. And Lewis, the most recent expedition member to be seriously injured (a rifle bullet through the buttocks in a hunting accident three weeks earlier), seemed to be safely on the way to total recovery. His wounds had forced him to ride supine and face down in his canoe while Clark ministered to his "worthy friend," but he declared himself well enough to hobble up Floyd's Bluff one more time.

At the grave site on this second visit, the two worrisome unknowns that had accompanied them to the Pacific and back could finally be laid to rest. Lewis, Clark, and everyone else now realized that Floyd was to be not just their first casualty, but their *only* one. And, safely past the land of the Tetons and back where black walnut trees flourished, they also realized that nothing stood in the way of their successful return from the continent's farthest shore. Whatever their lingering feelings of mourning for Floyd's passing, this must also have been a moment of great relief. (Ignorance is bliss, and happenstance bends the direction of history more than we care to admit. At that same moment—and unbeknownst to the expedition—a massive Spanish military force of six hundred Mexican and Indian troops reached the Pawnee villages only a few hundred miles to the southwest. The latest and biggest in a series of expeditions periodically dispatched by nervous Spanish authorities from Santa Fe to intercept and defeat the Corps of Discovery, this one came the closest and had the manpower to fulfill its mission, but for some reason it turned back when the Pawnees refused to join in the hunt.)

Yet even if the principal and most elemental suspense of their journey—involving survival and success—had now dissipated, as they departed Floyd's Bluff the men would have had other questions crowding into their minds. *What's happened "back in the States" during our long absence? How will we be received? And what will become of me?*

They already had a few answers to the first question. Only the night before, they had camped next to the boats of a fur trader named James Aird, a Scotsman who had recently declared himself an American in order to be licensed to do business with the Indians of the new Louisiana Territory farther upriver. Aird had given them an earful of news: Jefferson was still president (reelected in 1804, while they were wintering with the Mandans);

General James Wilkinson had been appointed governor of the territory; Vice President Aaron Burr had killed Alexander Hamilton in a duel; tensions with both Spain and Great Britain had resulted in separate naval engagements; fire had destroyed the home of their friend Jean Pierre Choteau; and two Indians had been convicted of murder and hanged in St. Louis.

Such encounters soon became an almost daily occurrence, as the explorers encountered boat after boat with other traders eagerly pushing upriver— nearly 150 of them before the expedition reached the Mississippi, the earliest possible evidence that Jefferson's dream of an orderly westward expansion would never come true. On September 6, one of the traders sold the captains a gallon of whiskey, which provided the men the first liquor they had tasted since July 4, 1805, at the Great Falls. Six days later, another trader "gave our officers wine and the party as much whiskey as we all could drink," according to Sergeant John Ordway, and "informed us that the people in general in the united States were concerned about us, as they had heard that we were all killed. Then again, they heard that the Spanyards had us in the mines [of Mexico]." They met Joseph Gravelines, who had interpreted for them among the Arikaras in the fall of 1804 and who, at their request, had gone to Washington with a delegation of chiefs; he was now on his way back to the tribe with a letter from Jefferson expressing the president's regret that the Arikara chief had died during his visit to the East.

On September 15 the big river turned sharply east at the site of present-day Kansas City, and two days later they were nearly halfway across Missouri. Another trader gave them some biscuits, chocolate, sugar—and more whiskey—and told them, Clark reported, "that we had been long Since given out [up] by the people of the U S Generaly and almost forgotton, the President of the U. States had yet hopes of us." The men were now so anxious to get home that when the biscuits ran out they told the captains there was no need to slow their progress to send out hunters for meat; they would gladly exist on the ripe papaws growing along the riverbanks if it meant putting more miles behind them each day. The building tempo was so great that Sergeant Patrick Gass apparently gave up writing in his daily journal after a short entry for September 19, which mentions that they saw wild turkeys on the shore "but did not delay a moment to hunt."

"The party being extreemly anxious to get down ply their ores very well," Clark noted dryly on September 20. Then something caught their attention. "We saw some cows on the bank which was a joyfull Sight to the party and caused a Shout to be raised for joy." *Cows in View! O! the joy.*

Around the next bend lay the tiny village of La Charette, the westernmost white settlement on the Missouri, and therefore the first to see the Corps of Discovery in two and a half years. "Every person, both French and americans seem to express great pleasure at our return, and acknowledged themselves much astonished in seeing us return," Clark reported. The next day they reached the more substantial town of St. Charles. (Clark: "The inhabitants of this village appear much delighted at our return and seem to vie with each other in their politeness to us all.") And on September 23 they steered their canoes south onto the Mississippi and landed them for the last time when they pulled into St. Louis at noon. (Ordway: "The people gathred on the Shore and Huzzared three cheers.")

With that, the second question had been repeatedly and uniformly answered. *How will we be received?* As heroes.

The answer to the third question—*And what will become of me?*—turned out to be more complicated.

The perfect ending for a Lewis and Clark novel might be the scene at Christy's Inn two nights after the Corps of Discovery's triumphant arrival, when the jubilant citizens of St. Louis hosted a ball for the newfound heroes and raised eighteen toasts in their honor; or perhaps at any of the series of other galas held in their behalf as the captains and their entourage worked their way east toward Washington, where the grandest ball of all was held on January 14, 1807—complete with more than two dozen toasts from the capital's social elite and the reading of an epic poem written especially for the occasion, which concluded with the recommendation that the Columbia River be renamed in honor of the nation's newest Columbus, Meriwether Lewis:

> Then hear the loud voice of the nation proclaim,
> And all ages resound the decree:
> Let our Occident stream bear the young hero's name,
> Who taught him his path to the sea.

But history isn't fiction. It has the messy habit of proceeding on past the scriptwriter's neat and tidy endings. And if the historical story of Lewis and Clark teaches us anything about heroes—*real* heroes as opposed to fictional ones—it is a lesson as mundane as it is profound, as self-evident as it is oft-forgotten: they're human. They were "not geniuses, not titans," the historian Donald Jackson observed, but "ordinary men performing feats beyond the ordinary."

For most of the Corps of Discovery, life "back in the states" meant a return to an ordinary existence decidedly less eventful and heroic than their epic quest for a Northwest Passage—so much so, that the answer to *And what will become of me?* has been lost to history for most of them.

Let the solid and dependable Sergeant Ordway stand in as their representative. He had begun the expedition with a touching letter to his parents in New Hampshire, expressing his excitement about the prospects of making great discoveries and receiving great rewards, but also revealing anxieties that he might not survive. With almost perfect symmetry he concluded his journey with this final journal entry, written upon the expedition's arrival in St. Louis: "And now we look for boarding in Town and wait for our Settlement, and then we entend to return to our native homes to See our parents once more, as we have been So long from them.—finis."

Ordway accompanied Lewis to Washington, visited his New Hampshire family, got married, and by the fall of 1807 had returned to Missouri to settle on the 320 acres Congress had awarded him. He apparently also used some of the double pay he had received to further increase his acreage. "There is no better land in the world," he wrote home that November from the New Madrid district in Missouri's bootheel, where he already had peach and apple orchards under cultivation. From intrepid explorer to yeoman farmer in a year's time. Though the records are sketchy about Ordway's subsequent life, his serenity and prosperity were undoubtedly upended in 1811, when the cataclysmic New Madrid earthquake devastated the region, shaking things violently enough to make the Mississippi momentarily flow northward. By 1818, court records list him as deceased.

Some of the men reenlisted with the Army. Some of them went to work for fur-trading companies. Some, like Nathaniel Pryor, would go on to marry Indians; others fought them—the German-born John Potts would be killed by the Blackfeet at the Three Forks of the Missouri, as was George Drouillard; George Shannon would lose a leg in a battle with the Arikaras, who became mortal enemies of the Americans once they learned their chief had perished during his visit to Washington. By the mid-1820s, Clark would list nearly half of the party as already dead; a few, notably Alexander Willard and Patrick Gass, would live to ripe old ages. Only one of them achieved greater renown *after* the expedition than during it: John Colter, whose exploits and adventures as a mountain man became the stuff of western legend, though he soon forsook the mountains for a home in Missouri, where he died of jaundice in 1813.

Much more is known about the post-expedition fates of the two main heroes of the tale, Lewis and Clark, perhaps the best examples of how human—and fallible—heroes can be. For two and a half years the two captains had displayed personal bravery, unselfish friendship, uncommon foresight and perseverance combined with remarkable flexibility, and at times inspired leadership. Those qualities had made it possible for what began as a ragtag corps of soldiers and backwoodsmen to cross a harsh and unforgiving continent—and not just survive, but return in glory with the loss of only one man. Like the men they led, however, "back in the states" the captains seemed far less glorious.

With epic poems written in his honor and a statue of his likeness placed in Independence Hall, Lewis would have been the nation's most eligible bachelor in the winter of 1806. But for some reason his several attempts at courtship all ended in failure. The decisiveness he exhibited on the trail was still evident (even if his motive was more selfish) when he moved quickly to suppress publication of Private Robert Frazer's journal, which would have greatly diminished prospective sales of Lewis's own much-advertised account. And yet for three years he was never able to bring himself to even *begin* his manuscript, while the world—and his mentor, Jefferson—eagerly waited. As governor of the Louisiana Territory, he proved to be clumsy at the politics necessary for success. He lost money in land speculations, sank into debt, drank too much, and may have overused opium.

Clark's description of the last time he saw his comrade—at the St. Louis wharf in September 1809, as Lewis set off for Washington—is almost too heart wrenching to read, both for the pain Clark expresses and for what it implies about the state into which Lewis had fallen. "I have not Spent Such a day as yesterday for maney years," Clark wrote his brother about Lewis's departure. "His Crediters all flocking in near the time of his Setting out distressed him much, which he expressed to me in Such terms as to Cause a Cempothy which is not yet off. . . . [I]f his mind had been at ease, I Should have parted Cherefully." *And what will become of me?* had obviously become a much different question for the undaunted hero who had once conquered the Continental Divide and confidently compared himself to Columbus. A month after bidding Clark farewell, Lewis would be dying at a lonely outpost in Tennessee from self-inflicted gunshot wounds.

In a memoriam to his protégé, Jefferson later described what he called "hypochondriac affections" and occasional "sensible depressions of mind" in Lewis. "During his Western Expedition, the constant exertion which that required of all the faculties of body and mind suspended these distressing affections," the president wrote, "but after his establishment at St. Louis in sedentary occupations, they returned to him with redoubled vigor and began seriously to alarm his friends." In the end, the tangled passages within his own tortured mind proved harder for Meriwether Lewis to overcome than an unexpected range of mountains eternally covered with snow.

Clark met a happier fate. At the start of the expedition, the government had refused to grant him the co-equal rank of captain which Lewis had promised—a disappointment the two men kept secret from their men throughout the journey. As they approached St. Louis, the *And what will become of me?* question for Second Lieutenant Clark may have centered on whether Jefferson's view that this had been the "Lewis Expedition" would become history's as well. To his everlasting credit, Lewis made sure otherwise.

Beginning with his first letter to Jefferson, written on the day of their safe arrival, Lewis pointedly referred to "my frind and colligue" as *Captain* Clark in every reference. "With rispect to the exertions and services rendered by that esteemable man Capt. William Clark," he wrote the president, knowing that every newspaper in the nation would repeat it, "in the course of [the] late voyage I cannot say too much; if sir any credit be due for the success of that arduous enterprize in which we have been mutually engaged, he is equally with myself entitled to your consideration and that of our common country."

A grateful Congress awarded Clark the same land grant of sixteen hundred acres as Lewis (although his double pay was based on his lesser rank and shorter service). Jefferson appointed him superintendent of Indian affairs for the Louisiana Territory and brigadier general of the militia. (Nearly two hundred years later, Congress and President William Jefferson Clinton would retroactively give him the official rank of captain for his service with the Corps of Discovery.)

Luckier in love than Lewis, Clark married Julia ("Judith") Hancock in January 1808 and with her had five children, including an eldest son named Meriwether Lewis Clark. (Ms. Hancock is remembered for Clark's naming the Judith River in Montana for her, although he also christened a stream "Marthey's river in honor to the Selebrated M.F."—a woman unidentified further. Maybe he was hedging his bets.) Unlike his tragic friend, Clark lived a long and full life—successful at business, territorial governor for several terms, renowned for the map of the West he had created (and continued to refine), friend and confidant to royalty, writers, and explorers who continually stopped to see him on their own way up the Missouri. True to the promise he had made to Toussaint Charbonneau and Sacagawea when they left the expedition at the Mandan villages, he oversaw the education of their son, Jean Baptiste, and later of their daughter, Lisette. He died in 1838 at age sixty-eight.

But just as the gravitational pull of Lewis's inner demons proved impossible for him to escape once he returned from the unknown, Clark found himself unable to rise above his times and his surroundings as much as we might have hoped from a hero. On the trail, Clark had shown remarkable skills at dealing with Indians—a directness coupled with more than a tinge of sincerity and compassion that the Native Americans seem to have recognized as distinctively as the color of his hair. When he became superintendent of Indian affairs, many tribes referred to St. Louis as the "Red-Headed Chief's town," and they looked to him for assistance and understanding at a time when the American nation was making its first push across the Mississippi and onto their homelands. There was little he was able to do. Many whites accused him of being "soft" on Indians, but the land grabs, wars, and waves of deadly epidemics that swept across the Indian world on Clark's watch were not much different in severity from those that continued throughout the rest of the century.

"In my present situation of Superintendent of Indian Affairs, it would afford me pleasure to be enabled to [help] the conditions of these unfortunate people placed under my charge, knowing as I do their wretchedness and their rapid decline," he plaintively wrote former president Jefferson in 1825. "It is to be lamented that the deplorable situation of the Indians do not receive more of the human feelings of the nation." There is a profound sadness in those words, a decidedly unheroic admission of defeat from the realization that he had been as helpless to protect the Indians in his care as he had been to save his best friend from self-destruction.

Clark's treatment of his slave York inspires less sympathy. Of all the members of the Corps of Discovery, its sole African American would have been most focused on *And what will become of me?* as they swept down the final miles of the Missouri. Among the Indians, who had never seen a black man before, York's color had earned him a level of prestige and fawning attention—"Big Medicine," they had called him. A few incidents reported in the journals suggest that some of the men may have considered York beneath them, but there are more entries that paint him as just another member of the group. And there is no question that on November 24, 1805, at the mouth of the Columbia River during the decision on where to spend the winter, a slave's vote was recorded openly and equally with every other person's.

York may not have found freedom on the trail, but he had certainly tasted a version of it. By the time the expedition was completed, he seems to have believed he rightfully deserved it in full. But freedom was not what William Clark had in mind for the human being he had owned since childhood.

A series of recently discovered letters from Clark to one of his brothers reveals that for a number of years after their return to St. Louis, in consideration of his services during the expedition, York persistently asked to be set free. "I did wish to do well by him," Clark wrote in one letter from late 1808, "but as he has got Such a notion about freedom and his emence Services, that I do not expect he will be of much Service to me again; I do not think with him, that his Services has been So great/or my situation would promit me to liberate him." Short of being freed, York asked at least to be hired out to work near Louisville, where his wife lived as a slave to another owner. Clark didn't like that idea either, although he eventually relented, telling his brother in early 1809, "perhaps if he has a Severe Master a While he may do Some Service . . . and give over that wife of his." Later letters indicate York's return to St. Louis, where Clark peevishly described him as so "insolent and Sulky, I gave him a Severe trouncing the other Day."

By 1811 it appears that York had been sent back to Kentucky and, in fact, was hired out to a master who treated him roughly; and by late 1815, nearly a decade after the expedition's completion, he was still a slave. Reportedly, Clark eventually granted York his freedom and helped him get started in the freighting business. According to this account, sometime before 1832 he died of cholera in Tennessee.

During the expedition, of the two captains it was William Clark who most consistently exhibited a fatherly concern for the plight of the men, who seemed capable of being touched by moments of familial emotion (Sacagawea's reunion with her people; the infant Baptiste's playful dancing), who impressed British fur traders and Indian chiefs alike as the less rigid and stubbornly trapped by preexisting prejudices. And clearly something had transpired by the time they reached the Pacific Ocean that prompted Clark to solicit and record his slave's opinion on an important matter—something, however subtle, that obviously gave York reason to assume their lifelong master-slave relationship had changed.

But "back in the states," the innovative and extraordinary wilderness leader proved himself to be a very run-of-the-mill slaveowner, incapable of seeing York—a man who had contributed mightily to Clark's greatest success, a man yearning for his own just rewards and aching to be reunited with his wife—as anything but a piece of property.

Like their own hero Thomas Jefferson, whose immortal words on the equality of man would inspire a slow but steady march of freedom across the centuries just as surely as his own private actions fell far short of those words, Lewis and Clark could point to a better future but were never quite capable of reaching it themselves. They were "ordinary men" again, fallible humans. They had weaknesses, failures, shortcomings. To pretend otherwise would not only create a sanitized history, it would detract from the lesson in heroism we can draw from their out-of-the-ordinary, truly inspirational moments of strength, success, and transcendence.

If only perfect people can be heroes, then there can be no heroes. But if imperfect people are capable of heroism, then aren't we all?

Floyd's Bluff teaches another lesson about history, heroes, and humans. Unlike historians, the human heroes of the past don't know how their story will end. Nearly every recounting of the Lewis and Clark saga, when it reaches the moment of Floyd's death early on the westbound journey, immediately informs the reader that his would be the expedition's only fatality. Armed with that reassurance, the armchair explorer travels the rest of the distance knowing not to expect the loss of any more members. The Corps of Discovery didn't have that luxury—just like every one of us, who begin and end each day of our ordinary lives not knowing what will happen next. The most any of us can do is try our hardest, admit our mistakes, learn from yesterday, and hope for a better tomorrow.

On a grassy and windswept knoll in 1804, as they buried one of their own, the men of the Corps of Discovery were vividly reminded of how mortal each of them was and what risks they all were taking in the uncertain journey they had embarked upon. Fresh graves have a way of focusing the mind on such thoughts. In that moment would have come the larger realization that they were all in this together, that none of them could make it on his own.

And with that, an unruly collection of individuals started on the path of becoming something greater than the sum of its parts. Just how much greater was made clear when the same group stood together at the same spot two years later, having achieved things none of them would ever come close to replicating once they went their separate ways.

In April 1810, as he prepared the captains' journals for publication, Nicholas Biddle interviewed William Clark and took notes elaborating on individual events from their journey, details not found in their daily logs. For September 4, 1806, he wrote: "Floyds grave. A chief of one of the Sioux bands encamped near it, lost one of his sons. He had Floyds grave opened & his son put in with Floyd for the purpose of accompanying him to the other world believing the white man's future state was happier than that of the Savages."

As with so many anecdotes from the expedition, this one is especially poignant with the hindsight of history: an Indian boy's corpse, placed in a grave alongside the first American soldier to die west of the Mississippi by a grieving father who could not possibly know how many more graves for soldiers and Indian boys were yet to come. But it also encapsulates something more. Like Floyd's grave, ours is a shared history, an imperfect monument to the irreversible fact that we're all human, imbued with an inextinguishable desire for a better world.

14

The View from the Home Front

In February 1997 I gave a brief talk to the Historical Society of Cheshire County in Keene, New Hampshire, in which I explored some of the following material about the feud between two local newspapers over the Louisiana Purchase. (As a former reporter and editorial writer for the *Sentinel*, I was quick to point out that the paper's editorial wisdom had clearly improved since its earliest days.) A few years later I met a descendant of one of Lewis's sisters, who told me of a quilt the captain's sisters had sewn while he was on his epic journey. It's now part of the grand bicentennial exhibition of Lewis and Clark artifacts put together by the Missouri Historical Society.

Something about the notion of the sisters quilting away while they waited for Lewis to return from the unknown got me thinking about all the others who would also have wondered what was happening to the expedition—and how hard it would have been at the dawn of the nineteenth century to find out.

In December 1803, in one of its first editions as a brand-new newspaper in the small village of Walpole, New Hampshire, the *Political Observatory* posted a short notice from Louisville, Kentucky. "Capt. Clark and Mr. Lewis," the news item said, in a dispatch dated October 29, "have left this place, in the prosecution of their expedition to the westward. They have been sent thereon by the president of the United States. The object of their travels has not transpired. They will, it is said, ascend the Mississippi and Missouri as far as possible. They have an iron frame of a boat, intended to be covered with skins, which can, by screws, be formed into one boat, or four boats, as may best suit their purposes. About sixty men will compose the party." And with that, the residents of the town that is now my home—nestled on the banks of the Connecticut River and about as far from the new Louisiana Territory as was possible in the nation's seventeen states at the time—began learning of the Corps of Discovery's progress for the next three years.

Within those six sentences rest a number of intriguing points: It was *Capt.* Clark and *Mr.* Lewis in Louisville (undoubtedly reflecting the bias of Clark's hometown). The goal of the mission was a little confusing—to reach the headwaters of either the Mississippi or the Missouri (for reasons of international politics, Lewis and Clark were being deliberately fuzzy to the public about their precise plans). The iron boat frame Lewis had personally designed was singled out for mention (proud as a father of his creation, Lewis probably couldn't help bragging about it—but was he exaggerating that it could be assembled into four canoes, or was that simply sloppy reporting?). And the size of the party seems to have mushroomed from the dozen men Congress thought it had approved to "about sixty" (another reportorial mistake, or had the two captains already decided that they would need more men than originally contemplated?).

What may be more significant is something less esoteric—a reminder that people "back in the States," two-thirds of whom lived within fifty miles of the Atlantic, were hungry for information about the new American territory beyond the Mississippi and about the expedition sent to explore it; and a reminder that in the early 1800s, news—and almost everything else— traveled at an agonizingly slow pace. In this instance the Louisville report had taken a month and a half to reach western New Hampshire. By the time the people of Walpole were reading about Lewis and Clark setting off down the Ohio, the Corps of Discovery was across from the mouth of the Missouri, constructing winter quarters at Camp Dubois on the Illinois side of the Mississippi.

"The acquisition of the country through which you are about to pass has inspired the public generally with a great deal of interest in your enterprize," Jefferson wrote Lewis in January 1804, throwing in a complaint that he hadn't heard from his protégé in two months. "The enquiries are perpetual as to your progress." So it would be for the next two and a half years as

Lewis and Clark made their way up the Missouri, over the Rockies, down the Columbia River to the Pacific Coast—and then back.

Besides the general public, a small but far-flung group of people shared a special desire to be kept informed as completely as possible. At Monticello and the White House, Jefferson of course was intently eager for updated reports on his pet project. Lewis's mother in Virginia, Clark's brothers and sisters near Louisville, and the families of the other expedition members, scattered throughout the young nation, would have been anxious for any word of their loved ones. And in Mexico and Santa Fe, nervous Spanish authorities, concerned that the expedition had more to do with American conquest than exploration, struggled to keep up with events, even hired a well-placed spy in the American government to keep them informed.

With no CNN to provide any of them with on-the-spot, up-to-the-minute reports, no telephones or telegraphs to quickly transmit information, no railroads and not even many good wagon roads to speed the mails, they all relied on the sparsity of letters—and occasional rumors—that slowly filtered back from the unknown. Out on the trail with the expedition, it was "we proceeded on." Back at the home front, it was "we waited and waited some more."

Sometime in the early summer of 1804, the Ordway family of Hebron, New Hampshire, would have rejoiced to receive a letter from their young son, John, a sergeant in the Army. The last they had heard from him, their boy was serving in the First Infantry in Indiana Territory and his principal concern was that some girlfriends back home had forgotten him. Now he had something of greater urgency to tell them. It's one of my favorite documents in the entire Lewis and Clark archives and worth, I think, repeating in nearly its full extent:

Camp River Dubois April the 8th 1804

Honored Parence

I now embrace this oppertunity of writing . . . to let you know where I am and where I am going. I am well thank God, and in high Spirits. I am now on an expidition to the westward, with Capt. Lewis and Capt. Clark, who are appointed by the President of the united States to go . . . through the interior parts of North America. We are to ascend the Missouri River with a boat as far as it is navigable and then go by land, to the western ocean, if nothing prevents, &c.

This party consists of 25 picked Men of the armey & country likewise and I am

So happy as to be one of them pick'd Men from the armey, and I and all the party are if we live to Return, to Receive our Discharge when ever we return again to the united States if we chuse it . . . we are to Start in ten days up the Missouri River. . . .

We expect to be gone 18 months or two years. We are to Receive a great Reward for this expidition, when we Return. I am to Receive 15 dollars pr. month and at least 400 ackers of first Rate land, and if we make Great Discoveries as we expect, the united States has promised to make us Great Rewards more than we are promised . . . For fear of exidants I wish to inform you that I left 200 dollars in cash, at Kaskaskias . . . and if I Should not live to return, my heirs can git that and all the pay Due me from the U.S. . . . Government.

I . . . will write next winter if I have a chance. Yours, &c.

John Ordway Sergt.

What a wonderful letter—and, since nothing at all like it has been recovered from any of the other men on the expedition, how lucky history is to at least have Ordway's charming message to his parents to stand in for everyone else. He's happy and obviously proud to have been selected to join the captains on a mission of presidential importance. His reasons for volunteering are clear: the pay, the land, and the likelihood of other "Great Rewards" (including some measure of fame) if they make "Great Discoveries." Bursting with expectancy, he assures his father and mother of his good health and promising future, but the potential danger is enough on his mind that he alludes twice to the possibility of not surviving the adventure. Then a dutiful promise to write "if I have a chance"—and he's gone.

How many more parents got similar letters from sons about to embark with Lewis and Clark that spring—prompting that many more mothers and loved ones to gaze westward and wonder each day where their child, brother, or boyfriend was at that moment? And would tomorrow's mail bring bad news or good news, or any news at all?

Clark managed to send off a letter to his family near the time of the expedition's departure in May, saying he hoped to see everyone in less than two years. "My rout is uncertain," he added. "I think it more than probable that Capt. Lewis or my self will return by sea, and the other by the same route we proceed, the time is uncertain." What letters from Lewis still survive from the time are more official in nature—he was busy arranging to send some maps, botanical samples, and a group of Osage chiefs back to Jefferson, among other things—but I would imagine he got something off to his mother and siblings before leaving.

By June, the American military commandant in St. Louis wrote to his superiors in Washington that Lewis had sent him a note from sixty miles up the Missouri. "He proceeds about 15 miles per day," the officer wrote, "a celerity seldom witnessed on the Missouri. . . . His men possess great resolution and they [are in the best] health and spirits."

Meanwhile, mail was crisscrossing the vast province of New Spain with the purpose of putting an early end to the expedition led by the man they often referred to as "Captain Merry Weather" or just "Captain Merry." In March, a paid informant in New Orleans had sent Spanish authorities a detailed description of Lewis and Clark's plans and urged them to "detach a sufficient body of chasseurs to intercept Captain Lewis and his party, who are on the Missouri River, and force them to retire or take them prisoners." (The informant was none other than General James Wilkinson of the United States Army, soon to become governor of the Louisiana Territory, and later a prominent player in the Burr conspiracy.)

Luckily for the Corps of Discovery, the Spanish mails were just as slow as the Americans'. The commanding general in Chihuahua received Wilkinson's message in May. He immediately ordered the governor of New Mexico to do anything possible to stop "the expedition of Merry" and suggested a party of Comanches might do the trick. By the time the governor in Santa Fe received the order and dispatched a force of soldiers, it was August 1; when the search party reached Nebraska, the calendar had turned to September and the "Merry" men were already safely moving upriver into South Dakota.

Back in New Hampshire during the summer of 1804, however, opposing forces had found each other and a different kind of confrontation had broken out. About twenty miles south of Walpole—and in response to a glowing article about the Louisiana Purchase in the *Political Observatory*—the *New Hampshire Sentinel*, based in Keene, had taken up the Federalist cudgels against Jefferson and his doubling of the nation's size. "FIFTEEN MILLIONS of DOLLARS," it shouted, had been spent in an act that threatened "the Liberty, the Happiness, the Peace, the Security, the Prosperity, the Glory of the Northern States, and *particularly* of New England." Even worse, according to the newspaper, expanding westward might lead to "the subversion of REPRESENTATIVE GOVERNMENT, and to the dissolution of THESE UNITED STATES." Jefferson, it concluded, was fostering a government "which bears more resemblance to a Monarchy than a republic."

The *Political Observatory* tried to steer the discussion back to the facts. In mid-July (two full months after the fact) it reported that Lewis was leaving St. Louis. "His boat is capitally manned, as well with stout Americans as with hardy Canadians," the newspaper noted, "and will no doubt winter this fall a little below the Mandanes, which is reckoned near 800 leagues from the mouth of the Missouri." The delegation of Osage chiefs, it added, was on its way toward Washington.

The *Sentinel* kept its oratorical guns trained on Jefferson and his spending. Fifteen million dollars, the paper explained to its readers, "if in silver would weigh something more than four hundred tons and would take the same number of waggons, each carrying twenty hundred weight, to carry it from the treasury—making a line of carriages of about six miles in length, all of them loaded with dollars."

A few weeks later the paper brought religion into the mix, hoping to galvanize Puritan doubts about the deist president. Jefferson, it reported, had been observed on at least four occasions traveling between Monticello and Washington on the Sabbath! "This appears pointed and pre-meditated," the paper warned ominously, and then drew the *Observatory*'s editor into the conspiracy: "The snivelling Ex-Priest at Walpole gave us as an excuse for one of these journies, that Mr. J. was called home by the sickness of one of his children! What forgery he will now resort to, is past conjecture."

Apparently turning the other cheek, the next week's *Observatory* contented itself with coverage of Jefferson's speech to the Osage chiefs. The paper reprinted the president's entire address, the editor noted, "with a confidence that the sentiments of good will it breathes towards the aborigines of the soil, will afford as much pleasure to the readers, as they confer honor on the government."

For his own part, Jefferson ended the year 1804 having won reelection. Despite Federalist complaints such as the *Sentinel*'s, his doubling of the nation's size without the firing of a gun had proved immensely popular. Already planning other explorations of the new territory, particularly up its southwestern rivers, the president waited expectantly for news of Lewis and Clark.

Near the end of the year, General Wilkinson forwarded to the War Department a report (probably from a fur trader coming downriver) that by August 4 the expedition had reached the mouth of the Platte River, "where two of their boatmen deserted" and "the others were much dissatisfied & complained of too regid a discipline." This account also vaguely alluded to "a difference between the Captains."

But Jefferson apparently had his own sources. In late November, long before Wilkinson's report arrived, he wrote Lewis's brother a short letter that confirmed the information about the expedition's reaching the Platte and suffering two desertions, but set a much cheerier tone. "All accounts concur in the entirely friendly dispositions of the Indians," the president wrote, "and that he will be through his whole course as safe as at home."

On January 4, 1805, Jefferson dispatched another short note to the captain's family, saying that by August 19 Lewis had made it 850 miles up the Missouri without accident. Jefferson assured the Lewises that the expedition would most likely winter with the Mandans, reach the Pacific in the summer of 1805, and return to the Mandan villages for the next winter. On January 26, 1805, in a one-paragraph notice, readers of the *Political Observatory* learned much the same information—reported in language so similar to Jefferson's letters to Reuben Lewis that it seems clear the president was drafting his own press releases. If there was anything to worry about, the president was keeping it to himself.

And then . . . nothing. The ice-choked Missouri had shut down communications, leaving everyone in the East with little to do except speculate or worry, depending on their temperaments.

Whether they subscribed to the *Political Observatory* or got their information via word of mouth, Private Alexander Hamilton Willard's parents, living in the town of Charlestown just ten miles north of Walpole, surely must have wondered who these Mandan Indians were with whom their son was reportedly wintering. How shocked they would have been to learn that the Mandan-Hidatsa villages were home to roughly forty-five hundred people—a population larger than that of Walpole or Charlestown—or even Washington DC—at the time.

What would John Ordway's parents have thought, riding out their own winter within sight of New Hampshire's White Mountains, if they had known that their boy, out on the unimaginable northern plains, was writing in his diary, "the weather is 12 degrees colder this morning than I ever new it to be in the States"? Would they have wanted to know that in late February, after a brief confrontation between some expedition members and a party of Lakotas, he was confiding to his journal, "They Say if they can catch any more of us they will kill us for they think that we are bad medicine"?

Herbal healer that she was, Lewis's mother might have been fascinated by the tale of her son assisting Sacagawea's childbirth by administering a dose of crushed rattlesnake rattle. But would she have wanted to know that by midwinter he was treating many of his men for venereal disease?

If Jefferson had known that the representatives of the Hudson's Bay and North West companies living among the Mandans were writing that they viewed Lewis as a pompous snob but considered Clark the better diplomat, would the president have second-guessed his decision on who should lead the expedition?

Perhaps no news was good news. If so, there was plenty of it. January, February, and March 1805 passed with nothing from the Corps of Discovery. The ice on the river melted. April went by, then most of May. Still no word. Then on May 20 the big keelboat arrived back in St. Louis, loaded down with maps, a copy of one of the men's journals, reports on the Indian tribes, soil samples, animal skins and skeletons, some live birds and a prairie dog, a delegation of Indian chiefs—and letters to Jefferson, Clark's family, and Lewis's mother. (For all we know, the other men sent letters back with the keelboat as well, but none have been found for history.)

Here at last was real news, and it soon spread in the manner of the time— from one newspaper (the most western one was in Kentucky) to another, finally reaching the *Political Observatory* in time for its July 20 edition. The report was dense with information. The land to the mouth of the Platte was fertile; beyond that to the Mandans, not so fertile, a flat and treeless plains covered with grass. One of the men, Charles Floyd, had died "much regretted" from a "cramp in his stomach"; a river had been named in his memory. The Indians "have been friendly, with but a few exceptions," notably the Teton Sioux, who were the "most troublesome." The Mandans were good corn farmers. "*Buffaloes* are said to be in great numbers, and of a large size. . . . Elks and goats are numerous. The grouse, or paire hen are in plenty. . . . Fish scarce, and those principally of the cat kind." The Missouri was still muddy and a mile wide at the Mandan villages, 1,609 miles from St. Louis—but only six hundred more miles west was a great waterfall "made by a ledge of mountains, called Rocky Mountain, in which it is presumed the Missouri terminates."

In town after town along the news report's route, imagine the buzz such facts touched off. ("We expect in a few days further particulars relative to this interesting voyage," the account concluded—a surefire way to boost circulation.) But for the families of the expedition's members, all eyes would have been riveted on a paragraph near the end. "The greatest friendship has existed with the party," it said, "and the men who have returned, speak in the highest terms of the humanity, and uncommon pains and attention of both Captains, Lewis and Clark, toward the whole of them." Everyone, the report said, was in "good spirits" and "enjoyed perfect health" when the keelboat had headed south while the main expedition pushed westward toward the Northwest Passage. Floyd was dead, but all the other sons and loved ones were healthy, happy, and in good hands. That was news worth waiting for.

A personal letter from Clark to his family told them that the land he was about to enter "is but little Known," but the information about it he had gleaned from the Indians was "entitled to some credit." Based on that, he said, "my return will not be so soon as I expected, I fear not sooner than about June or July 1806."

Lewis's letter to his mother was much longer, describing in detail the tricky current of the river ("we have experienced more difficulty from the navigation of the Missouri, than danger from the Savages"), the beauty of the land ("one of the fairest portions of the globe"), the abundance of game ("our prospect for starving is therefore consequently small"), and the sunny prediction for an easy ascent of the Missouri to its source, making a half-day portage, and descending the Columbia to the Pacific by summer.

"Give yourself no uneasiness with rispect to my fate," he wrote, "for I assure you that I feel myself perfectly as safe as I should do in Albemarle; and the only difference between 3 or 4 thousand miles and 130, is that I can not have the pleasure of seeing you as often as I did while at Washington." In other words, everything a mother wanted to hear.

The longest letter went to Jefferson, along with the boxes and trunks stuffed with curiosities from the West. (The letter and other dispatches reached Washington by July 10; the larger shipment arrived in mid-August.) Two lines in the letter would have registered with the president as he prepared to follow Lewis's travels in his mind. One said the captains expected to return "as far as the head of the Missouri, or perhaps to this place [the Mandan villages] before winter" and they would "meet you at Montachello in September 1806." The second was a sweetener to offset such another long wait for information. "I shall dispatch a canoe with three, perhaps four persons, from the extreem navigable point of the Missouri, or the portage betwen this river, and the Columbia river, as either may first happen," Lewis promised. "By the return of this canoe, I shal send you my journal, and some one or two of the best of those kept by my men."

Jefferson could now set his mental calendar: a canoe dispatched from the Missouri's headwaters in early summer, racing down the river with news from the farthest limit of the Louisiana Territory, could probably reach St. Louis in three months; another month for the mail to reach the East—he should expect the next message from Lewis in October or November. In the meantime, he had plenty of material to occupy his voracious intellect. There was Arikara tobacco seeds and Mandan corn to plant in his Monticello garden, the horns of a bighorn sheep and antelope skins and skeletons and sixty-seven dried plant specimens to study, a buffalo robe painted with battle scenes by a Mandan warrior to admire, soil samples to sift through, a tin box of dead insects and mice to inspect, even a live prairie dog to keep him company. He could read Clark's journal and peruse the map Clark had drawn of their route so far (with projections farther west based on Indian information). He could prepare for the delegation of western chiefs to arrive for their meeting with the "great father." And then, before the year was out, he could expect Lewis's next bundle of news—more journals and perhaps a map with the precise latitude and longitude of the Northwest Passage.

Not surprisingly, part of Lewis's letter immediately found its way into the Washington newspapers, and worked its way north to the *Political Observatory* in Walpole by early August 1805. It included Lewis's most optimistic words. "I can foresee no material or probable obstruction to our progress, and entertain therefore the most sanguine hopes of complete success," he wrote. He and his "inestimable friend and companion Captain Clark" were in better health than at the start of the expedition. "At this moment," he concluded, "every individual of the party is in good health and excellent spirits, zealously attached to the enterprise, and anxious to proceed; not a whisper of discontent, or murmur is to be heard among them, but all in unison act with the most perfect harmony. With such men I have every thing to hope and but little to fear." No doubt Willard's parents proudly cut out or copied this tribute to their son and read it aloud from time to time as August turned to September, then October, then November . . .

On November 9 the *Political Observatory* ran its next Lewis and Clark news. It was short and unsatisfying—a mere rehash from another newspaper saying the shipment from Fort Mandan had arrived in St. Louis in May, along with twenty Indians bound toward Washington. It's as if the editor wanted *something* about Lewis and Clark to fill his pages, and stale news was all he could find.

In December, another placeholder appeared—an extract from a letter by "an intelligent gentleman" in New Orleans, describing part of the Louisiana Territory along the Mississippi. "I have travelled upwards of two thousand miles through this vast national domain," it said, "and assure you that it equals, if not surpasses the most flattering description! . . . In a word it seems a second Eden, in which God has presented to man a second time, all the fruit thereof, as an inducement to him to be virtuous, happy, and free." A stirring—if anonymous—testimonial to President Jefferson's purchase to be sure. (And perhaps enough to keep the *New Hampshire Sentinel* quiet on the topic.)

But what about something a little more concrete from people with names? When would the next shipment arrive from Lewis and Clark with western curiosities, solid information, and letters filled with news for anxious parents and presidents alike?

I am at the head of the Missouri. All well, and Indians so far friendly. All fall and early winter of 1805, Jefferson waited for some such message from his young explorer. In preparation for the expedition in 1803, the president had devised a special code for Lewis in case a secret message needed to be sent to the White House. For training—and perhaps for good luck—Lewis had been instructed to practice the ciphers using those two sentences: *I am at the head of the Missouri. All well, and Indians so far friendly.* Jefferson, of course, was hoping for much more than that in the interim report Lewis had promised to send from the Missouri's headwaters, but as time passed without any news, even those two sentences, coded or uncoded, would have sufficed.

The winter wore on. The Missouri froze again. It became clear that no canoe was going to arrive in St. Louis from the foot of the far western mountains. In the place of facts, rumors seeped in. From Philadelphia, Benjamin Smith Barton wrote the president, "We are made uneasy here by a report, that Capt. Lewis and his party have been cut off. I hope this is not true."

By January, Jefferson bravely wrote Lewis's brother that some Oto Indians had told some Osage chiefs who in turn told the Indian agent in St. Louis that "Capt. Lewis & his party had reached that part of the Missouri near the mountains where the Indian tract leads across (in 8. days march) to the Columbia, that he had there procured horses and had, with his whole party entered on the tract." How much stock he placed in this Indian telegraph is hard to say, for at the same time Jefferson admitted in another letter that "We have no certain information of Capt. Lewis since he left Fort Mandan."

Optimist that he was, Jefferson preferred to assume the best. "We expect he has reached the Pacific," he wrote on February 11, 1806, "& is now wintering on the head of the Missouri, & will be here next autumn." He—and the world—would have to content themselves once more with waiting. "I do not expect we shall again hear from him or of him until he gets back to St. Louis," he advised Reuben Lewis, "because when he begins to redescend the Missouri, he will travel as fast as the news could come by any other conveyance."

The president had readjusted his mental calendar: with Lewis wintering at the headwaters of the Missouri, the expedition could set out with the spring thaw, reach St. Louis in, say June or July at the latest. A special dispatch could make it from St. Louis to Washington in a month—say July or August—and then Lewis himself would be arriving.

Early in 1806, the delegation of chiefs arrived. In his speech to them, Jefferson said, "I . . . sent our beloved man Capt. Lewis one of my own family, to go up the Missouri" to meet them. "Some of you who are here have seen him & heard his words. You have taken him by the hand, and been friendly to him. My children I thank you for the services you rendered him, and for your attention to his words."

On the one hand, the gathering of chiefs would have been pleasing to Jefferson—living, breathing proof that Lewis had been accomplishing part of his mission. But they had seen Lewis in *1804* and had arrived in St. Louis with the keelboat in May *1805*—and therefore were also stark reminders of how little was actually known about the fate of "our beloved man."

To reassure himself, perhaps Jefferson took out his copy of the coding matrix and tried his hand at the message he and Lewis had practiced so many times, seemingly such a long time ago. *I am at the head of the Missouri. All well, and Indians so far friendly.*

Because we have access to the expedition's journals, we now know that the reason Jefferson didn't receive a report from the Missouri's headwaters is because Lewis and Clark decided against sending a canoe back downriver in June 1805. They had reached the Great Falls—which turned out to be five cascades, not one—but believed they would need all available hands for the longer-than-anticipated portage as well as for surmounting the bigger-than-expected mountains looming to the westward. It was a wise decision, but there was no way to inform Jefferson of the change in plans.

We also know that a series of unanticipated delays—the portage, the final tough haul up the Missouri and its tributaries the Jefferson and Beaverhead, the long ordeal through the Bitterroots, the overall unruly expansiveness of a West that contradicted all of Jefferson's expectations—blew the captains' neat and tidy schedule for 1805 to pieces. From Fort Mandan to the Pacific and back in a season? Hardly. November was already upon them when they finally reached the ocean; the mountains between them and the Missouri were already blocked by snows. They decided—again wisely—to winter along the coast and would set off for home in March 1806 not from the Mandan villages or even from the source of the Missouri, but from the western edge of the continent. Again, there was no way to tell anyone back home what had happened.

And we now know that the Spanish, operating in the dark as much as Jefferson, would mount three more attempts to capture or destroy the Corps of Discovery—one in 1805, two even bigger ones in 1806. We further know that all three additional attempts would fail, just like the first one.

Ironically, knowing all this makes it that much harder to put ourselves in Jefferson's shoes, or in the eastern homes of worried family members, or even in the public squares and taverns where, as 1806 unfolded, people surely noticed that Lewis and Clark had not been heard from for quite some time. Because the journals allow us to accompany Lewis and Clark, we know where they were and know what was happening each day, which makes it easy to overlook what the people left behind *didn't* know. They didn't know anything. All they could do was wait and worry. For anyone in that position, time has a way of slowing down. Days and weeks seem longer. Months become eternities.

May 1806 arrived, marking one full year since the keelboat from Fort Mandan had pulled into St. Louis, one full year without word from the Corps of Discovery. The yawning void stretched into June, July, August. Still no word.

In Walpole, New Hampshire, August 3, 1806, marked a full year since the *Political Observatory* had reprinted Lewis's letter to Jefferson. In Washington it marked a full year since the arrival of the cornucopia of western wonders. (The prairie dog had long since been sent to Mr. Peale's museum in Philadelphia.) By this time, the silence in the press had become deafening and Jefferson's correspondence seems to have dropped the topic of Lewis and Clark almost entirely. Where were they? And what were people thinking about the expedition in the face of such a long absence of news?

Once again, the journals come to our aid. On September 17, as they were racing downriver on the Missouri, the homebound explorers met a trader heading west. "This Gentleman informed us that we had been long Since given out [up] by the people of the U S Generaly and almost forgotton," Clark reported, adding, however, that "the President of the U. States had yet hopes of us."

The sixteen-month gap of no news had apparently convinced most of the public that the expedition had disappeared, been captured, or perished—and with no reason to await word of its fate, people had shifted their attention to other things. But Jefferson still had faith that they might return. Or at least that was his public posture. No doubt mothers and fathers clung to similar hopes for their sons and put on brave faces for the smaller children, regardless of their private doubts and fears.

Just as Jefferson had predicted, Lewis and Clark were now paddling faster than news could travel, and so on September 23, 1806, when the Corps of Discovery pulled into St. Louis, no one was expecting them. *They* were the news. Displaying a knack for public relations as refined as his mentor's, Lewis immediately dispatched a messenger to hold the mail until he and Clark could send some letters. Lewis's was to Jefferson, of course, announcing the successful completion of their mission and touting the prospects for a western fur trade. Clark's was to his brother in Louisville, also covering the basic details of the expedition's success. Both were written in the certain knowledge that the letters would end up being reprinted in newspapers, as in fact they were.

Other letters were also sent that same day by excited townspeople eager to be first to break the news of the expedition's surprising return—and just as certain that their reports would find their way into print. (I get the impression of the expedition landing its canoes in the midst of huzzahs and celebratory rifle rounds, and then everyone immediately dispersing in a mad rush to get to a desk with pen and paper.) "Concerning the safe arrival of Messrs. Lewis and Clark," one letter began, which eventually appeared in several Philadelphia papers, "I have the pleasure to mention that they arrived here about one hour ago. . . . They really have the appearance of Robinson Crusoes—dressed entirely in buckskins. We shall know all very soon—I have no particulars yet."

By October 26, Jefferson had received Lewis's letter and was writing a reply: "I received, my dear Sir, with unspeakable joy your letter of Sep. 23 announcing the return of yourself, Capt. Clarke & your party in good health to St. Louis. The unknown scenes in which you were engaged, & the length of time without hearing of you had begun to be felt awfully." *Had begun to be felt awfully.* Those sixteen months without any word from Lewis had started to take their toll even on Jefferson, who the same day dashed off a note to Lewis's brother informing the family of the happy news.

New Hampshire being that much more distant from St. Louis, it would have been mid-November before any letter from John Ordway reached his parents in the lake town of Hebron. While no such letter has been found, it's impossible to believe he didn't write one. A son who ends his expedition journal with "we entend to return to our native homes to See our parents once more as we have been so long from them" would not let his mother learn of his fate through a newspaper.

On November 21, under the headline "Domestic Intelligence," the *Political Observatory* proudly reprinted Clark's letter to his brother, after a brief editor's note. "We congratulate the public at large and the particular friends of Mssrs. Lewis and Clark and their companions, on the happy termination of an expedition, which will, doubtless, be productive of incalculable commercial advantages to the western country," the paper said. "Whatever differences of opinion may exist on this point" (Are you paying attention, editors of the *New Hampshire Sentinel*?), "we are presuaded all think and feel alike, on the courage, perseverance, and prudent deportment displayed by this adventurous party. They are entitled to, and will receive the plaudits of their countrymen."

Just in case anyone had missed the big news, in December the *Political Observatory* prominently reprinted a story from a Washington newspaper proclaiming the expedition's safe return. Next to it, the editor placed a notice "To Our Patrons," celebrating three complete years of publication: "To those who have ever made regular and punctual payments we feel ourselves particularly indebted and assure them that no pains shall be spared to make it worthy of their future support. All persons indebted to us are requested to make immediate payment. Those whose accounts are of two years standing and upwards are informed that unless settlement is made immediately we shall be necessitated to put them into the hands of an attorney for collection."

With the lawyers called in, life obviously had returned to normalcy.

15

The Lewis and Clark Guide to Leadership

In the summer of 1998, after traveling part of the Lewis and Clark trail in Montana with me and my family and a group of friends, Van Gordon Sauter suggested that I more fully develop my thoughts about the captains' leadership qualities and turn them into one of the business advice books that keep turning up with great regularity, especially in airport bookshops. Other projects intruded on my life (perhaps I need to read some good time-management advice books), and I never got it finished—except for this essay.

Call them CEOs in buckskins if you wish, managers on the move, wilderness entrepreneurs, dynamic troubleshooters dispatched from the home office to investigate and consolidate a dramatic expansion of market share. But above all, call Lewis and Clark leaders. At a time when the rolls of history are being steadily culled for management case studies—from Lincoln to Shackleton, Ulysses S. Grant to the *Leadership Secrets of Attila the Hun*—it's time to give Lewis and Clark their due.

As explorers and commanders, they have few peers. In 1806 Zebulon Pike was sent to investigate the southwestern borders of the Louisiana Territory. He made it to the Colorado Rockies (though he failed to climb the peak that now bears his name) but was captured by Mexican cavalry, taken as a prisoner to Santa Fe and Chihuahua, and ultimately spent as much time in Spanish custody as he did exploring.

A generation later, John Charles Frémont—the Pathfinder—became America's most famous explorer (it helped to have Kit Carson for a guide and a celebrity wife to write his romanticized public reports; so did going west when thousands of Americans were already moving there). Whatever the assessment of his five expeditions in the 1840s, however, as a commander his record is spotty at best. The mapmaker and sole journalist on Frémont's first expedition—Charles Preuss, whose secret diary was not published until 1958—labeled him "childish" and "a foolish lieutenant" on the third day out; then, as the journey progressed, Preuss got really critical. One expedition, entangled in political intrigue, resulted in Frémont's military arrest and his being taken back to Washington in chains to face court-martial. Others were marked by a chronic and sometimes disastrous impulsiveness that cost lives—a third of his men in one expedition, a few of them by cannibalism.

But perhaps the exploration that puts Lewis and Clark's skills in greatest relief took place half a world away and half a century later. In 1860, fifteen thousand people gathered in Melbourne, Australia, for the departure of the Burke and Wills expedition, whose mission was to make the first overland crossing of the desert continent. Burke and Wills had sixteen men (including a doctor), twenty tons of supplies, a small herd of imported camels (equipped with special shoes to protect the camels' feet on rocky ground and inflatable air bags to help them cross deep rivers), and the advantages of fifty years of technological advances from the time of the Corps of Discovery. "Never," one local newspaper reported, "did an expedition set forth under, on the whole, brighter auspices."

And yet, as if it occurred in some parallel universe, the Burke and Wills expedition became the reverse image of Lewis and Clark's. In the Australian crossing, nearly everything went wrong. There was bickering and backbiting up and down the ranks, including between the two leaders. Moments of indecision were followed by rushes to judgment. Relations with the aboriginal people they encountered were badly handled. Before it was over, all but one of the crew had perished (including Burke and Wills), and a good portion of Australia actually received its most fruitful exploration by the search parties sent out to find them. To be fair, a small contingent actually made it to the continent's north shore and attempted to return, but the expedition was a disaster.

By contrast, the Lewis and Clark expedition crossed their continent, accomplished their mission, made more friends than enemies among the natives they met, collected valuable information, lost just one man (to a ruptured appendix; this was eighty years before the first appendectomy), and returned with the captains not only alive but having forged one of the great friendships of all time. Passed down through two hundred years of history, their success sometimes seems matter-of-fact, almost inevitable. In truth it was spectacular.

Leadership is what created Lewis and Clark's success, a quality of leadership that separates them so distinctly from all the others whose expeditions turned out so differently. It's also a style of leadership they're still willing to share with anyone who cares to read their journals and study their lessons. Embedded in the story of the Corps of Discovery are ten clear and commonsense rules: *The Lewis and Clark Guide to Leadership.*

RULE ONE

Have a clear goal and make sure everyone understands it.

If the expedition had been a corporation, Thomas Jefferson would have been its founder and chairman of the board. Even though he never left the boardroom to visit the factory floor, everyone recognized his central authority. It was Jefferson's idea to mount an American exploration in the international competition to locate the fabled Northwest Passage, the trade route that would unlock the wealth of North America for whichever nation discovered and controlled it. In fact, he had already—in 1783, 1786, and 1793—launched three "start-ups" that never got off the ground. By the time he became president in 1801 and found himself in the position to try again, he had given the strategic business plan a great deal of thought and could express its overarching goal in one clear sentence.

"The object of your mission," he wrote Lewis in his final instructions on June 20, 1803, "is to explore the Missouri river, & such principal stream of it, as, by it's course and communication with the waters of the Pacific ocean . . . may offer the most direct & practicable water communication across this continent for the purposes of commerce." Follow the Missouri and its tributaries to find the best way for future traders in boats and canoes to reach a navigable river flowing west to the Pacific—that was the mission statement of Lewis and Clark Inc.

To that strategic goal Jefferson added a long list of other instructions, some of them buttressing the central mission, some of them ancillary to it: take precise readings of longitude and latitude at important milestones so a good map could be made; keep accurate and legible records; make detailed observations of the soils, minerals, crops, animals, and weather; get to know the Indians along the route, learn about their customs, languages, populations, religions, food, and clothing, and persuade them through friendliness of the United States' peaceful intentions and eagerness to open trade relations.

In several passages, Jefferson admitted that he couldn't foresee every contingency the expedition would face and assured Lewis that he trusted the young captain's judgment in making the right decision—but he urged Lewis always to "err on the side of your safety" and to remember the importance of getting information about the expedition's discoveries back to Washington. In other words, while finding the Northwest Passage was the prime objective, simply doing so without collecting useful information *and* returning with it would be tantamount to failure.

Lewis needed to be reminded of all this only once. Slowly descending the Ohio River in his newly built keelboat in October 1803, he began to worry that the endless delays in getting started up the Missouri might be costing the project political support in Congress. "To keep them in a good humour on the subject of the expedicion in which I am engaged," he wrote Jefferson from Cincinnati, "I have concluded to make a tour this winter on horseback of some hundred miles through the most interesting portion of the country adjoining my winter establishment." He would scout southwest of the Missouri toward Santa Fe and possibly dispatch Clark on a similar jaunt in another direction. The information they gathered might "at least procure the further toleration of the expedition" by the stockholders who had authorized it.

When Lewis's letter reached the White House in mid-November, alarm bells went off in corporate headquarters. Chairman Jefferson sent a quick and firm reply to rein in the restless ambitions of his CEO in the field. Plans were already in the works for other explorations of the Louisiana Territory, he wrote back, but more to the point, any side trips by Lewis or Clark "will be more dangerous than the main expedition up the Missouri, & would, by an accident to you, hazard our main object." Just in case Lewis had forgotten it, Jefferson boiled it down even further: "The object of your mission is single, the direct water communication from sea to sea formed by the bed of the Missouri & perhaps the Oregon."

Lewis abandoned his winter sojourn, and from that moment on, virtually every decision he made kept Jefferson's instructions clearly in focus. Clark and the men became equally inculcated in the mission, as their own journals and letters and actions attest.

From the comfortable confines of the White House and Monticello, Thomas Jefferson nonetheless led the Corps of Discovery across a broad continent and back. Through simple clarity of purpose he was with them each day, pointing them forward, keeping them moving, and helping them measure their progress toward a goal they all shared.

RULE TWO

The advantages of advance preparation cannot be overstated.

A leader's clearly enunciated goal *points* everyone to the future, but reaching it successfully requires careful planning. This was especially true for the Corps of Discovery, an enterprise explicitly conceived to travel great distances across totally unknown territory, where communication and support from the home base would be unavailable. Both Jefferson and Lewis therefore put a premium on early preparation.

After two years of study and planning with Jefferson in the White House, Lewis was dispatched to Philadelphia to learn celestial observation, rudimentary medicine, and basic botany and zoology from the nation's leading academics. While there, he went through Congress's appropriation of $2,500, buying supplies from a lengthy list he had compiled in advance— everything from clothing for his men to trade goods for Indians, from expensive scientific instruments to 193 pounds of "portable soup" for the possible time when no other food might be available. At the government arsenal in Harpers Ferry he requisitioned more equipment and supplies, even supervised construction of a collapsible iron canoe frame he had designed that could be carried, in component parts, to the farthest reach of the Missouri and then be quickly assembled and covered by skins for use on the Pacific-bound leg of the journey.

Jefferson was equally dedicated to leaving as little as possible to chance. He circulated his proposed instructions to his cabinet to solicit their suggestions, gathered what few reports and maps already existed of western lands, and wrote out a special letter of credit pledging the full faith of the government to repay anyone whose goods or services might be needed in an emergency. He even devised a secret code (key word: artichokes) for Lewis to use in sending confidential messages back to Washington.

One of the most important early decisions occurred when Lewis realized that his original estimate of the number of men needed for the expedition was inadequate. He had assured Congress that roughly a dozen men would be plenty and had outfitted for a group of that size in Philadelphia. But sometime during the winter of 1803–4 at the camp on the Mississippi River— and probably at Clark's urging—Lewis more than doubled the size of what he called the "permanent party" and arranged for additional supplies in St.

Louis before setting off. Had he not shown such flexibility in altering his initial calculations, it's doubtful that a half-strength Corps of Discovery ever would have succeeded.

Some of the meticulous advance planning never paid dividends out on the trail. Jefferson's suggestion that Lewis keep one copy of his notes on birch bark "as less liable to injury from the damp than common paper," for instance, was of little use in a terrain devoid of birches; and his letter of credit and secret code seem never to have been used. But being prepared for something that doesn't happen is much better than being unprepared for something that does. For example, what if they had encountered a sailing vessel at the mouth of the Columbia but were refused supplies or passage back with their discoveries because they had no way to pay for it? Or what if they had been captured by the Spanish and desperately needed to get a secret message to Jefferson?

For his own part, Lewis would later regret that he had not purchased enough blue beads—the only color the Indians on the Pacific Coast prized for trade; the iron frame canoe never worked; and in the one recorded instance of dispensing the portable soup, "some of the men did not relish" it, according to Sergeant Patrick Gass, so they butchered one of their horses. On the other hand, there must have been many nights on the riverbanks when the men silently thanked their captain for his foresight in purchasing mosquito netting to make sleep possible.

And as Stephen Ambrose has pointed out, even though the whiskey was depleted in Montana and the last of the tobacco was used in Oregon, the Corps of Discovery never ran out of the four supplies most essential to their success and lasting fame: gunpowder and lead (for their survival), and paper and ink (for recording their discoveries). Upon their return to St. Louis, they still had enough of all four to repeat the whole journey over again.

RULE THREE

Pick good people and give them the opportunity to prove themselves.

In 1813, Jefferson wrote down the reasons he had put Lewis in charge of a project so dear to his heart: "Of courage undaunted, possessing a firmness & perseverance of purpose which nothing but impossibilities could divert from it's direction, careful as a father of those committed to his charge, yet steady in the maintenance of order & discipline, intimate with the Indian character, customs & principles, habituated to the hunting life, guarded by exact observation of the vegetables & animals of his own country, against losing time in the description of objects already possessed, honest, disinterested, liberal, of sound understanding and a fidelity to truth so scrupulous that whatever he should report would be as certain as if seen by ourselves, with all these qualifications as if selected and implanted by nature in one body, for this express purpose, I could have no hesitation in confiding the enterprize to him." In other words, the task required someone with a wide range of talents, and Lewis possessed them.

Jefferson didn't make a rash personnel decision. He was a friend of Lewis's family in Virginia and for two years had been able to take his young aide's full measure as they lived together in the White House "like two mice in a church." He understood Lewis's weaknesses as well as his strengths. "While he lived with me in Washington, I observed at times sensible depressions of mind," Jefferson admitted, but they did not seem overly serious. One of the president's cabinet members had pointed out a potential for impulsiveness (prompting Jefferson's stress on the safety issue in his list of instructions), and other acquaintances believed the expedition's contribution to knowledge would be greater if a formally trained scientist had been sent along.

But Jefferson never questioned his choice of Lewis for a simpler reason: trust. A leader's ability to delegate authority is important in any organization; it was even more essential for this expedition, which left Jefferson's direct control (except for a few letters of advice) almost from the minute Lewis departed Washington in July 1803. Jefferson placed his trust in Lewis—and equally important, Lewis understood and appreciated it, and strove to prove himself worthy of it, which in itself made him a better commander.

If Jefferson's choice of Lewis was wise and pragmatic, Lewis's choice of Clark was inspired. Clark's strengths—more practical experience as a field commander (Lewis had once served under him), a steadier temperament, mapmaking skills, better familiarity with Indians—so perfectly complemented Lewis's, it almost seems that Lewis somehow perceived in his older friend the antidote to his own potential weaknesses.

"Your situation if joined with me in this mission will in all respects be precisely such as my own," Lewis pledged, an astonishing offer of shared command that broke with all military protocol. The War Department apparently considered it too unorthodox, refusing at the last minute to grant Clark the promised rank of captain—an embarrassing disappointment the two leaders kept secret from the rest of the men and then totally ignored in their joint decision making throughout the expedition.

Any understanding of Meriwether Lewis or William Clark must take into account each young man's pride, personal ambition, and forceful energy—

traits that could easily have wrecked their joint command. That it instead worked so seamlessly (if the two disagreed on anything during the long journey, other than the taste of dog meat and the desirability of salt, the journals don't report it) is a measure not only of their unshakable friendship and mutual trust but their understanding that each one's success relied completely on the other's.

The two captains, however, could not have succeeded without a well-chosen crew. From the start, Lewis told Clark they should be looking for "stout, healthy, unmarried men, accustomed to the woods, and capable of bearing bodily fatigue in a pretty considerable degree." While the ability to bear fatigue turned out to be one of the most necessary attributes, it appears the leaders were also careful to assemble a wide range of critical skills in their subordinates: a gunsmith, blacksmith, carpenter, tailor, boatmen, hunters, cooks, interpreters—an amalgamation of specialties (overlapping the assumed basic competencies of soldiers) that would permit the Corps of Discovery to meet any contingency that crossing the continent might entail.

No personnel system is flawless. Two men had to be drummed out of the "permanent party"—one for desertion, the other for mutinous remarks—and were sent back to St. Louis after the winter in North Dakota. And journal entries about near disasters during the wild rides down the Clearwater, Snake, and Columbia Rivers reveal an unusually large number of men who couldn't swim, a skill a more careful recruiter might have insisted upon for an expedition whose mission was to follow an all-water route to the Pacific.

But like the captains who led them, whether the men of the Lewis and Clark expedition filled in each other's missing strengths or reinforced important attributes, in the end they created something that transcended their individual potentials.

RULE FOUR
Molding a team requires a variety of techniques; unity doesn't happen overnight.

The unruly collection of individuals that started up the Missouri River in May 1804 was a Corps of Discovery in name only. The group that returned in triumph two and a half years later was a well-functioning, cohesive unit. This dramatic transformation cannot be tied to a single moment. It was a steady progression, the result of patient leadership that used discipline and reward and creativity to mold a team that eventually thought—and acted—as one.

During the preparatory winter of 1803–4 at Camp Dubois in Illinois, the men got drunk and disorderly on a regular basis, fought with one another, openly disobeyed—even threatened—their sergeants. Things did not automatically improve once they got under way. Before the first year was completed, by my count the captains convened seven courts-martial to consider charges against ten different privates (two of whom appeared in two trials).

That means a third of the "permanent party" created discipline problems of one kind or another. Offenses included being absent without leave, talking back to an officer, being drunk on guard duty, sleeping on guard duty, "mutinous expression," and, the most serious, desertion. In every case the accused was found guilty; and in almost every case a jury of fellow servicemen recommended anywhere from twenty-five to a hundred lashes on the bare back as punishment. The deserter, Moses Reed, was forced to run the gauntlet of men (each with nine switches) four times, suffering what Clark estimated to be five hundred lashes.

The lashings seem excessively cruel by modern lights, even if they were not unusual according to military standards of discipline for their time. But what still translates easily across two centuries is how the captains clearly and consistently enunciated the rules they expected to be followed, how the men themselves calibrated the punishments according to the seriousness of the charges, how the example made by each court-martial seems to have marked the last instance of that particular offense, how some of the early offenders eventually became model soldiers and earned back their captains' full trust, and how Lewis and Clark proved themselves confident enough in their leadership not to become blindly hidebound in dispensing discipline. When Private Thomas Howard was court-martialed on February 10, 1805, for sneaking back into Fort Mandan after hours by scaling the palisades, the jury sentenced him to fifty lashes, but then recommended that the captains forgive the punishment. Apparently no longer worried about sparing the rod and spoiling the child, Lewis and Clark agreed. It turned out to be the expedition's last court-martial.

Teamwork, however, is much more than obedience to the rules, and unity cannot simply be imposed. Lewis and Clark used other techniques to forge the Corps of Discovery. They sensed the right moments to halt on particularly hard days and reward the exhausted men with an extra gill of whiskey, just as they seemed to know when Cruzatte should be asked to get out his fiddle around evening campfires. They encouraged celebrations on Independence Day, Christmas, and New Year's. They knew when to look the other way when the men were eager to accept the offers of companionship from native women, as well as when to prohibit it.

"The men complain much . . ." (about mosquitoes, excessive heat or constant rain, prickly pears, the toil of the portage) shows up in the journals often enough to suggest the captains knew when to let them bellyache and blow off steam. Among the Nez Percés on the return trip, impatiently waiting for the Bitterroot snows to melt, the captains kept the men happily occupied—and simultaneously got them in shape for the upcoming mountain crossing—by organizing footraces and games of prison base (a precursor of baseball) against their Indian hosts.

They displayed a willingness to grant the men second chances after human mistakes (Alexander Willard's forgetfulness of his tomahawk and, later, his horse comes to mind; so does young George Shannon's allowing himself to be separated for days from the main party)—giving them opportunities to prove themselves capable of contributing to the expedition's success.

Even though they were undisputed military commanders, Lewis and Clark also knew that simply giving an order was not always the best option for settling things. When Sergeant Charles Floyd died, the captains had his replacement chosen by a vote of the men. At an unexpected fork of the Missouri in north-central Montana, when Lewis and Clark were literally the only members of the expedition who believed the south fork was the one to follow, they gave the men's contrary opinion enough consideration to delay for scouting parties to search each option. The captains had been correct, and the delay was costly in time, but the incident cemented the men's respect for their commanders at a crucial stage of the journey, as Lewis reported when they moved on: "They said very cheerfully that they were ready to follow us any where we thought proper to direct."

And near the mouth of the Columbia River, when the men's exhilaration at reaching the Pacific Ocean had immediately been overwhelmed by relentlessly bad weather, a discouraging absence of supply ships, and the intense desire to turn back toward home, Lewis and Clark's decision to let the entire company vote on what to do next turned out to be their finest hour as leaders. The vote transformed what could have been a morale-destroying moment into a powerful demonstration to every member that the Corps of Discovery's destiny lay in their own hands. They would succeed or fail together.

It might be tempting to argue that a group that spent such a long time together, facing one challenge and obstacle after another, would naturally coalesce into a close-knit team. History, however, suggests otherwise, offering innumerable examples in which repeated tensions at close quarters had just the opposite effect. The difference is the quality of leadership.

The Corps of Discovery's teamwork—the hallmark of its success—did not occur by happenstance. Lewis and Clark created, nurtured, and sustained it.

RULE FIVE
Real men stop and ask directions.

For Lewis and Clark, not knowing what awaited them around the next bend of the river or over the next horizon was not a metaphor for the uncertainties of the future; it was the central fact of their journey. They were acutely and unabashedly aware of what they *didn't* know, recognized that others might have important information to impart, and took every possible opportunity to glean what they could from everyone they encountered. Asking questions and seeking directions or advice was not a sign of weakness, it was a critical component of their leadership.

On the way up the Missouri River in the summer of 1804 they met a number of fur traders heading downstream after wintering among the Indians. The captains already had a good map of the lower Missouri, but they grilled the traders to confirm their information, inquired about the big river's tributaries, and sought to learn about the tribes they would soon encounter. (They hired one trader, Pierre Dorion Sr., to accompany them back upriver and serve as an interpreter with the Otos, Missouris, and Yankton Sioux.)

Farther on, each tribe they came across would be peppered with questions about what to expect from the route ahead. Every answer armed Lewis and Clark with that much more information upon which might rest the fate of the expedition. The Yanktons warned that the Teton Sioux, or Lakota, might not be so friendly; so the captains were prepared for trouble. The Hidatsas drew lines in the dirt to describe the Missouri's course far beyond the limits of the expedition's maps and told of the Shoshones, a tribe rich in horses, at the river's headwaters; so the captains hired Toussaint Charbonneau and his young Shoshone wife in anticipation of the need for important negotiations. The Shoshones said the nearby river routes to the Columbia (via the Salmon and Snake) were impassable and traversed deserts without game; so the captains detoured to a mountain passage they were told were used by the Nez Percés, and brought along pack-bearing horses that could double as food. The Nez Percés said their river was navigable to the sea; so the captains had the Indians show them the best way to make dugout canoes from Ponderosa pines. The Clatsops said the hunting was better on the south side of the Columbia; so the captains looked there for winter quarters.

One of the "primary objects of human existence," Lewis wrote to himself on his thirty-first birthday, was to "advance the information of the succeed-ing generation." The future is created by the answers to the questions the present is willing to ask. Lewis and Clark showed an uncommon willingness and ability not only to ask the right questions but to sift through the answers and construct the right course of action.

RULE SIX
Be willing to adjust to new and unexpected situations.

Lewis and Clark's original plan for the summer of 1805 was to send a small contingent of men in a single canoe back to St. Louis from the Great Falls of central Montana, with updated reports to augment the maps, scientific discoveries, and Indian information they had already shipped downriver in the big keelboat. (The keelboat's cargo, in fact, included a letter to President Jefferson promising this additional dispatch.)

But the Great Falls turned out to be five cascades instead of one, and the portage around them was much harder and time-consuming than ex-pected. They were falling behind schedule. The Rocky Mountains—still snowcapped in midsummer—were visible in the distance, and there had been no sign of the Indians whose help they were counting on to cross the Continental Divide. Time to reconsider the plan of attack.

While the men celebrated the Fourth of July with music and the last of the whiskey supply, the two captains conferred privately. "We have conceived our party sufficiently small," Lewis wrote that evening, and had concluded not to make it even smaller by dispatching one of the canoes. "We fear also that such a measure might possibly discourage those who would in such case remain, and might possibly hazzard the fate of the expedition."

Keeping the group at full strength—and equally important, in good morale—was deemed more essential than getting an interim report to Jef-ferson, even if it meant not only disappointing the president but forgoing the last chance for communication before disappearing into the complete unknown.

Savvy leaders that they were, Lewis and Clark made this important mid-course adjustment in such a way that the men were totally unaware of their captains' growing concern about the turn of events. "We have never once hinted to any one of the party that we had such a scheme in contemplation," Lewis confided to his journal, "and all appear perfectly to have made up their minds to suceed in the expedition or purish in the attempt."

Only a few days later, Lewis had to face another unexpected setback more openly. The iron canoe frame that he had personally designed and brought all the way from Harpers Ferry was pieced together and covered with buffalo skins. Christened the *Experiment*, it was supposed to do the work of several dugout canoes, and Lewis—who was immensely proud of his creation— saw it as a great technological breakthrough that would make conquering the Northwest Passage all the easier. "Five men," he bragged, "would carry her with the greatest ease."

When the *Experiment* was first put on the river upstream from the falls, "she lay like a perfect cork in the water," but the seams soon leaked and it became clear that without a new covering and better caulking the canoe would be useless. "I need not add that this circumstance mortifyed me not a little," Lewis admitted in what must be his greatest understatement of the journey. Initially reluctant to give up on it entirely, he believed he had now figured out a better way to prepare the buffalo skins. But getting them ready would require additional delays. "To make any further experiments in our present situation seemed to me madness," he wrote, "and the season was now advancing fast. I therefore relinquished all further hope of my favorite boat."

Swallowing his pride in front of his men, Lewis ordered his "favorite boat" dismantled and buried in a cache—and then never mentioned it or his grand ambitions for it again. (Perhaps silently doubting his partner's original confidence in the boat—or simply out of prudent contingency planning— Clark had already scouted out two cottonwoods suitable for turning into the *Experiment*'s replacements. The expedition soon moved on.)

There would be many other instances in which the captains' plans collided with unanticipated obstacles. Fortunately, their ability to improvise and adjust to changing circumstances was one of their greatest strengths. At Lemhi Pass, for instance, where they had expected to find the Northwest Passage and a short portage to a river they could float to the Pacific, they instead encountered an endless jumble of daunting mountains. And having originally planned on reaching the Pacific in midsummer, being resupplied by a trading vessel, and perhaps making it all the way back to the Mandan villages in North Dakota by winter, they instead arrived at the ocean in November, at the onset of the annual storm season that kept ships away from the coast, and at too late a date to attempt heading back across the Rockies.

In every instance, Lewis and Clark adeptly responded to whatever new challenge presented itself, modifying or in some instances completely aban- doning their initial plans. All the while, however, the captains never forgot their mission: to trace the Missouri to its source, find its best link to the Pacific, and return with as much useful information as possible.

Understanding the difference between their all-important, unchanging strategic goal and the more disposable tactical plans for achieving it, Lewis and Clark navigated a winding path to success by always keeping their North Star in sight.

RULE SEVEN
Never give up.

Lewis caught his first glimpse of the Rocky Mountains on May 26, 1805, when he was still in the Missouri River Breaks of central Montana, roughly a hundred miles from the Front Range. The distant peaks "were covered with snow and the sun shone on [them] in such manner as to give me the most plain and satisfactory view," he wrote. "While I viewed these mountains I felt a secret pleasure in finding myself so near the head of the heretofore conceived boundless Missouri; but when I reflected on the difficulties which this snowey barrier would most probably throw in my way to the Pacific, and the sufferings and hardships of myself and party in them, it in some measure counterballanced the joy I had felt in the first moments in which I gazed on them; but as I have always held it a crime to anticipate evils I will believe it a good comfortable road untill I am compelled to believe differently."

Besides capturing the alternating current of Lewis's psyche (joy, dark foreboding, then a false bravado to shake off the darkness, all in quick succession), the passage also indicates that the captains were already sensing in the late spring of 1805 that the western mountains would be much bigger and more difficult to surmount than Jefferson—or anyone else in the East—had possibly imagined. Even so, at that moment even Lewis surely couldn't conceive that in the middle of September—nearly four months after this first sighting of the Rockies—he and his crew would still be in the mountains' grip, half-starved and stumbling through wet snows in the bewildering Bitterroots. "A good comfortable road" it most assuredly was not.

On a journey in which nearly every expectation blew up in their faces, the ability to persevere in the face of continual discouragement was crucial. The members of the expedition had been chosen partly for their toughness and wilderness skills, but the Corps of Discovery was repeatedly called upon for something more than "bearing bodily fatigue in a pretty considerable degree." Lewis and Clark had to imbue them with a *mental* toughness, a psychological discipline that allowed them to keep their distant goal of crossing the continent in mind while focusing on the innumerable tasks required to progress a mere fourteen miles a day.

Whatever new obstacle presented itself, if it worried the captains, they kept the disappointment to themselves and immediately organized the group to surmount it in manageable steps. They reconnoitered, reconsidered, adjusted, but most of all they made decisions and acted on them. They kept everyone moving forward.

For the men, each measurable success undoubtedly instilled a little more confidence—in themselves as well as in their captains—that surely helped the next time they discovered yet another potential discouragement across their path. "We proceeded on" became the most recurrent phrase in everyone's journals for good reasons.

Just how ingrained this became can be seen during the return journey, when the expedition began its recrossing of the dreaded Bitterroots. "Every body seems anxious to be in motion," Lewis wrote on June 14, 1806, "convinced that we have not now any time to delay, if the calculation is to reach the United States this season. This I am detirmined to accomplish if within the compass of human power." Despite summer weather, in the higher elevations they encountered what Lewis called "winter with all its rigors"—numbing cold at night and snowdrifts twelve to fifteen feet deep. The packed snow supported the men's horses, but it covered any possible grass for feed and obliterated any traces of a trail.

"If we proceeded and should get bewildered in these mountains," Lewis wrote on June 17, "the certainty was that we should loose all our horses and consequently our baggage inst[r]uments perhaps our papers and thus eminently wrisk the loss of the discoveries which we had already made if we should be so fortunate as to escape with life."

The captains concluded that trying to continue would be "madness" and begrudgingly ordered everyone to turn around and head back to a previous campsite at a lower elevation. "This is the first time since we have been on this long tour that we have ever been compelled to retreat or make a retrograde march," Lewis noted ruefully, and "the party were a good deel dejected." Sergeant Patrick Gass described them as "melancholy and disappointed"; Sergeant John Ordway wrote of their "sorrow." As if to mark the sad occasion of retreat, hail and freezing rain began falling.

After a week of impatient waiting, with Nez Percé guides to show them the way, they were finally able to resume their homeward journey. The mountain passage was still cold, difficult, and full of hunger, but no one complained. They were doing what the Corps of Discovery did best—"proceeding on."

RULE EIGHT
Lead by example.

Organized as a military unit, the Corps of Discovery had a well-defined ladder of hierarchy, with Lewis and Clark indisputably at the top. No one expected the captains to man the oars on the keelboat, set up tents, or take a turn as night guard. Rank had its privileges—and besides, they had other things to attend to.

But in the meting out of danger and hardship and sheer misery throughout the long journey, both leaders accepted more than their full share. When the men went hungry, Lewis and Clark went hungry. The snows, hail, pelting rains, and sweltering sun beat down with the same force on everyone. Mosquitoes attacked captains with the same relish they attacked lowly privates. So did grizzly bears.

Over the course of two and a half years, Lewis and Clark were afflicted with many of the same ailments—fevers, dysentery, "cholics" (though not venereal disease)—as the enlisted men, and were equally subjected to the explosively purgative treatment of Rush's Thunderbolts. Lewis's gunshot wound in the buttocks was one of the expedition's most serious injuries. After an exhausting reconnaissance had left him suffering from chills, high fever, a festering boil on one ankle, and both feet badly lacerated and infected from constant puncturing by prickly pear cactuses, Clark's weakened condition at the Three Forks of the Missouri was alarming enough that all the journalists made concerned and repeated note of his agonies.

The men surely must also have noticed how the captains responded to these adversities: with fortitude. In the initial moments after being shot, Lewis disregarded his wound in favor of rallying his small hunting group for what he presumed was an Indian attack (it turned out that one of his own hunters had mistaken him for an elk). Clark's ailments had already been evident when he nevertheless insisted on going back out on the scouting mission that ultimately left him unable to walk for several days.

The captains set equally clear personal standards of bravery. When the Lakotas were demanding one of the expedition's canoes in exchange for passage up the Missouri, it was Clark who stood his ground in the shallow water, hand on his sword, and adamantly refused while hundreds of warriors notched their arrows just a few feet away. And when sixty mounted

Shoshones thundered up, ready for battle near Lemhi Pass, it was Lewis who laid down his rifle and coolly approached with an American flag.

The two leaders proved themselves in other ways. Having saved himself from certain death in the first weeks of the journey when he used his knife to stop his slide off a three-hundred-foot-high cliff in Missouri, Lewis put his experience to use a year later when he and Private Richard Windsor were scouting along the rain-slicked bluffs of Montana's Marias River. "I heard a voice behind me cry god god Capt. what shall I do," he recounted in his journal, and turned around to discover that Windsor had slipped and was lying on the edge of the precipice with half of his body already dangling in space.

"Altho' much allarmed at his situation I disguised my feelings and spoke very calmly to him and assured him that he was in no kind of danger," Lewis wrote, "to take the knife out of his belt behind him with his wright hand and dig a hole with it in the face of the bank to receive his wright foot which he did and then raised himself to his knees; I then directed him to take off his mockersons and to come forward on his hands and knees holding the knife in one hand and the gun in the other. this he happily effected and escaped." (Windsor deserves some credit here. Simply following Lewis's complicated instructions would have been difficult in any circumstance, let alone in the midst of a life-or-death situation.)

A few weeks later, during the portage of the Great Falls, Clark saved the lives of Sacagawea and her baby. Caught at the bottom of a ravine during a tremendous cloudburst, he pushed the mother and child up the embankment as a flash flood rose to his waist. "I Srcely got out before it raised 10 feet deep with a torrent which [was] turrouble to behold," he wrote, "and by the time I reached the top of the hill, at least 15 feet of water." A compass, gun, tomahawk, and other items were swept away by the flood, but Sacagawea and little Baptiste, not to mention Clark, were safe—and the men had been given another practical demonstration in the meaning of courage by their captains.

One more thing they demonstrated every day to the men: the meaning of friendship. The respect they gave each other in their shared command, the brotherly concern they openly showed when the other needed help, the confidence they so unequivocally placed in the other's judgment and competence—all that was in plain view and must have rubbed off to some degree on the rest of the group. At the very least it presented the highest possible standard of mutual trust and cooperation for the others to strive toward.

From the quality of their writing styles—Lewis with his elegance, Clark with his directness—it seems reasonable to conclude that the captains were capable of delivering effective and occasionally stirring speeches to their charges. But the journals provide few examples of them resorting to oratory to motivate the Corps of Discovery. Lewis and Clark led not by words but by something much more powerful—the unambiguous example of their actions.

RULE NINE
Be ready to take calculated risks.

As leaders, Lewis and Clark were careful not to needlessly endanger their mission or their men. But sometimes success *requires* taking chances, and at other times a little extra risk can enhance success with large dividends. The trick is knowing the difference between a calculated risk and a rash gamble.

On the way west, the captains would occasionally split small crews off from the main expedition for days at a time to explore the route ahead, seek food when game was scarce, or search for (hopefully friendly) Indians. Whatever risk was involved in those cases the captains usually considered minimal, and it applied to the smaller groups, not the expedition as a whole.

Private George Shannon, the expedition's youngest member, twice found himself separated from the main group long enough to seriously worry the captains. In his desperate attempt to find the Shoshones, Lewis pushed ahead toward the Continental Divide with only three men, intending to be gone for a month, if necessary, and leaving behind written instructions for Clark "lest any accident should befall me on the long and reather hazardous rout I was now about to take." And in the Bitterroots, Clark and a few men left the others behind in order to blaze a trail out of the mountains and secure food for the starving men. Scouting and hunting parties, of course, were standard procedure for a military unit on the move, and even in the more dangerous instances, the potential rewards (in some cases, survival itself) made dispatching them a straightforward decision.

On the Snake and Columbia Rivers, the risk taking took a different turn. Hurtling down the raging rivers in six awkward dugout canoes (and with a sizable contingent of men who couldn't swim), Lewis and Clark grew concerned when a series of spills not only endangered some of the crew but also delayed their progress to thirty miles a day. Stopping to portage around every rocky rapid, however, would delay them even more. Winter was fast approaching and they wanted to reach the Pacific as soon as possible, yet the rivers kept throwing more obstructions in their way.

Weighing their options, the captains decided to shoot through as many of the rapids as possible—even some that the local Indians, who were much more skilled on the water, considered impossible to navigate. "We Should make more portages," Clark admitted on October 13, 1805, "if the Season was not So far advanced and time precious with us." Less than three weeks later, they passed the final barrier and noticed their first tidal motion in the river.

The greatest risk Lewis and Clark purposefully took was on the way home, immediately after the successful recrossing of the Bitterroots. At Travelers' Rest (near modern-day Lolo, Montana), they began splitting the Corps of Discovery into increasingly smaller units. Lewis and nine men headed due east toward the Great Falls to explore a shortcut the Indians had described; at the falls, while some of his party retrieved the material buried there during the portage, Lewis and only three men headed north to reconnoitre the upper reaches of the Marias River, which he believed would mark the new Louisiana Territory's northern border. Meanwhile, Clark and the rest of the expedition returned to Camp Fortunate on the Beaverhead River, where they had cached their canoes and other supplies; but then this group, too, would be divided—half to paddle the canoes down the Missouri to connect with the men at the falls, while Clark and the other half traveled overland to the unexplored Yellowstone River. At the Yellowstone, yet another division would take place—Sergeant Nathaniel Pryor to take a few men with the horse herd (for trade) directly to the Mandan villages; Clark to build canoes, float down the Yellowstone, and meet everyone else at its confluence with the Missouri.

The plan was as risky as it was complicated. Having worked so hard to keep the Corps of Discovery in one piece across an unforgiving landscape, and having finally surmounted the Bitterroots, the last substantial barrier between themselves and home, the captains were suddenly dividing the expedition into five small pieces and sending some of them into unknown territory controlled by potentially hostile tribes. My friend Stephen Ambrose always considered this an "excessively dangerous plan" and believed "the captains were taking chances they should have avoided." While I would normally defer to him completely on such matters—he's the military historian, not me—I'm not sure I totally agree on this issue.

Consider this from the perspective of Lewis and Clark. It certainly wasn't a rash decision—they had started working on the plan more than a year earlier. Their canoes and important supplies and records were cached at Camp Fortunate; additional critical material was buried on both sides of the Great Falls (and farther down the Missouri at the mouth of the Marias). Those were fixed, unavoidable stops for the return trip.

But if everyone simply retraced the route they had taken westward, what about the tantalizing prospect of a shortcut to the falls? The Indians said it was only a four-day journey going directly overland, versus the fifty-three torturous days the expedition had consumed the previous year, getting between the same two points along an oxbow-shaped route that followed the meandering Missouri and then looped north from Lemhi Pass. Not to have sent someone to confirm the Indian promise of a faster route would have been tantamount to ignoring the expedition's central mission to find the most direct and practical route from the Missouri to the Pacific.

Lewis's scouting party took eight days—including a delay for hunting— along the shortcut, and his final report to Jefferson recommended it as the best route to take. Without this shortcut, the failure to find of an easy Northwest Passage would have been even more of a disappointment to present to the president; without his firsthand exploration, Lewis could not have been confident enough to mention it.

And could the captains legitimately resist exploring the Yellowstone River, the Missouri's principal tributary in the far West? From her childhood, Sacagawea was familiar with the area between the Missouri's Three Forks and the Yellowstone, and she assured them it was a short and easy distance (only forty-eight miles, Clark would discover, all but eighteen of them along a navigable stretch of the Gallatin River). By making his reconnaissance, Clark was able to employ actual measurements and observations to fill in an important gap in his western map, the most valuable single document the expedition produced in terms of immediate usefulness to the young nation. Further, this scouting mission persuaded the captains that the Yellowstone (with its easy connection to the beaver-rich Three Forks) would be the key to an American fur empire.

Sending someone to retrieve the canoes and all the other things stashed at different points along the Missouri was essential and unavoidable; scouting the shortcut to the Great Falls was central to the prime mission; and exploring the Yellowstone gave the expedition tremendous added value. Temporarily dividing into smaller groups to accomplish all three certainly added an element of risk, but they were justifiable risks, balanced against their payout.

It's the two extra missions—Lewis's trip to the Marias's headwaters, Pryor's horse journey to the Mandans—that were questionable. Questionable because their smaller size (groups of four) automatically put them at much greater peril, and equally questionable because the potential benefits were much smaller, too. As it turned out, they were also the least successful.

Fixing the latitude of the northernmost drainage of the Missouri (and therefore of the nation's new boundary) would have been interesting and marginally helpful to Jefferson, but it was hardly crucial information in the summer of 1806. Lewis set out anyway—and with only three men, even though he was headed into the homeland of the most powerful tribe on the upper Missouri, the Blackfeet, about whose fierceness the expedition had been repeatedly warned.

When Lewis reached Cut Bank Creek, the north fork of the Marias, cloudy weather prevented him from taking the necessary celestial observations that were the reason for the trip in the first place, so he named the spot Camp Disappointment and prepared to return to the Missouri. The next day he encountered a band of eight Blackfeet warriors, warily made camp with them, and awoke the following morning to sounds of a fight that had erupted when his men caught the Indians attempting to steal rifles and horses. Two Blackfeet were killed in the struggle. Fearful that the survivors who escaped would soon return with a war party bent on revenge, Lewis's group made a harrowing 120-mile ride south to the river, met the canoes, and paddled off as quickly as possible.

A mission of negligible importance had resulted in the only act of bloodshed during the entire expedition, the death of two Indians, and the enduring enmity of an important tribe. (It could just as easily have also ended with the death of Lewis and his three men.) Even if the skies had been clear at Camp Disappointment and Lewis had been able to make the proper observations he sought, it still wouldn't have been worth the cost.

Pryor's mission was perhaps even more doubtful. He and three other men set off from the Yellowstone with two dozen horses, planning to reach the Mandan villages before everyone else, prepare the tribes for the expedition's return, and present a British fur trader with a letter asking him to persuade some chiefs (particularly the Lakotas) to return to Washington with Lewis and Clark. Since the expedition's supply of trade goods was depleted, the horse herd would be used for barter and gifts.

This hardly seems like a mission essential to the expedition's success. It's almost tempting to suspect the real rationale was trying to get something in return for the horses, rather than simply abandoning them. Whatever the potential benefits, Pryor's small team was being sent nearly five hundred miles across some of the most lethal territory on the Great Plains, an area jealously contested by a half-dozen warring tribes and the future site (remember the Little Bighorn) of some particularly bloody battles.

Fortunately for Pryor and his men, their mission ended in farce instead of tragedy. The second night out, some Crows stealthily relieved them of their entire herd. They walked back to the Yellowstone, made Indian-style bull boats out of buffalo skins, and floated downriver, catching up with Clark's group on August 8. Lewis's full contingent arrived on August 12, and everyone was reunited once more.

Had the captains followed a simpler—and more strategic—three-part division of tasks from Travelers' Rest, they would have returned with just as much valuable information, a blood-free record of relations with Native Americans, and two fewer moments when the lives of their men might easily have been lost. (The Crows were the ones who benefited. Admittedly, they would have gotten the expedition's horses anyway if Clark had simply turned his herd loose once his canoes were made on the Yellowstone. But that would have denied some young warrior the chance of counting coup by leading a successful horse raid—and returning to *his* home with palpable proof that he was a leader who knew how to assess risks and benefits.)

Second-guessing decisions from the distance of two hundred years, of course, is a patently risk-free enterprise. The real test of leadership takes place in the crucible of the moment when the risks are weighed and the decisions are made, when leaders set events in motion painfully aware that they are acting without the luxury of hindsight and yet will be held accountable for their future consequences.

Lewis and Clark were not perfect—which the fatal incident with the Blackfeet particularly demonstrates. As the expedition wore on and they became more confident in themselves and their men, they understandably showed an increasing willingness to take greater risks, with mixed results. But the larger picture is clear. In a long journey fraught with danger at every turn, Lewis and Clark successfully accomplished their mission with the loss of only one man, and his death by illness was unavoidable. That simple statistic speaks for itself.

RULE TEN
Be lucky.

If Lewis's four-man reconnaissance along the Marias had encountered fifty Blackfeet instead of eight, or if a major village had been close enough to be quickly alerted by the survivors of his dawn fight, the nation might now be commemorating the bicentennial of the famous Clark Expedition. If Pryor's group had met a war party—of Crows, Atsinas, Cheyennes, Hunkpapas, or Oglalas—seeking to count more coup than a string of horses could provide, our view of the captains' leadership skills would be greatly diminished.

If the Shoshones had left their homeland for their annual buffalo hunt two weeks earlier and weren't at the Continental Divide (with their horses) when Lewis arrived, the expedition would either have had to turn back or push into the mountains without pack animals and most probably perish without a trace in the Bitterroots. In the first instance—turning back from the headwaters—Lewis and Clark would now rank in fame with Freeman and Custis, whose expedition in 1806 to the upper reaches of the Red River was also sponsored by President Jefferson. In the latter instance—disappearing without even leaving behind the journals—perhaps today a solitary historian might be writing a doctoral dissertation called *Speculations on the Fate of the Mysterious Corps of Discovery.*

Over the course of three years, the viceroys of New Spain (tipped off by a highly placed spy in the United States government) dispatched a number of small armies from Santa Fe with the express order to capture or destroy "Captain Merry" and his men. The last one included five hundred troops, one hundred Indian allies, and a pack train of more than two thousand animals, the largest Spanish military party the Great Plains had ever seen. If just one of those Spanish forces had been able to locate the Americans . . .

If, if, if, if . . . The point is that even the best leaders are never in complete control of outside forces that can spell success or failure. (An ancillary to that truth is that those who succeed usually credit themselves; those who fail often blame bad luck.) Study any success story long enough and it's virtually impossible not to come across moments when just one more click of the cosmic wheel of fortune would have turned everything to disaster. It helps to be lucky once in a while.

Lewis and Clark got their share of breaks, the most famous of which occurred the moment they sat down near Lemhi Pass to begin the all-important negotiations for horses with Cameahwait, the Shoshone chief. To help with the translating, they called for Sacagawea, a native Shoshone who had been captured by the Hidatsas five years earlier. "She came," Clark wrote, "sat down, and was beginning to interpret, when, in the person of Cameahwait, she recognized her brother. She instantly jumped up, and ran and embraced him, throwing over him her blanket, and weeping profusely." They soon had all the horses they needed. The captains didn't name the spot Camp Fortunate for nothing.

This was certainly one of the greatest coincidences in American history and a providential stroke of luck. But think back a second. Shortly after their arrival at the Mandan and Hidatsa villages a year earlier (in fact only a day after construction of Fort Mandan commenced), the fur trader Toussaint Charbonneau had presented himself to Lewis and Clark, offering his services as an interpreter. He said he spoke Hidatsa (which would be helpful to the captains during the upcoming winter) and that his two wives were Shoshones. Before the day was out, Lewis and Clark had hired him not only for the winter but "to go on with us and take one of his wives to interpet the Snake [Shoshone] language." Busy as they were with the details of building winter quarters amidst surroundings in which everything was new and challenging, in their minds the captains were able to project themselves one year and a thousand miles into the future—to mountains they had never seen and people they had only heard of, who owned horses they thought would be useful. At the time, when the dream of a Northwest Passage still substituted for hard facts, they had no way of knowing just how useful, how absolutely crucial, those horses would be; just as they had no way of imagining that in Charbonneau's wife, Sacagawea, they would be returning a young chief's long-lost sister to her homeland. They simply recognized what seemed to be a good opportunity and jumped at it. And in that decisive act of forward thinking, they *made* their luck.

No one is immune from the random whims of fate, good or bad. Understanding that, what leaders do is try to minimize the chances for bad luck to strike, or at least make preparations to contain the damage if it does. At the same time, they try to create situations for good fortune to smile upon them, and when that occurs they squeeze the absolute most out of it.

Lewis and Clark may have been lucky, but don't look to that as the secret of their success. Look to their leadership.

16

We Proceeded On

When I first met Gerard Baker in 1983, he was near the bottom of the rung of the National Park Service's career ladder and I, having recently become unemployed, was on a freelance writing assignment that I had secured by pretending to know more about Lewis and Clark than I actually did. Over the next twenty years I've watched Gerard steadily rise in the NPS—including a stint as superintendent of the Little Bighorn Battlefield National Monument—and I'm happy to report that I've somehow found steadier work myself.

One of the great honors of my life came in January 2003, at the official ceremonies launching the Lewis and Clark bicentennial at Monticello, when I got to introduce my old friend as the superintendent of the Lewis and Clark National Historic Trail and as the head of the Corps of Discovery II, the federal government's traveling exhibit that will spend three years retracing the expedition's route and retelling its story. I can't think of a better person with whom the nation could entrust such an important assignment.

One January afternoon years ago, I found myself huddled around a fire inside an earth lodge near Stanton, North Dakota. The temperature outside had managed a high of only three degrees below zero. A north wind howled across the prairies. The sun was slipping below the horizon, to be followed by nearly sixteen hours of darkness. The word "cold" does not begin to express where the night was clearly headed.

Across from me, patiently feeding the fire with cottonwood logs, sat Gerard Baker, a Mandan-Hidatsa and park ranger for the National Park Service. He had built the earth lodge as a "living history" demonstration for the Knife River Indian Villages National Historic Site, where three Hidatsa villages once stood when Lewis and Clark wintered in the area. I was retracing the explorers' route, trying to connect their experience with my own over a gap of nearly two centuries, and had asked if I could spend a night in the earth lodge, which with a dusting of snow looked something like a sod igloo. Gerard had seemed bemused by my request, but he agreed to accompany me, even provided our supplies.

First he smudged the interior in all four directions with the smoke from a bundle of sweetgrass. "For the spirits," he explained. Then, in an iron pot, he boiled potatoes, onions, red peppers, and buffalo tripe, the spongy membranes of a buffalo stomach—a rubbery meal that we ate with our hands. I told him tales about my trip upriver from St. Louis, about all the changes I had seen compared to what the captains had described in their journals. He shared stories of his ancestors and sang some Hidatsa chants. Outside, the northern lights began to dance while the temperature kept sinking. It was time to go to bed.

Gerard had brought along five large buffalo robes, and he advised me to place one of them, fur side up, on the dirt floor as my mattress. The other four, he said, would provide more warmth stacked on top of me, fur side down.

"But what about you?" I asked, thinking that he was taking Indian hospitality to a foolish extreme. In the back of my mind, I recalled Clark's journal entry about the two Indians who had stayed out all night on the frozen prairie and survived—proof, he wrote, that the "customs and habits of those people have inured them to bear more cold than I thought possible for a man to endure." The smudge ceremony, the meal of buffalo, the stories around the campfire, *and now this*, I thought. History was repeating itself.

"Are you sure you'll be OK?" I insisted.

Gerard smiled at me, his eyes twinkling in the firelight. "I'll be all right," he answered, and he unrolled a fancy down-filled sleeping bag next to my buffalo robes. "This one's guaranteed to twenty below."

I have traveled the Lewis and Clark trail many times since that evening in the earth lodge with Gerard. Yet every time my path has crossed theirs, I have wondered what the two captains would think if somehow they were magically transported back to life in the modern world and were sent out as, say, a Corps of Rediscovery. What would they recognize? What would confound them? What would they regret? What would they appreciate?

Certainly, a frigid night on the northern plains would be almost painfully familiar to them. These were two Virginia-born gentlemen, accustomed to the mildest of winters; I doubt they could ever forget their experience at Fort Mandan, where they were exposed to one of the harshest weather extremes this continent has to offer. I, too, have stood on the banks of the Missouri and been awestruck by its raw power as huge chunks of ice floated relentlessly downstream, only to be even more stupefied the next morning on finding the mighty river frozen solid, conquered by the coldness. It's something you remember. In the column headed "Unchanged," place a big check mark for the ferocity of winters on the upper Missouri.

Nor would the captains find anything new in a meal of buffalo, or in a Mandan's willingness to share it with a stranger. But Lewis, I imagine, would be fascinated by Gerard's sleeping bag—so lightweight, yet so warm; just the kind of scientifically advanced equipment he had scoured Philadelphia to find when outfitting his expedition. Whether the captain would appreciate the irony that in this case it was an Indian showing off the latest in technology to a white man—and poking a little good-natured fun in the bargain—depends on your own assessment of Lewis's psyche. Personally, I doubt it. In my mind's eye, I see him bristling silently as he tucked himself in between the buffalo robes. Clark's the one who might have enjoyed the joke, even if it was on him. But he would also have been the one most troubled by a story Gerard had told as the embers turned crimson.

In 1836, while an aging Clark was still Indian agent for the territory, the government sent two doctors up the Missouri with instructions to vaccinate all the tribes along the river against smallpox. They inoculated most of the tribes until winter turned them back, before they had reached the Mandans, Arikaras, and Hidatsas. For some reason, the secretary of war did not dispatch them to finish the job the next spring (and even misled Congress into believing the project was completed). That summer, catastrophe struck.

When a fur-trading boat filled with supplies paid its annual visit, it unintentionally also brought the smallpox virus, which quickly spread among the unprotected Indians. Gerard has read all the eyewitness accounts, as well as listened to oral history passed down through the tribes' generations. Smallpox, he says, causes a "very, very ugly death"—sores that ooze and burst on the victim's skin, swelling, aching, vomiting, delirium, and finally loss of life. In the villages, people began dying at a rate of eight to ten a day. Corpses piled up; the stench of rotting bodies could be smelled for miles.

Fearing their protective spirits had abandoned them, some Mandans sought escape through suicide. After debating the bravest way to die, one warrior cut his own throat while another forced an arrow into his own lungs. Some drowned themselves in the Missouri.

Among those struck by the sickness was Four Bears, a Mandan chief of some note. As a warrior, he had killed five chiefs of other nations in hand-to-hand combat, wrested a knife from a Cheyenne warrior and used it to kill its owner, taken many prisoners, and survived an enemy arrow and six gunshot wounds. But like the rest of his people, he had always felt nothing but friendship for the white man. When the fever first hit him, he put on his ceremonial garments, mounted his horse, and rode through his village singing his sacred songs.

And then, as he, too, began to succumb to the dread disease, he gave a final speech to his people. A fur trader transcribed it, and it's preserved in a book of tribal history that Gerard lent me:

Ever since I can remember, I have loved the whites. . . . To the best of knowledge, I have never wronged a white man. On the contrary, I have always protected them from the insults of others, which they cannot deny. The Four Bears never saw a white man hungry, but what he gave them to eat, drink and a buffalo skin to sleep on in time of need. . . . And how they have repaid it! With ingratitude! I have never called a white man a dog, but today I do pronounce them to be a set of black-hearted dogs. They have deceived me. Them that I have always considered as brothers have turned out to be my worst enemies.

I have been in many battles, and often wounded, but the wounds of my enemies I exalt in. But today I am wounded, and by whom? By those same white dogs that I have always considered and treated as brothers.

I do not fear death, my friends. You know it. But to die with my face rotten, that even the wolves will shrink with horror at seeing me, and say to themselves, "That is the Four Bears, the friend of the whites."

Along with Four Bears, 90 percent of the tribe perished in the epidemic. The once-prosperous nation, whose villages had constituted the biggest city on the plains during Lewis and Clark's time, was reduced to barely a hundred individuals, huddled together with remnants of the Arikaras and Hidatsas.

Word of the devastation would have reached Clark in St. Louis shortly before he died. He was experienced in the loss of friends, but it must have greatly saddened him, "the Red-Headed Chief," to ponder the fate of the people who had so warmly welcomed the expedition thirty years earlier. Showing up in Gerard's earth lodge nearly two centuries later would undoubtedly flood him with even stronger emotions. Outside, the three villages once teemed with life and noise, and the smoke of cook fires once curled from the tops of hundreds of earth lodges, and neighbors and explorers alike shared food, music, and laughter to ward off winter's chill. Now there are only large, circular depressions in the ground marking where each lodge stood, like so many supplicating palms outstretched on the barren plain.

My guess is that Clark would have had the same trouble sleeping that I did that night, hearing echoes of Four Bears' words whenever the night wind hissed or a cottonwood groaned as it shook in the gale. And I imagine that he, too, would have uttered a silent prayer that Gerard had adequately appeased the spirits of friendship with the smudge of his sweetgrass.

"We proceeded on" is the most recurrent phrase in the journals of the Lewis and Clark expedition. Charles Floyd wrote it several times in the brief diary he kept before he died far from home—the first United States soldier to die west of the Mississippi, but certainly not the last. His comrades Patrick Gass, Joseph Whitehouse, and John Ordway used it all the time as well. So did the captains.

With three matter-of-fact words they could describe the act of getting up each morning, facing an unknown horizon whose only certainty was another day of hard work, and pushing forward with, if not confidence, then at least dogged determination to move at least a little farther toward that horizon before the sun went down.

"We proceeded on." It became, in effect, the Corps of Discovery's unofficial motto, a mantra that kept them going in the face of every obstacle. When I travel in their footsteps, I usually adopt it as my own. It reminds me that they didn't have the luxury to look backward, to pause and contemplate the past. And it helps me conjure up their spirits to join me on my modern journey.

The captains in particular were Jeffersonian men, imbued with the Enlightenment notion of steady progress. "We proceeded on" could summarize their view of how the universe works. It would also influence their reaction to many of the starkest changes to be found along their route across the continent.

Lewis, who devoted so much time to scientific descriptions, would no doubt be enthusiastic about the agricultural transformation of the Louisiana Territory. The Missouri, he had written his mother from Fort Mandan, "waters one of the fairest portions of the globe, nor do I believe that there is in the universe a similar extent of country equally fertile." He would probably nod his head, as if to say "I told you so," when he learned that the area is now the food basket for the nation and much of the world.

Clark, with his keen eye for terrain, had marked locations on his map as likely places for future forts and settlements. The mouth of the Kansas River, where the Missouri bends sharply toward the east, was such a spot. He would enjoy, I think, the vista from his old campsite. Where once two rivers met in the wilderness, now rises the skyline of Kansas City, the largest city along the Lewis and Clark route west of St. Louis. Other cities, like Omaha and Bismarck and Portland, grew up at strategic places he had identified. "We proceeded on," he might say.

More changes. A series of dams, built to prevent flooding and to provide irrigation and hydroelectricity, has turned much of the Missouri into more lake than river. The "sublimely grand spectacle" of the Great Falls, which Lewis described so ecstatically, is now dominated by a concrete barrier that holds back the Missouri; except in times of unusually high water, the falls themselves are dry rocks. The same goes for the Columbia. Celilo Falls, the Long and Short Narrows, the Cascades—places that Clark noted for their "horrid appearance of this agitated gut swelling, boiling & whorling in every direction"—are now entombed under reservoirs.

What would the explorers think of the two mighty rivers now? To them, the raging cataracts were uncommonly magnificent, but they were also impediments. I can imagine Lewis noting ruefully at the Great Falls that their majesty had once reduced him to wishing for better words to adequately describe their beauty—and then walking excitedly into the powerhouse to see how the turbines work. On the Columbia (and its tributary, the Snake), Clark would be wide-eyed at the sight of deep-draft vessels blithely carrying cargo toward the twin cities of Clarkston and Lewiston, now officially designated as *sea*ports though they are four hundred miles inland from the Pacific.

It would not escape their notice that the same dams that tamed the Columbia for boat traffic, and that generate electricity used as far away as California, have also virtually eliminated the salmon. The number of salmon, Clark wrote in 1805, was "incrediable to say." Even attempting to estimate their numbers seemed preposterous. I think he would be equally speechless today if he went with me into one of the deeper recesses of the Bonneville Dam. There one employee literally—and rather easily—counts each adult salmon that manages to swim past a window looking out on the dam's fish ladder.

Lewis and Clark would have questions about wildlife. They would remember beaching their canoes for hours as a buffalo herd forded the river;
going for several months in which encountering a grizzly bear was almost
a daily event; seeing enormous elk herds and packs of wolves; being kept
awake at night by the slapping of beaver tails; witnessing a midday sky
darkened by huge flocks of wild geese; filling their journals with description
after description of animals they had never seen before, in numbers beyond
imagination; passing through a landscape in which, as they wrote, "the
Game is getting so pleanty and tame in this country that Some of the party
clubbed them out of their way." Some of the species they recorded have
vanished entirely; others are struggling back from the brink of extinction.
Another side of the same coin upon which the nation emblazoned, "We
proceeded on."

Likewise, we would encounter fewer Indians. Lewis and Clark had been
the first to tell them they had a new "great father." In their speeches the
captains promised that he "has offered you the hand of unalterable friendship, which will never be withdrawn from your nation." But on the modern
trail, moving from reservation to reservation, they would hear instead tales
of lands lost and promises broken. For the Lakotas, the Nez Percé, the
Shoshones, the Blackfeet, and the tribes along the Columbia, the offered
hand had turned into a fist. And even for those tribes that never experienced
war with the United States—like the Salish and Hidatsas and Mandans—the
handshake of friendship proved a bad bargain.

"Follow these councils," Lewis had concluded his first speech to western
Indians, "and you will have nothing to fear, because the great Spirit will
smile upon your nation, and in future ages will make you to outnumber
the trees of the forest." Even by the standards of the Virginia gentry, Lewis
was acutely sensitive about matters of honor; seeing how his word was so
cavalierly disregarded would start him sputtering, and then, perhaps, send
him into dark despair. Clark's face, I think, would turn as crimson as his
hair, out of both anger and shame.

To cheer them, I'd take the captains through the White Cliffs of the Missouri in north-central Montana, protected by Congress from damming and
development, and now further protected by President Clinton as a national
monument. This is another place where Lewis waxed rhapsodic, writing for
pages about "seens of visionary inchantment." I'd invite Lewis to do what
friends and I have done on several occasions: read passages from his journal
and then look up from our campsite or canoe to see precisely what he had

struggled so hard to describe. With luck, we might even see a bighorn on the cliffs.

On our journey together, the captains would learn that the western sky is still as big as it was for the Corps of Discovery, the horizons still as simultaneously intimidating and exhilarating. Nothing has changed the broiling summer heat on the plains or the startling fury of a prairie hailstorm—not to mention the maddening persistence of mosquitoes up and down the Missouri. And the mountains? To Clark they were the "Shineing Mountains." Lewis called them "tremendous . . . covered with eternal snows." Snow still covers their peaks in midsummer; from a distance they still shine. Farther west, winters on the Pacific coast are still sodden with rain.

It was on the coast that the Corps of Discovery got into the habit of carving their names into tree trunks. Reading between the lines, I get the impression they emblazoned the date and their names and initials with particular gusto, relief, and pride, as the most tangible evidence they could think of to prove they had actually crossed the continent. But mixed in with those emotions was also a tinge of fear—fear that they might not make it back to their homes, that they would never be heard from again, that they and their remarkable achievements would be lost to history.

The tree markings have long since disappeared. But other things now bear their names. On our hurried return toward St. Louis, I would point some of them out: towns, counties, and national forests, rivers and mountain passes, high schools and colleges, campsites and cafés, the Lewis and Clark Search and Rescue Association and the Lewis and Clark 24-Hour Wrecking Service. Where they ran out of whiskey, there is a Lewis and Clark Distillery. And where they switched from eating horses to eating dogs, there is the Lewis and Clark Animal Shelter.

Federal highway signs mark the "Lewis and Clark Trail" all the way from the Pacific to the east bank of the Mississippi, where they had embarked on their epic journey. Near St. Louis I would drive them over the Lewis Bridge and then the Clark Bridge before I dropped them off on the Illinois side, at the Lewis and Clark Motel. "We proceeded on," I would tell them on behalf of their nation, "but you weren't forgotten."

There would be much for them to report on to Mr. Jefferson, some of it with great pride, some of it with profound sorrow. Before we parted, I would add one more story, about what happened back in North Dakota on the morning after the cold night in the earth lodge with Gerard Baker.

Thanks to his sleeping bag, Gerard woke up warmer than I did. My feet felt like blocks of ice, and it took some time near the fire to restore them. Gerard teased me, saying that in honor of my experience he might give me an Indian name. What did I think of "Man Who Sleeps in Buffalo Robes" or "Smells Like Tripe"? Once more we shared stories over the fire. He invited me back for the summer, promising that we could visit a traditional sweat lodge he had built along the banks of the Missouri. A friendship was forming that has now lasted for twenty years—despite the distances between our homes and the differences of race and culture.

We have learned that we have many things in common. Among them is a passion for history, not just out of intellectual curiosity but based on a more practical belief: that the journey to a better future must include discovering the past and learning from it. And while our approach is to explore history by being clear-eyed about its darker moments, we both try to pay attention and respect to the spirits of those who came before us, and search for lessons that might call upon the better angels of our nature.

Gerard's desire to honor his ancestors and keep alive the traditions of his people had led him to the journals of Lewis and Clark, one of the best written records about the Mandans and Hidatsas before the cataclysmic epidemic that nearly ended the tribes' very existence. My search to understand my nation, by retracing its pursuit of the next horizon, had led me to the same source. Along the trail of the Corps of Discovery, our paths had crossed, and if I could meet their spirits I would thank the two captains for bringing us together.

That morning was as cold as the morning before. The sun was rising, but the temperature was not going to reach zero. The north wind still howled. We had planned on hiking to the site of Fort Mandan, a walk guaranteed to be both bone-chilling and fatiguing. For a moment we considered staying put, near the warm comfort of our fire. But like Lewis and Clark, we were moved by the spirit of discovery. We packed up our gear and stepped out to face the new day. And then we proceeded on.

17
"O! The Joy":
Trail Advice for the Modern Explorer

I'm often asked by people contemplating a trip along the Lewis and Clark trail for tips and information. I tell them there are a number of good guide-books that can help them with specifics, but what follows is my broader advice. To it, I would add a few pleas: Be respectful of the land—and the local people already living there. Tread lightly, so that your children's children can have the same experience, and two hundred years from now what Jefferson would call "the most distant posterity" can experience it, too.

From the dramatic bluffs of Cape Disappointment, at Washington's Fort Canby State Park, the vista was quite the opposite of disappointing. For as far as my eyes could reach, the rolling swells of the Pacific Ocean marched toward me, line after endless line beginning at the farthest western horizon, building in size and form as they approached, wave after wave arcing forward with white caps flashing in the sun, only to crash and atomize into sparkling foam on the rocks far below my perch.

If I were looking for a spot that states with utmost finality, "Continent Ends Here," this would be it. And I couldn't help repeating out loud William Clark's most famous journal entry: "Ocian in view! O! the joy."

For two months I had been retracing Lewis and Clark's historic route from the mouth of the Missouri River, near St. Louis, to the mouth of the Columbia. My main means of travel had been my sister's aging Volkswagen camper, which I had named the *Discovery* in honor of the two captains and their Corps of Discovery, the first American citizens to cross the continent and reach the Pacific by land.

My car (and the passage of nearly two hundred years) had made my journey both faster and easier than theirs. For much of their journey west— as they fought the Missouri for its entire twenty-five-hundred-mile length, then trudged through the snowy Bitterroot Mountains—Lewis and Clark would have defined substantial progress as making fourteen miles a day. Shooting down the Snake and Columbia Rivers in their dugout canoes for the final stretch must have seemed like hyperdrive, although in fact it only increased their speed to thirty or forty miles per day. No wonder it took them a year and a half to reach Cape Disappointment. Without breaking any speed limits, and allowing plenty of time for unhurried stops and leisurely side trips, my Volkswagen camper covered the same distance in sixty days.

Needless to say, I also hadn't suffered the hardships the Corps of Discovery routinely faced—the backbreaking toil, the loss of a comrade to illness, dangerous encounters with enraged grizzlies, near-starvation in the ordeal across the Bitterroots, demoralizing coastal rains that rotted the clothes on their backs, and so much more. Compared to their experience crossing the continent, mine was (thankfully) a summer vacation. They had been *making* history; I was merely retracing it.

And yet, on that sunlit afternoon as I stood mesmerized by the rolling breakers arrayed at my feet, I felt a special kinship with the explorers I had been following. Like them, I had chased one sunset after another, moving steadily west across a constantly changing, perpetually awe-inspiring landscape. Like them, along the way I had encountered new people, seen new sights, learned new things around each bend of the trail. And like them, I had finally reached the spot where that trail could go west no farther.

Standing there at the coast, I could share in their sense of satisfaction. ("Great joy in camp," Clark had written. "We are in *View* of the *Ocian*, this great Pacific Octean which we [have] been So long anxious to See. and the roreing or noise made by the waves brakeing on the rockey Shores . . . may be heard disti[n]ctly.") But retracing their route had also permitted me to share something more, something that a mere reading of their journals would never have revealed: an indelible, visceral sense of the sheer *largeness* of the country.

Lewis and Clark and their Corps of Discovery were the first to truly comprehend that fact at the very core of our national being. In November 1805, as they prepared to make their winter camp near the Pacific coast, they understood—as no other Americans at the time could possibly understand—

just how big, how rugged, how mind-bogglingly varied this country really is. They understood because they had crossed it at fourteen miles a day.

The Lewis and Clark expedition is significant in many ways—for science, geography, ethnology, the politics of empire; for providing (through their journals) an unparalleled description of the West at the dawn of the nineteenth century; for offering enduring lessons in bravery, perseverance, and the success that comes only from working together; for leaving behind what the novelist Larry McMurtry has called "our first really American adventure . . . our only really American epic" and "the essential elements of a national myth."

But equally significant is the journey itself. They had crossed the continent and survived, simultaneously learning how much more difficult it was than their sponsor, Thomas Jefferson, had imagined, yet proving that it could be done nonetheless. For the rest of the nineteenth century, Americans followed their footsteps west, taking their nation with them. Much of American history, much of who we are as a people—for good and for ill—is bound up in that larger journey.

We take it for granted now, spanning the continent. By that I mean we take for granted that the United States reaches from sea to shining sea. And we take for granted, traveling as we normally do in jet planes, that getting from one coast to the other is no big deal. In both instances, Lewis and Clark remind us otherwise.

When their expedition was originally conceived, the United States ended at the Mississippi River. Thanks to Jefferson's Louisiana Purchase, by the time they set off from the east side of the Mississippi in 1804, the nation's boundaries had been stretched to the Rocky Mountains, but the Southwest and the Pacific coast were still claimed by others. There was nothing self-evident at the time that our nation would one day embrace it all. Lewis and Clark's arrival on the western coast helped make what we now consider inevitable, possible.

Likewise, in taking the nation's first transcontinental "road trip," they symbolically set in motion what has become an American tradition—a belief that the only way to really get to know this country is to hit the road and go find it. These are experiences unavailable to those who peer out their airplane windows at thirty-five thousand feet and idly wonder what it must be like down there in all those seemingly endless, open, and empty spaces.

The airline traveler is, is some ways, not much different from Jefferson two centuries ago. Sophisticated and educated as he was, fascinated in the

West as he might have been, Jefferson never ventured more than fifty miles west of Monticello and therefore relied on his two "road warriors" to fill him in on the details. I'm sure he nodded his head when they returned and told him of the immensity of the Great Plains, or the daunting majesty of the Rockies, or the startling change from desert to rain forest at the Columbia Gorge, but since he hadn't been there himself, do you think he ever fully understood what they were trying to convey?

Lewis and Clark, the president informed Congress upon their safe return in 1806, had "learnt the character of the country." Coming from Jefferson that's high praise—and perhaps a trace of envy.

Every year in the course of two decades since my moment of reverie at Cape Disappointment, I've gone back to the Lewis and Clark trail—retracing it in its entirety or revisiting some segment of their route. I've done it alone, I've done it with friends, I've done it with my family. With the expedition's bicentennial now under way, I expect to be doing it some more. During those travels, I've learned two important secrets about retracing the Corps of Discovery's trail.

The first is: Don't Get Hung Up on Your Mode of Transportation. Lewis and Clark traveled by keelboat, canoe, horse, and foot. You have more options—and each one is as valid as any other in trying to connect with the United States' first expedition to the farthest horizon.

Besides my sister's Volkswagen camper, I've done it in a rusty old Saab and a borrowed GMC Suburban. I've paddled canoes in certain stretches (*always* downstream, unlike the explorers), ridden a tugboat on the Missouri, a barge and a crab boat on the Columbia, and all manner of other motorized vessels in between. I've gone by horseback over the Bitterroot Mountains and hiked up many of the expedition's mountain passes. (I've climbed Lewis and Clark Pass, which Clark himself never saw and never hiked; then again, I've also hiked to the top of Pompey's Pillar, which Lewis never saw and never climbed—so by my count I'm one up on each of the captains.) Along the way I've seen people following the explorers on bikes, motorcycles, Winnebagos, jet boats, and reconstructed keelboats and pirogues. Many of them—like me—spent more nights in motels than under the open sky.

My first point is that you should choose the mode of travel that makes the most sense to you. That's what Lewis and Clark did, after all. They didn't drag that big keelboat up the Missouri, paddle those canoes against two rivers' currents, haul those dugouts around the Great Falls, and straggle across the Bitterroots with horses that sometimes doubled as dinner as some sort of early-nineteenth-century Outward Bound test. They did it that way because at the time it was the best way to proceed on. Traveling in the *spirit* of Lewis and Clark is more important than getting too literal about how you get there. (Although if you choose a motor home or standard car, there are certain segments you should definitely avoid; and, personally, I don't think a jet boat is a wise choice.)

The second secret is in the same vein as traveling in the spirit of Lewis and Clark: Don't Confine Yourself to the Past. Reconnecting with history is obviously a crucial reason for retracing the trail and full of its own rewards. But remember, Lewis and Clark's mission was not chronicling the past. It was discovering what was then the present: learning about the land's geography and wildlife and, equally important, getting to know the people who already lived there.

A few years ago, I took Dianne and our two children, Emmy and Will, along part of the trail in southwestern Montana and decided we should stop for the night in the tiny, remote town of Jackson, where Clark had written about a hot spring on his return trip. That hot spring now feeds a big swimming pool connected to a small motel/restaurant, and after we checked in and luxuriated in the warm waters for an afternoon we learned that Jackson was holding its "Old Timers' Celebration" that weekend. The band, we were told, would crank up around 10 P.M.; the dance would go until 2 A.M. or later; and Jackson's population was soon expected to start skyrocketing and reach its peak right around the time we weary travelers had planned on going to sleep.

What to do? We took Lewis and Clark as our guide. In Indian village after Indian village, the captains recorded in their journals not just the clothing, food, dwellings, and medicine of Native Americans, but their customs as well. Including dancing. The journals tell us that many a night was spent not only watching Indians dance, but dancing *with* them (and sometimes, for the Indians' amusement, dancing *for* them). It was something the men always looked forward to—and no doubt it formed one of their fondest memories when they returned to their homes.

By ten o'clock that night in Jackson, my entire family was already bone tired. But we couldn't have slept, even if we wanted to; the country band was blaring, the beer tent was open for business, cars and pickups kept streaming into town, the ballooning crowd was getting raucous and noisy. So we headed out of our room and into the party, where we danced and laughed and whirled and laughed some more, surrounded by dancing and laughing natives. Sometime deep into the night, we finally collapsed into bed.

The party itself had nothing to do with Lewis and Clark—though following the explorers' trail had brought us to it, and surrendering to their spirit of adventure and discovery had moved us onto the dance floor. And now, years later, it's still one of our fondest "Lewis and Clark" memories.

Each time I've traveled in Lewis and Clark's footsteps, their trusted journals in hand, I've learned something more about them and their remarkable adventure. In those few places where little is different from Lewis and Clark's time, I've appreciated how the journals can put me in their company. In those places where little is the same, I've relied on the journals to transport me back across two centuries of unremitting change to see the land with the same fresh eyes of my favorite explorers. Equally important, with each successive trip I've learned something more about the character of my country, its people, and its history.

Traveling in the spirit of Lewis and Clark—with curiosity and wonder and a determination that learning something new is always an adventure, that *each day* is a day of discovery—is the most satisfying way to connect with their experience. I recommend it to anyone who finds in their story a personal itch to head out toward the next horizon and discover what lies beyond.

If you take that journey, do what I do. Whenever a jet passes overhead, I look up and think that the passengers inside don't know what they're missing. And whenever I reach the coast, I still can't help exclaiming, "Ocian in view! O! the joy."

Note on Sources

The headwater source for all Lewis and Clark scholarship is the thirteen-volume *The Journals of the Lewis & Clark Expedition*, edited by Gary E. Moulton and published by the University of Nebraska Press. Donald Jackson's *Letters of the Lewis and Clark Expedition*, published by the University of Illinois Press, is also indispensable for primary documents. Virtually all of the quotations relating to the expedition in this book come from those two works.

Back issues of *We Proceeded On*, published by the Lewis and Clark Trail Heritage Foundation, were helpful in finding facts (the total number of grizzlies the expedition encountered, for instance) and exploring different aspects of the journey. I would encourage anyone interested in Lewis and Clark to become a subscriber by joining the foundation: Lewis and Clark Trail Heritage Foundation, Inc., P.O. Box 3434, Great Falls MT 59403.

Bernard DeVoto's quotation originally appeared in "Passage to India: Christmas to Christmas with Lewis and Clark," *Saturday Review of Literature* 15 (December 1936); republished in *Voyages of Discovery: Essays on the Lewis and Clark Expedition*, edited by James P. Ronda (Montana Historical Society Press, 1998). Clark's post-expedition letters about Lewis and York first appeared in an article by James J. Holmberg in *We Proceeded On* and are now included in his book *Dear Brother: Letters of William Clark to Jonathan Clark* (Yale University Press, 2002). Larry McMurtry's quotes can be found in his wonderful book *Sacagawea's Nickname: Essays on the American West* (New York Review Books, 2001).

I am, of course, indebted to many other Lewis and Clark authors and scholars who have preceded me. They are too many to name here, but I particularly want to add John Logan Allen and Stephen E. Ambrose to those listed above.

Acknowledgments

An Unsatisfied Curiosity: The speech upon which this was based was reprinted as "What the Lewis and Clark Expedition Means to America" in *We Proceeded On*, the official publication of the Lewis and Clark Trail Heritage Foundation, Inc., Vol. 23, No. 3, August 1997; and later in *Columbia: The Magazine of Northwest History*, published by the Washington State Historical Society, Winter 1997–98.

The Alexander Hamilton Willard Expedition: This first appeared, in very slightly different form, as the introduction to *The Men of the Lewis & Clark Expedition*, by Charles G. Clarke, University of Nebraska Press, 2002. Reprinted here by permission of the University of Nebraska Press. © 2002 by the University of Nebraska Press.

Of Hearths and Home: The speech upon which this was based was reprinted as "The Chimneys of Fort Mandan" in *We Proceeded On*, Vol. 25, No. 3, August 1999.

"This Long Wished for Spot": The speech upon which this was based first appeared in *Proceedings: Fur Trade Symposium 2000*, published by the Fort Union Association, Williston ND, 2001.

Meriwether Lewis's "Curious Adventure": The speech upon which this was based was reprinted, under the same name, in *We Proceeded On*, Vol. 24, No. 4, November 1998.

"Toilsome Days and Wristless Nights": The speech upon which this was based was reprinted, under the same name, in *We Proceeded On*, Vol. 26, No. 4, November 2000.

Hallowed Ground: The speech upon which this was based was reprinted in *Columbia: The Magazine of Northwest History*, Spring 2001.

We Proceeded On: This essay first appeared, under the same name, in *Lewis and Clark: The Journey of the Corps of Discovery*, by Dayton Duncan and Ken Burns, Alfred A. Knopf, 1997.

"O! The Joy": Trail Advice for the Modern Explorer: Parts of this essay first appeared in *Washington Journey* and a number of other magazines associated with the American Automobile Association in the spring of 2003. Other parts first appeared in *America's Millennium Trails: Pathways for the Twenty-first Century*, edited by Kathleen Cordes and Jane Lammers, published by the American Association for Leisure and Recreation, in partnership with The White House Millennium Council, 2002.